T0265909

SYRIA

● Tyre

MEDITERRANEAN SEA

Mt. Arbel
● SEA OF GALILEE

GALILEE

● Caesarea

SAMARIA

● Sebaste

JUDAEA

Jerusalem ● Jericho
●
Bethlehem ● ● Callirrhoe
Herodium ●

● DEAD SEA

Ascalon ●

IDUMEA

Masada ●

NABATEA

HEROD

&

MARY

THE TRUE STORY OF
THE TYRANT KING
AND THE MOTHER OF
THE RISEN SAVIOR

KATHIE LEE GIFFORD
WITH DR. BRYAN LITFIN

W PUBLISHING GROUP

AN IMPRINT OF THOMAS NELSON

Published in Nashville, Tennessee, by W Publishing, an imprint of Thomas Nelson.

Published in association with United Talent Agency.

Thomas Nelson titles may be purchased in bulk for educational, business, fundraising, or sales promotional use. For information, please email SpecialMarkets@ThomasNelson.com.

Unless otherwise noted, Scripture quotations are taken from the New King James Version®. Copyright © 1982 by Thomas Nelson. Used by permission. All rights reserved.

Scripture quotations marked NIV are taken from the Holy Bible, New International Version®, NIV®. Copyright © 1973, 1978, 1984, 2011 by Biblica, Inc.® Used by permission of Zondervan. All rights reserved worldwide. www.zondervan.com. The "NIV" and "New International Version" are trademarks registered in the United States Patent and Trademark Office by Biblica, Inc.®

Scripture quotations marked NLT are taken from the Holy Bible, New Living Translation. Copyright © 1996, 2004, 2015 by Tyndale House Foundation. Used by permission of Tyndale House Ministries, Carol Stream, Illinois 60188. All rights reserved.

Italics added to Scripture quotations are the author's emphasis.

Any internet addresses, phone numbers, or company or product information printed in this book are offered as a resource and are not intended in any way to be or to imply an endorsement by Thomas Nelson, nor does Thomas Nelson vouch for the existence, content, or services of these sites, phone numbers, companies, or products beyond the life of this book.

ISBN 978-1-4003-3665-4 (audiobook)
ISBN 978-1-4003-3664-7 (eBook)
ISBN 978-1-4003-3662-3 (HC)
ISBN 978-1-4003-4518-2 (ITPE)

Library of Congress Control Number: 2024931229

Printed in the United States of America
24 25 26 27 28 LBC 5 4 3 2 1

*This book is dedicated to two of my favorite men on the planet:
Ray Vander Laan, my first rabbinical teacher in the
Holy Land, who lit a fire in my soul once again for the
Scriptures and the epic stories behind them.
The other person I want to acknowledge is my son, Cody,
who first encouraged me to take this newfound fascination
with the ancient stories and turn it into a modern-day
thriller for a whole new generation of readers.*

CONTENTS

HERODIAN CHRONOLOGY

73 BC	Birth of Herod
64 BC	Herod flees to Petra during the Jewish civil war
63 BC	General Pompey captures Jerusalem for the Romans and enters the temple
48 BC	Pompey is executed by beheading in Egypt
47 BC	Antipater I helps Julius Caesar in Egypt; he appoints Phasael and Herod as governors in Judea and Galilee; Herod marries Doris
44 BC	Julius Caesar is betrayed and murdered in Rome
43 BC	Antipater I is murdered by Malichus
42 BC	Herod divorces Doris; he gets betrothed to Mariamne I
40 BC	Parthians invade Roman Syria and Judea under Pacorus and Barzapharnes; Phasael is killed in prison; Hyrcanus is sent into exile in Babylonia; Herod flees to Masada, Egypt, and Rome; he is named king of the Jews by the Roman Senate
39 BC	Herod returns to Judea and fights Antigonus to claim his kingship
38 BC	Herod defeats the robbers at Mount Arbel
37 BC	Herod marries Mariamne I; he captures Jerusalem as its king; he appoints Ananel as high priest and brings Hyrcanus back from exile; Cleopatra is given Herod's palm groves at Jericho
36 BC	Herod replaces Ananel with Aristobulus II, the brother of Mariamne I; he drowns Aristobulus at Jericho

35 BC	Mark Antony summons Herod to explain the drowning of Aristobulus
33 BC	Mark Antony divorces Octavian's sister to free himself to pursue Cleopatra
32 BC	Herod initiates a war against Malchus and the Nabateans
31 BC	An earthquake shakes Judea; Herod delivers an inspirational speech; Octavian defeats Mark Antony at the Battle of Actium; Antony flees with Cleopatra to Egypt
30 BC	Mark Antony and Cleopatra commit suicide; Octavian is triumphant as Rome's sole ruler; Herod executes Hyrcanus on suspicion of treason; Herod pledges allegiance to Octavian at Rhodes
29 BC	Herod executes Mariamne I
28 BC	Herod executes Alexandra; he initiates a long-term building campaign in Israel
27 BC	Octavian is renamed Caesar Augustus; the Roman Republic becomes the Roman Empire; Herod builds up Sebaste in the emperor's honor; he marries Malthace
25 BC	Famine in the land; Herod provides relief
23 BC	Herod marries Mariamne II
22 BC	Construction is begun on Caesarea by the Sea and the new palace at Masada; Herod sends his sons Alexander II and Aristobulus III to Rome for education
20 BC	Mary is born to Joachim and Anna
19 BC	Construction begins on the new Jewish temple

17 BC	Herod goes to Rome and brings back his sons
15 BC	Marcus Agrippa tours Judea and is impressed with Herod's abilities
14 BC	Herod tours Asia Minor with Marcus Agrippa
13 BC	Antipater II goes to Rome with Marcus Agrippa
10 BC	The new Jewish temple is dedicated for use
9 BC	Herod initiates a second war with the Nabateans and falls out of favor with Caesar Augustus
8 BC	Nicolaus of Damascus reconciles Herod with Augustus
7 BC	Herod's sons by Mariamne I, Alexander II and Aristobulus III, are tried and executed by their father
6 BC	Mary receives the announcement of her virginal conception at Hanukkah (December)
5 BC	Antipater II goes to Rome but falls out of favor and hurries home; he is tried and imprisoned; Mary visits her aunt Elizabeth; the magi visit Herod; Mary gives birth to Jesus during Sukkot (October); Herod punishes the student protest about the eagle on the temple
4 BC	Antipater II is executed on Herod's command; the baby Jesus is presented in the temple; the magi visit Mary and Joseph in the Bethlehem house; the holy family flees to Egypt; massacre of the Bethlehem boys; Herod dies in late March or early April; the holy family returns to Nazareth via Jerusalem

HERODIAN FAMILY TREE

THE HASMONEAN HOUSE

Alexander Jannaeus

(great-grandson of the clan's founder)

Aristobulus I   John Hyrcanus

Alexander I **+** Alexandra

Aristobulus II   Mariamne I

THE IDUMEAN HOUSE

Antipater I **+** Cyprus

Phasael   **Herod**   Joseph   Pheroras   Salome I

Berenice

HEROD'S WIVES & CHILDREN

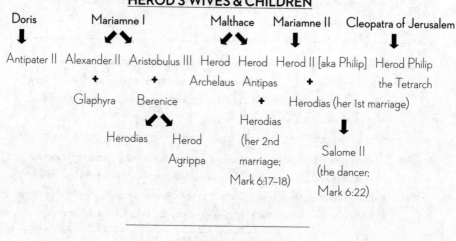

Doris   Mariamne I   Malthace   Mariamne II   Cleopatra of Jerusalem

Antipater II   Alexander II   Aristobulus III   Herod   Herod   Herod II [aka Philip]   Herod Philip

+   **+**   Archelaus   Antipas   **+**   the Tetrarch

Glaphyra   Berenice   **+**   Herodias (her 1st marriage)

Herodias   Herod   Herodias   Salome II

Agrippa   (her 2nd   (the dancer;

marriage;   Mark 6:22)

Mark 6:17–18)

+ = MARRIAGE

↓ = OFFSPRING

I, II, III = DIFFERENT PERSONS (same number = same person)

x

THE ROMAN EMPERORS

Julius Caesar

↙　　　↘ (via Adoption)

Pompey the Great + Julia Major　　Octavian (remamed Caesar Augustus)

↙　　↘ (via Adoption)

Julia the Elder　Tiberius

+　　↓ (via Adoption)

Marcus Agrippa　Caligula

Claudius (grandson of Octavia + Mark Antony)　　　　Octavia
(sister of Octavian)
↓ (via Adoption)　　　　　　　　　　　　　　　(divorced)

Nero　　　　　　　　　　　　　　　　　　　　+

↓　　　　　　　　　　　　　　　　Mark Antony

etc.　　　　　　　　　　　　　　　　+

Egyptian Queen Cleopatra

PROLOGUE

I have been completely fascinated by the historical figure of Herod the Great—known mostly to the world for the few references to him in the biblical narrative of Jesus' birth—since I went on my first rabbinical-guided trip to the Holy Land in 2012 with my brilliant, passionate teacher Ray Vander Laan. Ray changed everything for me when he set fire to my faith by explaining what the Scriptures—written originally in Hebrew and Greek—really meant.

He explained that the Bible has been translated incorrectly for centuries and, as a result, all kinds of damage has been done. For example, on the first day of our study we stood at the site of David's famous confrontation with Goliath the Philistine.

"How many of you know what Jesus and his earthly father, Joseph, did for a living before Jesus became a rabbi at the age of thirty?" Ray inquired.

Every member of our group answered, "He was a carpenter."

"Actually," Ray responded, "he wasn't a carpenter. The word in the New Testament used to describe their profession is *tekton*, and it means an architect or builder."

Well, first century AD Israel was a desert and still technically is. There was practically no buildable wood available in Jesus' time. The cedars of Lebanon had to be cut down and made into rafts and floated along the Mediterranean coastline to Joppa (Tel Aviv), broken apart, and then carried to the various construction sites all over the country. Jesus and Joseph would have worked with small trees (balsam, olive, sycamore, and so on), but the rest of their work would have been with stone.

At this point in the tour I was thinking, *Oh no! I'm stuck for ten days with a guy who doesn't even know the Bible!* But Ray explained the critical point: when King James commissioned an English translation in 1604, the translators of the New Testament were all English and had never been to Israel. So they understandably assumed that the word *tekton* meant "carpenter" because their reference point was their own verdant, lush English countryside.

Then Ray leaned in and spoke four astonishing words that set my heart on fire: *Jesus was a stonemason!*

Suddenly all the scriptures I had learned about rocks and stones came to life: "Let the one who has never sinned throw the first stone!" (John 8:7 NLT); "Upon this rock I will build my church" (Matthew 16:18 NLT); "The stone the builders rejected has become the cornerstone" (Matthew 21:42 NIV); and so many more.

"Ray," I asked, "if we can get something as simple as that so wrong, what more are we getting wrong?"

He smiled at me and with a twinkle answered, "Everything."

Later we visited the magnificent ruins of so many of Herod's brilliant architectural wonders, and Ray began to tell us more about the unbelievable life story of King Herod, the self-proclaimed king of the Jews. One site in particular was Herod's palace in Bethlehem, named Herodium, where he was eventually buried following an excruciating death as a broken, defeated, and horribly disfigured man.

Suddenly, Ray took off his trademark "Michigan Ray" hat and threw it on the dirt around him. "*Herod!*" he screamed into the wind, creating an echo that reverberated through the ruins. "*Herod! Herod! Herod! Was it worth it? Was it worth it?*"

Herod's life was marked by triumph, tragedy, murder, debauchery, and political intrigue. For me, the story of Herod the Great is the "greatest story *never* told," while Jesus' is the greatest story *ever* told.

In this book you will learn why I believe both to be true.

What follows is the story of evil personified in King Herod, contrasted with the living hope of Jesus told through the story of Mary, the mother of Jesus, who will forever be known as the young virgin who was chosen to give birth to the architect of creation and the builder of all things righteous and good.

To the *true* King of kings, our Lord and Savior, Jesus the Messiah.

Kathie Lee Gifford
Franklin, TN

HISTORICAL NOTE

Though this book isn't a work of fiction, it nonetheless has all the elements of a good novel: plot arc, dialogue, characterizations, conflict, turning points, and so on. King Herod's biography forms a powerful, instructive, sometimes-thrilling but often-tragic saga. You will encounter his story of bluster and bloodshed in all its bleak detail. But interwoven into the macro narrative is a quieter, humbler thread of hope and redemption—the backstory of a teenaged girl named Mary who gave birth to God's Messiah.

The primary sources for Herod's biography are two works by the ancient historian Josephus: *Jewish Antiquities* and *The Jewish War*. My quotations of these sources normally come from Harvard University Press's volumes in the Loeb Classical Library, which have the advantage of printing the original Greek across the page from the English for easy reference. I have also consulted G. A. Williamson's edition of *The Jewish War* (Penguin Classics, 1959; revised, 1981), as well as William Whiston's standby edition of *The Works of Josephus*, the origins of which go back to 1736.

The main source of information about Mary, of course, is the New Testament. My Bible quotations in this book typically come from the New King James Version, but other versions such as the New International Version (NIV) or New Living Translation (NLT) are sometimes used if they make more sense in context. For the ancient church traditions about Mary's backstory, I have made frequent reference to the handy anthology by J. K. Elliott, *A Synopsis of the Apocryphal Nativity and Infancy Narratives*. Among the ancient sources that Elliott has collected about Mary's parents and early life, the most helpful text that he included (because it was the first to be written after the time of the apostles) is *The Original Gospel of James*. Though this text has some legendary aspects to it, even so, its recollections about Mary reflect ancient Christian spirituality and may contain nuggets of historical truth.

Usually, I have quoted these ancient documents the way I found them translated into English in whatever book I was consulting. However, since those translations were sometimes unclear, I have freely adapted them in this book for the sake of giving you the best possible reading experience. Other times, I have availed myself of artistic license to paraphrase the sources or imagine things that the ancient characters might have said. Always, my quotations and imaginations are grounded in historical texts and my expertise about the way ancient people thought and spoke. As I said previously, while this book isn't a work of fiction, it is a narrative, so it should read like a good one.

Of the many modern biographies written about Herod, I consulted a select few and found myself returning again and again to the one I consider the best of them: Michael Grant's *Herod the Great* (Weidenfeld and Nicolson, 1971). Some other books that I found helpful, and so should be listed here, are:

- Adam Kolman Marshak, *The Many Faces of Herod the Great* (Eerdmans, 2015)
- Bieke Mahieu, *Between Rome and Jerusalem: Herod the Great and His Sons in Their Struggle for Recognition* (Peeters, 2012)
- Ehud Netzer, *The Architecture of Herod, the Great Builder* (Mohr Siebeck, 2006)
- Albert Pietersma and Benjamin G. Wright, *A New English Translation of the Septuagint* (Oxford, 2007)
- Peter Richardson, *Herod: King of the Jews and Friend of the Romans* (Fortress, 1999)
- Samuel Rocca, *Herod's Judaea* (Mohr Siebeck, 2008)
- Mark Toher (translator), *Nicolaus of Damascus: The Life of Augustus and The Autobiography* (Cambridge, 2017)

Although I have composed the "historical" aspect of this book, bringing my expertise as an ancient church scholar, university professor, and historical novelist to the table, the truth is that Kathie Lee Gifford was the book's driving force from beginning to end. Not only was the original idea hers, as well as the format, but she and I also had extensive (and prayerful) consultations along the way. Her heart, vision, and insight are on every page.

To provide the reader with a sense of how our collaboration worked, Kathie and I recorded some of our conversations. We have attached edited versions of those lively exchanges at the end of the book. Like a musical composition that adds a "coda" to bring the work to a fitting conclusion, we intend these codas to put finishing touches on the chapters. Perhaps the reader will sense a symmetry between the dramatic events of the Roman past and the challenges of modern life. People often say that history repeats itself. The struggles within Herod's household—as well as God's redemptive work behind the scenes— have many parallels today. The codas remind us that God is just as active now as he was in biblical times. Kathie's reflections on the chapter topics will help our readers process the story on a deeper level and take away lasting insights and relevance for daily life.

All of us from a certain generation (and I am one of them) have Kathie Lee Gifford's voice in our heads. Her bubbly personality, warm spirit, quirky humor, and distinctive verbal inflections are part of our everyday lives. Never did I type a word of this book without an awareness of what she wanted to say, how she wanted to communicate it, and what impact she wanted to achieve. If there was ever a collaborative book in which two people unified their distinctive gifts into a single offering, this is it. I hope you hear Kathie's voice as you read—her wisdom, warmth, and most of all, her love for the Messiah. May this book enlighten, entertain, and bless you from cover to cover.

Dr. Bryan M. Litfin
Lynchburg, VA

CHAPTER 1

A KING IS BORN

The terrible pains weren't what drove King Herod to raise the knife above his flabby, bloated breast in a final act of suicide. True enough, there was pain in him—an agony that never relented. Coughs and convulsions wracked his aged body. A fire burned inside him. His entrails were ulcerated along their entire length. Though hunger gnawed at his belly, Herod couldn't satisfy his appetite lest eating food kindle the fires anew. His feet ached constantly, for they were engorged with fluid and swollen like ripe melons. Gangrene had even caused his genitals to rot away. The man-part that Herod had so proudly considered a sign of his virility was now engulfed in cankers where flies laid their eggs and maggots wriggled as they emerged. Pus oozed where potency once had been. Yes, there was pain in Herod's body. But that was not what drove him to raise the deadly blade above his breast.

It was the itching.

So maddening was this itch that Herod believed he could no longer stand it. The prickly tingle radiated from his blackened groin until it tormented every part of his skin. Though no amount of scratching could relieve it, the red stripes on his flesh and the blood beneath his fingernails showed that he had tried. *I can't take it anymore*, Herod finally decided. *Now I commend my soul to God!*

With great effort, the obese king raised himself up on his sweat-soaked bed. His hand loomed above his head. The blade glinted in the lamplight. Somewhere, deep in the fog of his madness, Herod wondered if the little fruit knife that the servants had brought him could strike a deadly blow. He was determined to do the deed nonetheless. By the force of his will, he would make it work. It would be a dramatic and fitting conclusion to his long reign. For thirty-three years, he had ruled Judea and built great monuments that would stand for centuries. His whole life had been spent helping God's chosen people learn to live with Rome's power and glory. Now the Jews would remember his tragic end as well. Perhaps they would even admire his courage and forti-tude. Herod would become one of those celebrated men of the past, men like Samson, Saul, or Socrates, who had committed noble suicide.

But before Herod could go through with the great and memorable deed, a man entered the room. It was Achiabus, Herod's cousin. Surely he would try to prevent the suicide, lest he be accused of the crime himself. Herod quickly lowered his hand and hid the knife in the rumpled bedclothes. The sheets were made of silk imported from the East—the finest in the world. Now they were fouled with pus and blood, and probably much urine too. Herod wasn't quite sure what was happening down there. But no matter. Soon he would be dead. Then God would usher the king of the Jews into a blessed paradise.

The news that Achiabus had come to report actually comforted Herod. Caesar Augustus, the emperor of Rome and mightiest man on earth, had replied to Herod's letter. All the facts about the rebellion of Herod's son had been reported to Augustus, and he had ruled in Herod's favor. "Your son Antipater is guilty of treason," the letter declared. "I leave it to your judgment whether to execute him or send him into exile."

Exile? Such a fate was too good for so despicable a traitor!

Herod's thoughts turned to Antipater, who was locked in a cell not far away in the royal palace at Jericho. He was named after Herod's beloved father. Long ago, back before everything took a dire turn, the young Antipater had shown great promise. Herod had hoped his firstborn son might one day rule Judea as next in the royal line.

But then, like everyone else in Herod's clan, Antipater had turned treason-ous. Instead of honoring his father like a good son should do, he had plotted and caroused with Herod's enemies. Antipater even had the audacity to com-plain about Herod's longevity! "I'll be an old man by the time I gain the throne," he had grumbled. "I wish my father would hurry up and die." And to make sure that he did—sooner rather than later—Antipater had imported deadly poison from Egypt. But the assassination plot had been discovered. Now the despicable backstabber was locked up in chains, awaiting trial for his crimes.

Herod shook his head at the colossal mistake he had almost made.

I can't believe I ever wanted that wretch to inherit my kingdom! I need to put him to death very soon . . .

The truth was, no one in the Herodian house could be trusted. One by one, each of their hearts had grown corrupt. Their lust for power had consumed them. To survive, Herod had been forced to kill them all. His beloved queen Mariamne: executed and embalmed, though never forgotten. Her brother: drowned in a swimming pool. Her two sons: strangled like a pair of dinner fowl in a Samaritan dungeon. And there were more. So many, many more. Deaths beyond count since the first day Herod began to rule. It was a level of bloodguilt beyond remission. Perhaps God wouldn't be so merciful after all.

Perhaps I am not worthy to be called the king of the Jews?

It was time to find out. Achiabus had stepped away from the bed. He now stood across the room, whispering with one of the doctors. Both men covered their noses with kerchiefs, for the stench of Herod's fecal leakage bothered those who didn't dwell in it. Herod, however, had grown used to the smell.

You can do this, he told himself, probing his swollen heart to find enough courage to go through with the heroic deed. He wiped pus from his fingers on the silken sheets, then gripped the knife's hilt in his pudgy fist. It was only a paring knife, intended for an apple that the servants had brought. Its blade wasn't meant to pierce through so much fat. But it would be enough. Herod would make it so. With a sudden jerk, he yanked the knife from its hiding place and raised it again above his head.

Yet the king who had ordered so many deaths couldn't decree his own.

"Stop!" shouted Achiabus as he darted across the room and seized Herod's wrist in an iron grip.

The blade hung poised for a moment, savage like a demon's fang, not caring whether it stabbed a Judean apple or the king of the Jews. With all his ebbing strength, Herod struggled to plunge the knife into his chest. Achiabus refused to let go.

The two men were locked in mortal combat. It would be a fight to the death. But like all the wars in Herod's life, this was a battle he did not intend to lose.

Not far from the Jericho palace where Herod lay dying, a young woman likewise reclined in severe pain upon a bed. But unlike the king, she felt no silken sheets beneath her sweaty back, nor was she surrounded by a host of doctors and servants. In fact, she wasn't lying on a true bed at all. When her hands spasmodically clawed at her surroundings, seeking something to grip when waves of agony threatened to overwhelm her, all she could find were clumps of scattered straw. Her betrothed had made this simple pallet for his pregnant fiancée in a cave that served to shelter animals.[1] The day had come for Mary of Nazareth to give birth.

While all of Judea waited to find out what would happen to King Herod—whether he would recover, or, if he died, who would succeed him—Mary labored in total obscurity. No one who passed the cave's entrance bothered to notice the Jewish teenager struggling to deliver the baby in her womb. Not far away, the city of Bethlehem bustled with visitors, for the great Caesar Augustus had commanded a census to be taken in his Roman realm. Every man was required to return to his hometown to register. Joseph had recently arrived with Mary, at first seeking lodging with a local family member. But since that house's guest room was already occupied, the travelers had to settle for more humble accommodations. Desperate to find shelter, Joseph had carried his wife into a nearby cave where Passover lambs were birthed by priestly shepherds. There, in a place that no one noticed, a child would be born whom the world would never forget.

Though King Herod feared that some other king of Israel might supplant him, he never could have imagined that a ruler's beginnings could be so humble. Certainly, Herod himself didn't start out that way. The tormented invalid with a dagger in his hand and a death wish in his heart was once a man of power and prestige. He had brimmed with the energy and confidence that befitted a king. "Herod's genius was matched by his physical constitution," wrote his ancient biographer, the Jewish historian Josephus. "As a fighter he was irresistible; and

---

1. Mary was a virgin engaged to be married to Joseph at the time of her Son's birth. We know this because Scripture says they were still "betrothed" when they journeyed to Bethlehem (Luke 2:5). Nevertheless, they were essentially spouses at that time. Ancient Jewish betrothals were more binding than modern-day engagements. Back then, the engaged couple was considered legally married in every way except for sexual consummation and cohabitation. To break the betrothal agreement would actually require a "divorce" (see Matthew 1:19, where the Greek word for divorce, *apoluo*, is used). Joseph was acting as Mary's husband when he brought her to Bethlehem, even though they had not had any sexual union (Matthew 1:25).

at practice [the] spectators were often struck with astonishment at the precision with which he threw the javelin, the unerring aim with which he bent the bow." Herod had "pre-eminent gifts of soul and body." Everyone considered him to be "blessed by good fortune."

Josephus recorded an early glimpse of Herod when he described how the future king sojourned in Petra as a boy. Herod's world at the time was in turmoil, for a civil war had broken out in Judea. His father, Antipater—the man for whom Herod's firstborn son was later named—found himself caught in a whirlpool of violence and aristocratic intrigues. The Jewish throne was up for grabs and two Judean princes wanted it. Though Antipater wasn't a contender, he was second-in-command to John Hyrcanus, one of the two brothers who could lay claim to the royal title. If Hyrcanus won, Antipater would have a lot to gain. But a conniver named Aristobulus hoped to take out his elder brother and seize the throne instead.

Soon, Aristobulus began to prevail. When Antipater perceived that his friend Hyrcanus was about to be destroyed, taking his own fortunes down with him, he sprang into action. A safe haven had to be found for the imperiled aristocrat. Fortunately, Antipater knew where to find one. He convinced Hyrcanus to take refuge among the Nabateans. Antipater also sent his wife, Cyprus, and their five children—four sons and an infant daughter—to this adjacent kingdom. The family slipped out of Jerusalem at night and traveled 150 miles across the desert to the stronghold of Petra. There, they would be cared for by Aretas, king of the Nabateans and Cyprus's relative. That king's mighty army would soon march to Jerusalem and dethrone the evil Aristobulus.

As the nine-year-old Herod approached the city of Petra, his boyish eyes gazed in wonder at his surroundings. What he encountered impressed him beyond belief. He never had seen a city like this before. Petra lay in the red-rock desert of Arabia, a region that today is in the country of Jordan. The Nabatean capital was nestled in a cleft surrounded by mountains. Its easiest entry route was through a narrow canyon with towering walls. At times, the gorge was so tight that the four sons of Antipater could join hands as they walked through it with the outermost boys brushing the walls on either side. Eventually, the narrow defile opened to reveal the city's stark and austere beauty, all of it hidden from the eyes of outsiders. It was a secret haven reserved for the chosen few.

Though Petra was a remote and exotic place deep in the desert, it was also lush and luxurious—an artificial oasis made possible by clever Nabatean waterworks. Dams controlled the flash floods and cisterns retained the water for future use. Pipes distributed the water wherever it needed to go. Dazzled by what he saw at Petra, Herod would spend the rest of his life creating well-watered desert strongholds. Verdant gardens had no business existing in such arid places unless a man of great genius birthed them out of the sands. As Herod looked upon these wonders, he vowed to become that kind of man.

Yet the invincible security of Petra, while comforting to those who lived within its natural walls, turned out to be an illusion. The young Herod soon gained a valuable lesson about who held true power in his world. Never, through all his later years, would he forget it. This early revelation marked Herod so deeply that it became the core tenet of his future foreign policy. What had he learned?

King Aretas came slinking back to Petra with a wounded army after being booted from the confines of Jerusalem. His men were demoralized. Along the route of their retreat, Aristobulus's forces had ambushed them, slaying six thousand Nabatean soldiers. Though Herod's father, Antipater, had survived the attack, many others had been killed.

Why did the once-triumphant army of Aretas suddenly pick up and leave Jerusalem?

What iron pry bar had been strong enough to dislodge them?

It was no army that kicked the Nabateans out of the Holy City, at least not by the direct application of force. Nor was it a plague among the troops, nor a hefty bribe, nor a sudden change of political allegiance. It was something that everyone had long feared. Now, at last, it had come true.

The Romans had arrived in Judea.

And they were there to stay.

The new power in Judea had ordered King Aretas of Petra, "Withdraw, you trespasser, or you shall become our enemy and face our wrath."

Immediately, Aretas obeyed, for he understood what had just happened. Jerusalem's future was now intertwined with the distant city of Rome. The Jewish homeland had just become occupied territory. Once again, God's chosen people would have to learn how to live under foreign rule.

Yet the Romans weren't content only to conquer Judea. Down in the Arabian desert, Petra presented another enticing target. The lucrative spice trade that King Aretas controlled was well worth possessing, so the Romans decided that the Nabateans needed to come under their thumb like everyone else. The Roman war machine kicked into motion and marched south to capture Petra.

At this critical moment, Antipater gave his son the lesson he would never forget. The Roman legions found they couldn't penetrate the canyons to capture Petra, so they began to ravage the surrounding countryside. Soon the troops devastated the Nabatean kingdom in their search for food. They ransacked the local farms and date groves until even what meager supplies the peasantry had managed to stockpile ran out. So what did Antipater do? Even though he was married to a woman of the Nabatean aristocracy, he rounded up wagonloads of precious grain from Judea and supplied the Roman troops—the enemy!—with the victuals and matériel they needed to finish the job at Petra. Thus he betrayed the people and place that had provided refuge to his wife and five children.

With the Roman army reenergized, King Aretas had no choice but to parlay for peace. Young Herod could only watch, astounded, as his father informed the king that even impregnable Petra would be no match for Roman might. "You must buy them off or your country will be destroyed," Antipater told his friend. "Three hundred gold talents is their price. You'd be wise to pay it."

Cornered and out of options, King Aretas gave in. He paid the enormous ransom so the legions would retreat to Judea. Yet now the Nabateans, like the Judeans before them, carried the weight of defeat on their shoulders. They no longer possessed absolute freedom. The shadow of eagles' wings loomed over them.

This boyhood lesson about the contours of power was one that Herod took to heart. Its implications would determine every facet of his future reign. When Rome decided to get serious, the savvy leader—as Antipater had so quickly shown—learned to play nice and make the best of the new situation. Fighting for independence was a fool's errand. Why bang your head against a brick wall? The wall wouldn't crack but your forehead surely would. Far better to get along with Rome; for the man who could give that city what it wanted could live very well indeed.

Perhaps he could even live like a king.

CHAPTER 2

THE GLORY OF ROME

What Herod learned from watching his father's political maneuvers at Petra—that cooperating with the Romans was a lot smarter than fighting them—was the exact opposite of what most Jews believed. Whereas Antipater showed his son how to make deals with the new overlords, the typical Jewish father taught his boys to detest foreign domination. Several centuries later, a rabbi would urge his people to take a more collegial approach by offering the advice, "When you enter a city, follow its customs." But back in the days of Herod, few Jews thought that way. The Jews hated what Rome had to offer. Herod, on the other hand, found himself fascinated by it.

As loathsome as it was to the Jews for their land to be conquered by the Romans, the worst affront of all was a specific act of desecration and blasphemy that occurred in 63 BC. This fateful deed struck a terrible blow to the collective consciousness of worldwide Jewry. When the victorious Roman general Pompey the Great walked into the Most Holy Place of the Jerusalem temple, a line of no return was crossed.

The battle to possess the temple mount had been fierce. When its largest tower finally came crashing down, the Roman legionaries poured in like a biblical plague of locusts. The holocaust that day was complete. Twelve thousand Jews fell before the stabbing swords of the invaders. Surrounded by the bodies of the fallen—some of them dead, others still dribbling out their life-blood onto the pavement—General Pompey approached the temple itself. He crossed the sacred precincts and ascended the stairs of the sanctuary. This foreign conqueror, a devotee of the pagan gods, intended to see for himself what was inside. "Not light was the sin committed against the sanctuary," the historian Josephus later remarked, "which before that time had never been entered or seen."

The religious taboo that Pompey was about to violate carried the weight of the centuries behind it. The idea of the Most Holy Place—also referred

THE GLORY OF ROME

to as the holy of holies—goes far back in biblical history. Before there was a fixed temple in Jerusalem, the Israelites had their tabernacle, a portable temple made of poles and fabric that could be collapsed and moved from place to place. It was carried by the wandering Israelites until they finally settled in the Holy Land.

The heart of the tabernacle—and later, the temple—was its inner sanctum where the Lord dwelled in all his burning, blazing glory. God instructed Moses that the priest "is not to come whenever he chooses into the Most Holy Place behind the curtain . . . or else he will die" (Leviticus 16:2 NIV). Only one thing could allow the Jewish high priest to stand before God and live: an animal offering that made atonement for one's sins. The pathway into God's presence was stained red with the blood of sacrifice.

None of these restrictions, however, bothered Pompey when he opened the curtain that screened the Most Holy Place. He walked straight inside. Pompey didn't die that day, for the ark of the covenant had been captured by the Babylonians many centuries earlier, so the divine presence no longer dwelled above the mercy seat. Instead, Pompey found some other ritual implements in the temple's inner sanctum: a golden table, a menorah, sacred pitchers and vessels, spices, and a huge sum of money. Surprisingly, and much to his credit, the victorious Roman general didn't take any of this for himself. He merely ordered the temple to be cleansed and to resume its services the next day.

When General Pompey left the sanctuary after a quick inspection, he wasn't thinking about the blood of animal sacrifices upon an altar. Pompey had a different kind of blood on his mind. Someone had to dispose of the twelve thousand Jewish corpses that now littered the temple precincts. It was time to clean up the city and get it working again. Pompey was in Jerusalem to install a new regime.

From then on, Judea would no longer be a free kingdom with its own ruling family. Rome had arrived on the scene. And wherever Rome went, so did domination, oppression, and a constant flow of tribute to the most powerful city on earth. A new lord had taken up residence in the Holy Land of God—a lord who would shed the blood of his enemies without blinking an eye. Herod's only question was: Will I have the courage to do the same when the time comes?

Rome. Its very name signifies august majesty and timeless glory. The Roman army, comprised of highly trained legionaries with the finest weapons and equipment, is synonymous with brutality and conquest. Ancient Rome was a city of which no one in the Mediterranean world could be unaware—or unafraid.

In 63 BC, when Pompey walked into the Most Holy Place and young Herod was still hiding in the Arabian desert, an important event happened in the distant capital city. A child named Octavian was born on Rome's Palatine Hill to a father of modest political standing. No one at the time could have guessed how great a destiny lay ahead of this newborn baby.

Despite the obscurity of Octavian's family, legends about his miraculous birth eventually developed. One account says that some sort of omen in Rome predicted that "nature was pregnant with a king for the Roman people." To prevent the arrival of this predicted king, the senate issued a decree of death against every male child who was born that year. However, a few senators made sure the decree was never enforced. Each of these men hoped that perhaps his child might be the promised one.

Another legend recounts the story of Octavian's conception. When Octavian's mother visited the temple of the sun god Apollo, she fell asleep there. In the dark of night, a snake glided up to her bed, remained for a while, then left. Upon awakening, she felt she needed to ritually cleanse herself as if she had had sexual intercourse. A snakeskin mark appeared on her body, so visible that she never again went to the public baths where it would be seen. Nine months later, she gave birth to Octavian. His father dreamed that the sun had risen from his wife's womb.

The original sources of these legends were independent of the four Gospels of the New Testament. Even so, they recorded similar omens.

A prophecy of a coming king . . .
A death decree against innocent boys . . .
An otherworldly conception . . .
A symbolic dawn.

What dark forces inspired these stories that so closely—yet falsely—imitated the accounts in Scripture?

Mystery now shrouds the events that happened at the time of Octavian's birth. Myth and folklore obscure the origins of this great man. What historians know for certain is what happened next. The boy grew up to become the most powerful man on earth: Caesar Augustus, the first ruler of the Roman Empire.

Little did Herod suspect that one day, the great Augustus would be his intimate friend. The boy hiding in Petra had no way of knowing that his fate was bound to the emperor's. Nor could Herod have imagined the great deeds he would achieve on the Roman stage: that he would build a mighty fortress to honor Mark Antony, face the seductive powers of Queen Cleopatra, or navigate the schemes of countless politicians and princes who each left their mark on the Roman world. All Herod could know was the one indubitable truth he had learned in Petra: that try as he might to hide in a desert stronghold, no place on earth was beyond the reach of Rome's bloodstained hands.

CHAPTER 3

A FATEFUL CHOICE

Herod, the son of Antipater, was the ripe age of twenty-six when he finally stepped onto the public stage and embarked on a political career. By then he was a much different person than the boy who had taken refuge among the Nabateans at Petra. He was a grown man, ready to assume leadership. His father had just made him the governor of Galilee, a real prize for a rising politician. Herod would soon find himself put to the test. How he handled that test would determine what kind of ruler he would be.

In many ways, the young Herod looked to his father as a role model, taking his cues from Antipater's combination of audacity, ruthlessness, and charm. Antipater had surely prospered under the Roman occupation. After Pompey the Great stabilized Jerusalem, he left the region in the care of local underlings. Jerusalem was just as glad to see Pompey take his pagan feet elsewhere. The Jews buried the bodies of their kinsmen and tried to pull themselves together after years of civil war—the very infighting that had caused the Romans to intervene in the first place. Although the new Roman overlords had reduced Jerusalem's dominion, Antipater grew increasingly powerful in the reconfigured politics of the remaining kingdom. Soon he would even find himself at the epicenter of Roman affairs, providing salvation at a key moment. That timely favor would not be forgotten. Rome had a very long memory.

In the years after Pompey conquered Jerusalem, he got caught up in a deadly struggle against the great military genius Julius Caesar. Although the two of them used to be confederates, and Caesar was even Pompey's father-in-law, their relationship had soured and now only one man could be left standing. Pompey took a bad loss in battle and fled to Egypt. There, the local pharaoh, thinking he would win the favor of the victorious Caesar, apprehended Pompey and had him decapitated. The pharaoh's henchmen allowed Pompey's headless body to wash about in the sea before finally burning it.

Though Caesar was disgusted when Pompey's severed head was presented to him as a gift, the news of Pompey's death caused rejoicing among the Jews. They had not forgotten how the insolent conqueror had profaned their temple. An unknown Jewish poet even wrote a psalm to celebrate his death. What was the essence of Pompey's crime? "He did not consider that he was a human, nor did he consider the hereafter. He said, 'I will be lord of earth and sea,' and he did not recognize that God is great."

With his rival Pompey out of the way, Julius Caesar turned his attention to Egypt's internal affairs. His romantic dalliance with Queen Cleopatra became the talk of everyone across the Roman world. By one account, the flirty twentysomething queen even snuck into his palace while rolled up in a bed quilt to seduce him.

Soon, however, an urgent threat emerged in the Egyptian city of Alexandria. An army led by the pharaoh, Cleopatra's brother (who was also her husband), arose against the two lovestruck politicians. Although a faraway king named Mithridates was on his way to provide relief, his troops got held up along the route. Now, Julius Caesar was in great peril. He didn't have enough soldiers to defend himself. That was when an unexpected savior swooped in to help: Antipater, the father of Herod.

Antipater marched down the sea road from Judea to Egypt, bringing not only three thousand heavily armed Jewish soldiers but many Nabateans too. At first, the local Jews of Egypt didn't want to support Caesar, but Antipater convinced them to cast their lot with the new man in town. Instead of opposing the invaders, the Egyptian Jews agreed to resupply Antipater's army.

Mithridates and Antipater now advanced into Egypt. When the city of Pelusium put up resistance, Antipater was the first attacker to tear down a section of the wall and leap through the gap at the head of his troops. Pelusium succumbed to the onslaught. Continuing farther into the Nile Delta, Antipater's men fought bravely against Caesar's enemies. At one point in the battle, Mithridates's right wing broke and his troops fled before the Egyptians. Antipater wheeled around from the left and came crashing into the pursuing army. Though Mithridates was saved that day, he lost eight hundred men; Antipater lost only eighty.

Now the tide had turned. The invaders struck the Egyptians hard and annihilated the enemy. Total victory belonged to Julius Caesar. Once all the facts were discerned, Antipater came out looking like a hero. It was said that every part of his body bore scars from his acts of valor. When one man had the audacity to accuse Antipater of disloyalty, Antipater threw off his garments and displayed his many wounds. Each scar proved his devotion to Rome. From then on, Caesar held Antipater in high esteem. This led to Antipater being made the chief minister of Judea, serving under John Hyrcanus, whom Pompey had restored as the rightful high priest.

Antipater immediately began to deploy his newfound power to help his family. In 47 BC, he made two appointments. His oldest son, Phasael, was put in charge of Jerusalem. And of course, up in Galilee, the young and promising Herod was given the reins. This was Herod's first step into what was about to become a lifetime of rule over God's chosen people.

The Galilee of Herod's day was famous for its fruitful lands and productive agriculture. Unlike in the more arid south, the Mediterranean rains fell often in Galilee, making it a desirable place to grow crops and cultivate orchards and vineyards. Under good governance, the region ought to thrive. Herod intended to make that happen.

Of course, the most famous part of Galilee was its inland freshwater sea. This lake is almost completely surrounded by mountains, which subject it to terrible gales that sweep down unexpectedly from the heights. But when the weather is tranquil, the Sea of Galilee is very productive. Fishermen have plied its waters since before recorded history. Herod, the new regional administrator, soon found that the export of salted fish, with its associated taxation, piled up heaps of money. Though the commoners in this region had to work hard, whoever ruled Galilee was bound to get rich. It was the perfect place for an up-and-coming governor to get a good start.

Yet it didn't take long before Herod found himself facing a major challenge. He discovered a gang of bandits, led by a man named Ezekias, roaming the countryside. Herod was determined to destroy them. Who were these outlaws?

The ancient historian Josephus, whose narrative typically favors the Roman point of view, used the Greek word *lestes* to describe them. This term often refers to robbers, as when the New Testament describes the men who were crucified on either side of Jesus. But depending on one's perspective, Ezekias's bandits could be viewed as freedom fighters with a kind of Robin Hood status—outlaws who lived on the margins of society and tried to overthrow the dominant power that was oppressing the common people. On the other hand, let's not romanticize these men. This was no merry band in the forest but a group of violent insurrectionists who weren't afraid to shed blood for their cause. In Jesus' day, the Zealots were men like this, and the revolutionary Barabbas was also called a *lestes*.

Herod ruthlessly uprooted these outlaws plaguing his territory. He used overwhelming force to round them up and bring them into custody. But he was faced with a dilemma, for he was a man of two worlds. His father, Antipater, descended from the Idumeans, who had accepted Judaism as their faith. That made it Herod's religion as well. Yet in those days, Antipater was acting more like a traditional Roman, mowing down all opponents without remorse. Which path would his son take? Would Herod act like a Roman or a Jew? The ancient Jewish law didn't authorize the death penalty for the crime of robbery. Even the crime of murder required witnesses, and the bar for capital punishment was high. Such serious matters were supposed to be brought before Israel's judges. Only if a man was found guilty by the religious court was a penalty inflicted on him.

Herod opted for the more violent path. Roman brutality, not the law of Moses, had taken hold of his mind. Instead of giving the captured men a fair trial, he ordered the whole gang to be executed. No doubt, Herod debated this course of action before issuing the order. The decision to kill would come with consequences, and the young ruler knew it. The captured men were Jews like him. They were his spiritual kinsmen, fellow children of the Lord. Herod held their fate in his hands. All eyes looked to him—some pleading for mercy, others eager for the carnage. Absolute silence hung over the crowd. Then, with a flick of his fingers, Herod ordered the slaughter to commence. The swords came out. With a flash of shiny metal, the bandits' blood stained the soil of Galilee.

Herod's quick and decisive action against the bandits earned him praise in the Roman province of Syria. The outlaws had been raiding there, so the Roman authorities were happy to have them gone. Hymns were even sung in the Syrian cities and villages about Herod's exploits. But down in Jerusalem, trouble was brewing. News of the slaughter had reached the streets. The bandits' grieving mothers made such an outcry in the temple courts that the populace turned against Herod. Now, the Sanhedrin—the great Jewish council led by its high priest, John Hyrcanus—summoned Herod to a trial.

Though Herod came, he brought along a sizable bodyguard—one big enough to protect him yet not so big as to look like an invasion force. His militarized presence intimidated the Sanhedrin, causing the councilmen to dither about what to do. Then one Jewish elder named Samaias stood up and complained about Herod's arrogance. Usually, he said, people who are tried before the Sanhedrin appear humble and fearful. "But this fine fellow Herod, who is accused of murder . . . stands here clothed in purple, with the hair of his head carefully arranged and with his soldiers round him." It was like nothing they'd seen before. Samaias even predicted that one day, Herod would come back and get revenge on the Sanhedrin and its high priest.

Though it was clear that Herod had violated the Jewish law with his summary execution of the bandits, the Romans exerted strong pressure on Hyrcanus to let Herod go. The Sanhedrin, however, finally found its backbone. The Jewish elders decided to put Herod to death. He had broken the commandment "You shall not murder" (Exodus 20:13). To avoid his looming execution, Herod fled Jerusalem with his bodyguard. After he was gone, the Sanhedrin stripped him of his rule over Galilee. Yet far from humbling Herod, the decision inflamed him all the more. A single driving emotion burned within Herod's soul: an unquenchable lust for revenge.

Herod took refuge in Damascus with the Roman governor of Syria, who was still basking in relief that the bandit raids had been eliminated in his realm. As a reward, he gave Herod a prestigious government post in Samaria. Newly empowered again, the vengeful Herod raised up an army and returned to attack Jerusalem. But Antipater and Phasael rushed out of the city to calm Herod down. "You are a great success," Herod's father and brother reminded him. "Why ruin it by starting a war against the high priest? God might not favor you, and you might lose." Begrudgingly, Herod agreed to sit tight and wait for his day of revenge to come.

Antipater's advice to let fate take its course turned out to be wise. The Syrian governor who admired Herod was the cousin of Julius Caesar. This local official made sure that his powerful Roman relative heard all about the exploits of the rising superstar in the east. Caesar hadn't forgotten the timely aid rendered by Antipater's army in Egypt. The Jewish troops' bravery on the battlefield had made a huge difference. Now, here was the son of Antipater doing the same thing: getting the job done in good Roman fashion—ruthless and efficient. Herod had gained a powerful patron in Rome.

Unfortunately, though, this newfound favor wouldn't last long. A secret conspiracy was rising against Julius Caesar.

Et tu, Brute?

Most people have heard this imaginary Latin quote from the playwright William Shakespeare. It occurs in his play *Julius Caesar*, first performed in 1599. Shakespeare imagined that this question—"And you, Brutus?"—was what Caesar exclaimed when a gang of conspirators surrounded him on March 15, 44 BC, and stabbed him to death. Brutus had been Caesar's close friend, as dear to him as a son. Now, like Judas Iscariot at a later time, Brutus betrayed his master to mortal enemies.

Though no ancient source records that Caesar uttered these exact Shakespearean words, apparently he said something similar.[1] Whatever Caesar may have said, the fact remained that he was dead. The news shocked everyone, perhaps no one more so than the Jews. They had cast their lot with this Roman leader. He had been grateful for their support and therefore was benevolent toward them. Who would rise up to take his place? And whoever it was, would he be so favorable to the Jews as his predecessor?

Over in Galilee, Herod followed his father's example and scrambled to adjust to the new political reality. And adjust he did, for malleability in the hands of his overlords was one of Herod's foremost traits. He somehow managed to get everyone to like him, even when those same people didn't like each other.

---

1. Suetonius, in his *Lives of the Twelve Caesars*, recorded the assassination like this: "When [Caesar] saw that he was beset on every side by drawn daggers, he muffled his head in his robe, and at the same time drew down its lap to his feet with his left hand, in order to fall more decently, with the lower part of his body also covered. And in this wise he was stabbed with three and twenty wounds, uttering not a word, but merely a groan at the first stroke, though some have written that when Marcus Brutus rushed at him, he said in Greek, 'You too, my child?'"

And yet, who was Herod now?

The conspirators against Julius Caesar had resorted to the age-old tactic of bloody violence to achieve their political aims. Twenty-three dagger strokes had fallen on Caesar's helpless form. But how many slashes of the sword had been required to slaughter the bandits of Galilee? The bloodshed that day was far greater than what happened to Caesar. Like any good Roman, Herod had proved himself willing to murder his enemies. A shadow had darkened his bright future. Herod understood that sometimes—perhaps often—a king had no business being a prince of peace.

CHAPTER 4

RULER ON THE RISE

For someone so gifted and accomplished, Herod surprisingly suffered his whole life with an inferiority complex. His finger was always on the pulse of the people. Their thoughts about him—for good or ill—never strayed far from his mind. The young and rising Herod knew that if he intended to be viewed as a respectable ruler in Israel, he needed a pious wife. Every Jew believed in the divinely ordained goodness of marriage. After all, the first thing God recognized after he made Adam was the complete inadequacy of Adam's situation. When the Lord saw that the original man was alone, he declared it to be "not good" (Genesis 2:18). So God promptly created a woman. And if Adam required Eve, clearly Herod needed a good wife too.

He found one in a woman named Doris. Little is known about her except that she was a native of Jerusalem. Was she a noblewoman? Hardly. At the time of the wedding around 47 BC, Herod didn't see himself as someone who could marry into the Judean royal house. Doris is described somewhat ambiguously by the historian Josephus as "from the common people" yet "not undistinguished." Of course, as Josephus pointed out, Herod himself was still a commoner at this time, an Idumean from outside the Jewish royal family. Evidently Doris possessed sufficient social rank—as well as physical attractiveness, which Herod never failed to consider—to seem like a good match. Before long, she bore Herod his firstborn son, Antipater, named after his grandfather. The new family now had the sign of God's favor upon them.

Marriage and childbearing are deeply ingrained in the Jewish mind, as they reflect the blessing of God. The Hebrew Scriptures overflow with this theme. "Behold, children are a heritage from the LORD," declares Psalm 127:3, and "the fruit of the womb is a reward." God set forth his primordial arrangement for human flourishing in the book of Genesis: "So God created man in

His own image; in the image of God He created him; male and female He created them. Then God blessed them, and God said to them, 'Be fruitful and multiply; fill the earth and subdue it'" (1:27–28).

Of course, like all ancient men, Herod wouldn't have understood the biological mutuality that God had designed into the procreative process. Certainly he couldn't have known about the equal genetic legacy that each parent bequeaths to the child. When Herod looked down at newborn Antipater, still unwashed and bloody in the swaddling cloths, the proud father wouldn't have recognized much of Doris's contribution at all. The ancients viewed the male role in reproduction as sowing seed. This was quite literally their mindset. The Greek word for seed is *sperma*, and the Latin counterpart is *semen*. Ancient fathers believed they sowed their seed in a woman's uterus, where it took root and grew into what it would become. As everyone knew from the agricultural world, organisms drew their essence from their seeds. Sure, the soil in which a plant grew might be influential, as when wine from a certain vine could gain some flavors from the soil. But the main thing was the seed. It was the man's job to create life. The woman was only a passive receptacle for what the man had made.

This was not, of course, the way God actually designed things. The God of Israel had set things up so that salvation would come from the Seed of a woman. God made this clear in Genesis 3:15 after Adam and Eve fell into sin. Speaking to the Serpent, that great enemy of humankind, God declared, "I will put enmity between you and the woman, and between your seed and her Seed; He shall bruise your head, and you shall bruise His heel." No one yet knew who this Seed of the woman would be, least of all Herod. Nor did anyone yet know who would crush the Serpent's head underfoot. All they knew was that God would someday send his deliverer to Israel. That the Savior might be born from a peasant girl in a cave used for birthing animals never crossed anyone's mind!

Yet Herod did know one thing about his seed, and the evidence tells us it began to bother him soon after his wedding. Doris was no blue-blooded queen, which meant Antipater was no highborn prince. Their bloodlines were humble, unremarkable, lacking in nobility. When the marriage was originally contracted, such ancestry had seemed to be enough. But then, as Herod's power grew, he found himself wanting more. A man like him deserved more! Herod wanted to acquire the one name in Judea that signaled royalty . . . prestige . . . Jewish glory from days gone by.

Herod wanted to be a Hasmonean.

The great Hasmonean family had come to power through force of arms, but they were by no means the first Jews to fight in wars. The Israelites had been warriors from the beginning. One of the most prominent themes in the Hebrew Scriptures is *conquest*. Sometimes, God's people were the conquerors, as when they took the promised land from the Canaanites around 1400 BC. But more often they were the conquered. The Philistines, Hittites, Egyptians, Assyrians, Babylonians, and Persians all number among the peoples whom Scripture records as oppressing the Israelites. One of their most formidable conquerors of all appeared after the Old Testament writings had come to an end: Alexander the Great, who lived in the 300s BC. Though that man was enlightened and typically lenient after a victory, the Greek regime that arose in his wake became one of Israel's most hated and oppressive enemies. They were known as the Seleucid Empire.

For a century and a half, the Jews simmered under Seleucid tyranny, until at last God raised up a deliverer. History knows him as Judas Maccabeus, a charismatic and ruthless freedom fighter from a priestly family. The hard-fought guerrilla war, called the Maccabean Revolt, is described in Jewish writings that are included in Catholic Bibles but not Protestant ones. The outcome of the war is what matters: total victory by the rebels and the replacement of the Seleucid regime in Judea with a new Jewish dynasty that installed the Maccabean family as high priests and, eventually, as kings. The Jewish temple in Jerusalem—which the Greeks had terribly profaned by sacrificing a pig in the Most Holy Place—was cleansed and put back to proper worship in 164 BC. Today, the celebration of this glorious restoration is known as Hanukkah.

By Herod's time, the descendants of the Maccabees had taken up the name of their earliest ancestor, an obscure fellow named Hasmoneus. Now the so-called Hasmoneans shone like the brightest light in all of Judea. This family alone could rule over the Jews, possessing august titles such as high priest, king, or ethnarch. Their tangled family tree had wound its way down to

Herod's day through a figure we've already met: the high priest John Hyrcanus (who was the second in the family of that name). Herod's father, Antipater, was one of Hyrcanus's most visible supporters. But the same couldn't be said for Herod. He would eventually kill Hyrcanus—though not before making him his grandfather-in-law and forcing his way into the Hasmonean dynasty. That was Herod's ultimate dream: to be included in the royal family by marriage since he hadn't gotten there by birth. And the person who made this dream possible was Hyrcanus's royal granddaughter, Princess Mariamne.

————————

When the opportunity presented itself to make a match with such a high-ranking aristocrat as Mariamne, Herod jumped at the chance. But one thing stood in his way: Doris, the wife he had already married. Now he faced another thorny moral dilemma. *Can I just cast her aside? What will the people think of me? My fellow Jews hate divorce! Will I be criticized? Judged by them? Or worse, by the hand of God himself?* Though Herod surely debated his options for a time, in the end, the lure of the royal family proved too strong. He shattered Doris's world by sending her out of his household, along with little Antipater. Not until many years later would they be invited back into Herod's presence. Doris was a ruined woman. But no matter. Herod's policy was "out of sight, out of mind." Mariamne represented the future.

Most of what can be known about Mariamne comes from the time after her marriage to Herod. Yet something of her youth can be reconstructed. Certainly it was a youth of elite privilege. She was royal on both sides of her line, since her parents were Hasmonean cousins. Mariamne's good looks were legendary, rivaled only by those of her brother, Aristobulus. This golden pair was the talk of Jerusalem—rich, attractive, glamorous, and powerful. Like figures out of epic mythology, this brother-sister duo had the sheen of a bright future upon them.

Was Mariamne excited about being betrothed to Herod? Almost certainly not. Herod was no illustrious Hasmonean. In fact, he wasn't even a Judean. His family was Idumean on his father's side, while his mother was an Arab—a Nabatean. Who were the Idumeans? These people were known as "Edomites" in the Bible—ancient enemies of Israel. Their territory around the southern end of the Dead Sea had shifted over time. In Herod's day, it consisted of semi-fertile hill country south of Jerusalem, stretching into full desert where it adjoined Arabia.

Though the biblical Edomites had worshiped their own gods, the later Idumeans were forced to convert to Judaism after the Hasmoneans conquered them. This meant, in theory, that Herod was Jewish. One ancient critic remarked that Herod was a "commoner and Idumean, that is, a half-Jew." In other words, as an Idumean latecomer to the faith of Israel, Herod's Jewish credentials were suspect. All of this meant that Mariamne held her fiancé in a measure of contempt. He was by no means her social or religious equal, and both of them felt it acutely. Yet if the blue-blooded Mariamne could somehow gain the Judean throne through her lowborn yet powerful husband, would that make the sacrifice worth it? Perhaps. In any case, this marriage was surely destined for something other than tranquil wedded bliss.

———————————

Mariamne's grandfather, the esteemed John Hyrcanus, was a direct descendant of the original Maccabees. This lineage brought with it a measure of privilege; but in the Jewish royal house, power always came with danger. Murder lurked in the hallways, and backstabbings happened often—not just the metaphorical kind.

During the tumultuous time of Herod's engagement to Mariamne, another bout of violence occurred in his life. The Hasmonean family had all gathered at the same mansion, and Herod's father, Antipater the senior, had taken lodging there too. Unknown to Hyrcanus, the palace seethed with plots and intrigue. A minor political schemer named Malichus convinced Hyrcanus's butler to poison Antipater, who seemed to be the real power behind the throne. The attack succeeded in killing Antipater, not only eliminating the great Idumean general but providing a handy culprit for murder mysteries ever since: "The butler did it!"

Upon hearing the terrible news of his father's assassination, the shocked and furious Herod raised up an army to destroy Malichus. But once again, Herod's more cautious elder brother talked him down from the tree. "The Romans will think you're starting a civil war," Phasael warned. "Let's get our vengeance in secret." Herod grimaced but agreed.

An elaborate charade ensued in which Malichus publicly bewailed the loss of Antipater and Herod cleared him of all suspicion. Herod then gave his father a lavish funeral with much praise for the great man. At the Feast of Tabernacles in Jerusalem later that year, Malichus still fretted that Herod was out to get him, so he secured a bodyguard in case trouble arose. But Herod treated Malichus with friendliness and accepted him as a fellow mourner for Antipater.

Secretly, however, Herod bad-mouthed Malichus to a powerful Roman official who gave Herod permission—along with a squad of legionaries—to carry out his retribution. They attacked Malichus during a seaside stroll near the city of Tyre and "stabbed him through and through." At the sight of the flashing blades and flying blood, the genteel Hyrcanus fainted. When his servants finally managed to bring him around, Hyrcanus shakily asked who had given permission for the brutal carnage. After learning it was the Romans, he decided it was probably for the best.

Now Malichus was dead and Herod had his revenge. But he had also lost his father, a steadying force in his life. According to Josephus, Antipater was "a man of great energy in the conduct of affairs" and "distinguished for [his] piety, justice, and devotion to his country."

Did Herod grieve the loss of his father? Yes, but it's complicated. For a man like Herod, grief and fury formed two sides of the same coin. When Herod was hurt, the pain caused him to lash out like a wounded animal, injuring in return the one who had caused him pain. The deeper the trauma, the more vicious the retaliation. Eventually, this dysfunctional pattern would play itself out not only among Herod's enemies but also his most beloved family members.

With a violent background like this—not to mention Hyrcanus's longstanding jealousy at all of Herod's deeds and honors—it might seem strange that the high priest would offer his granddaughter in marriage to a potential rival with such eagerness to shed blood. Yet in the chaotic intrigues of those times, it was always best to follow the adage, "Keep your friends close and your enemies closer." By betrothing his only granddaughter to Herod, Hyrcanus, the wise patriarch of the Jews—who had no son of his own—was telling everyone that Herod was now his heir. The people of Judea could serve their current ruler with the confidence of knowing that after he passed, his capable replacement would be waiting in the wings.

The only question was, Would Herod be willing to wait?

CHAPTER 5

DISASTER AND DESTINY

At age thirty-three, the young Herod's hopeful prospects of a royal marriage and eventual rulership over the Jews as a new Hasmonean prince took a sudden turn for the worse when a powerful enemy invaded Syria and began to make incursions into Judea. During the first century BC, eastern Mediterranean regions like Syria and Judea served as buffer states against Rome's most worrisome enemy: the Parthians. In 40 BC, Rome's deepest fears began to come true on its eastern frontier. The Parthians—a people of Iranian ethnicity—rose up from their lands beyond the Euphrates River and invaded Roman territory. This event in world politics would have dramatic implications for Herod and his family.

Two prominent Parthians led the invasion: Pacorus, an ambitious young prince, and his devious military commander, Barzapharnes. Now the politics grew complex as some Jewish factions sided with the invading Parthians, believing they would be better overlords than the Romans. Meanwhile, the Hasmonean leadership resisted the invaders, though not without intrigue from within their own clan. Antigonus, the nephew of John Hyrcanus, decided now was the time to curry favor with the enemy and get himself installed as the Judean ruler in place of his uncle. He offered the Parthians a bribe of a thousand gold talents and five hundred women to serve as a harem. Included among those unfortunate sex slaves would be all the elite Hasmonean women. Many of the Jewish peasantry liked this idea, siding with Antigonus and putting their swords at his disposal. But the Hasmonean loyalists resisted the invasion. Jerusalem turned into a killing zone with bloody skirmishes every day.

As Herod considered what to do, he found himself at odds with his elder brother and future grandfather-in-law (Mariamne's father wasn't part of the picture since he had died before Herod's political career began). Phasael and

Hyrcanus believed they could bargain with the Parthian invaders. "We can offer them more money than what Antigonus has put on the table," Phasael reasoned. "Let's buy our way out of this. Let's pay them to leave."

But when the Parthian prince Pacorus urged Phasael and Hyrcanus to make a friendly visit to Barzapharnes up in Galilee, Herod grew suspicious. It sounded like a trap. Though he urged his two relatives to kill Pacorus and give no ground, they departed anyway and left Herod in tumultuous Jerusalem.

Though Barzapharnes received his guests and played nice, his devious intentions soon became apparent. The Parthians put a secret guard on Phasael and Hyrcanus, waiting to arrest them only until after they had captured Herod as well, lest a premature arrest give Herod enough warning to escape. When Phasael learned of this, he confronted Barzapharnes directly. The Parthian commander protested his innocence and went off to join his master, Pacorus. As soon as he left, Phasael and Hyrcanus were slapped in chains. Though they bitterly resented the barbarians' treachery, there was nothing they could do now but await their fate.

Down in Jerusalem, Herod realized he needed to take matters into his own hands. When the Parthian cup-bearer (a proxy for Pacorus) tried to convince Herod to come outside the city walls for a parlay, Herod suspected foul play and refused. Princess Mariamne and her widowed mother, Alexandra, came to Herod and pointed out that they were all trapped in the city. Persuaded by their urgings, Herod made the tough call to flee Jerusalem with his extended family.

The refugees found the journey into the desert to be arduous and not without tears of grief at the tragic turn of events. Behind them, the Parthians followed in hot pursuit. At one point, a wagon overturned and Herod's mother was injured. Struck by guilt and despair, he drew a sword and prepared to plunge it into his breast. Only the intervention of his many attendants prevented the suicide. "It isn't right for you to abandon your family and leave them in the power of your foes," they reminded him. "It isn't the act of a noble man to free yourself from danger and disregard the danger to your friends."

Stung by the criticism of his ignobility, Herod pulled himself together. With renewed vigor, he fought off the continual attacks from Jewish supporters of Parthia and managed to stay ahead of his pursuers. At last, the refugees reached the safety of Masada.

Even today, the citadel of Masada looms above the Dead Sea in splendid isolation. The region is a desert environment where besieging armies cannot encamp without an extensive supply chain. The walls of the plateau rise straight from the lowest point on earth. Yet Masada's top is flat, which had allowed earlier Hasmonean rulers to construct a fortress on the level surface. Later, Herod would expand those fortifications and build a lavish palace for himself in this desert refuge. No doubt, the possibilities that he noticed during his flight from the Parthians inspired those future plans. For now, though, Masada simply provided a safe place to leave his family, ensconced atop the impregnable plateau with plenty of food and water. Eight hundred men were appointed to guard them under the command of Herod's younger brother, Joseph. Herod then dispersed his remaining ten thousand troops throughout the Idumean countryside.

Desperate for cash with which to ransom Phasael, who was still imprisoned by Barzapharnes, Herod pressed on to their boyhood home of Petra, capital of the Nabateans. There he hoped for a warm welcome but was met instead with a rebuff. Parthian messengers had gotten there first and warned the royal family not to give refuge to Herod. When he realized the Nabateans wouldn't receive him, Herod immediately did an about-face and headed straight for Egypt. The mighty kingdom of Queen Cleopatra would be his last resort.

Arriving at the eastern edge of Egyptian territory, Herod received some terrible news. In a Parthian prison, his brother Phasael had committed suicide. Knowing he was destined for torture and slaughter, Phasael decided to deny that pleasure to his enemies. He chose the only means of death available to him in his chains: he dashed his head against a rock. By some accounts, Antigonus, the usurper who had bought his rulership over Judea from the Parthians, pretended to send a doctor to heal Phasael. But the doctor actually poisoned the wound and hastened Phasael's death.

To make matters worse, Antigonus ordered that John Hyrcanus's ears should be cut off. Some versions of the story recount that he actually bit off his uncle's ears with his teeth. Whatever brutal method was used, the mutilation meant Hyrcanus could no longer be the Jewish high priest, for the Mosaic law strictly prohibited it. Leviticus 21 recounts how God told Moses to inform Aaron the priest, "No man of your descendants in succeeding generations, who has any defect, may approach to offer the bread of his God. For any man who has a defect shall not approach: a man blind or lame, who has a marred face or any [other such defect]. . . . No man of the descendants of Aaron the priest, who has a defect, shall come near to offer the offerings made by fire to the LORD" (vv. 16–18, 21).

Since the mutilated Hyrcanus was no longer a threat, he was banished to faraway Babylonia. His nephew, Antigonus, now felt secure as the new ruler of Judea, confident in his pro-Parthian foreign policy. Everything was going his way. Herod, the former undisputed ruler of Judea, was on the run. His family cowered in a desert hideout and his bleak future lay in the hands of Egypt's whimsical queen. Every enemy had been vanquished. After spilling a lot of blood, Antigonus had pulled off a successful Hasmonean coup.

All of this wrangling for the right to rule the Jews had little effect on the day-to-day lives of the common people, unless by chance the military skirmishing happened to come their way. But for most of the peasants—especially those in the countryside villages—the great conflicts happened at the faraway level of palace intrigues and political maneuvering. Though professional soldiers and patriotic rebels did see violence, most Judeans went about their daily lives unaffected by the brutal infighting at the top of the social pyramid.

So it was for a Jewish woman known to history by the simple name of Anna. She was no famous princess like Mariamne, no great mover and shaker of her society. We learn about Anna's life especially in a text called *The Original Gospel of James*, which purports to have been written by Jesus' half brother, the author of the New Testament epistle that bears his name. Though this authorship probably isn't true, nor are some of the details recorded in this text and others like it, the stories nonetheless provide a valuable window into the world of Jewish women in ancient times. Through the figure of Anna, we can imagine the lives of many women just like her—humble and faithful servants of God, yet utterly overlooked by the rich and powerful of their times.

Anna herself wasn't poor, for her husband, Joachim, owned many flocks and herds. He was a pious man who gave to the Lord a double tithe: one portion for himself and another for the whole people of God. Yet despite the couple's wealth, a great sadness hung over them, for they were childless. When Joachim came to bring his sin offerings to the temple, he was rebuked by the priests and forbidden to offer his gifts first because he had "begotten no off-spring in Israel."

Heavyhearted, Joachim searched the record books and found that, indeed, all the righteous patriarchs of the twelve tribes had borne children. His own lack of offspring felt like a curse. Yet Joachim received encouragement from the memory of Abraham, who likewise was childless for a long time until God gave him Isaac in his later years.

In this sad yet hopeful frame of mind, Joachim decided to retreat to a wild and remote mountaintop for forty days and nights. "I shall not go down either for food or drink until the Lord my God visits me," the godly shepherd vowed. "Prayer shall be my food and drink."

With her husband gone, Anna found herself doubly saddened, as if she had lost a second male in her life. The cry of her heart was twofold: "I will mourn my widowhood and grieve for my childlessness." Yet Anna refused to give in to despair. Eventually, she put away her mourning garments, cleansed her face, and even donned her wedding dress as a remembrance of happier times. And then, at the ninth hour, Anna entered her garden to pray.

Anna's choice of the ninth hour (about 3:00 p.m.) for prayer holds great biblical significance. What does Scripture reveal about the ninth hour? First and foremost, it was when the Lord Jesus Christ finished his saving work on the cross. This was a moment of great sorrow, yet also the dawn of new hope. Angelic visions happened at this time. Divine healings happened as well. The ninth hour is an appropriate time to cry out to God and expect great things to unfold.[1]

---

1. Consider what important events happened at the ninth hour in the Bible: "And about *the ninth hour* Jesus [on the cross] cried out with a loud voice, saying, 'Eli, Eli, lama sabachthani?' that is, 'My God, My God, why have You forsaken Me?'" (Matthew 27:46).

 "Now it was about the sixth hour, and there was darkness over all the earth until *the ninth hour*. Then the sun was darkened, and the veil of the temple was torn in two. And when Jesus had cried out with a loud voice, He said, 'Father, into Your hands I commit My spirit.' Having said this, He breathed His last" (Luke 23:44–46).

 "Now Peter and John went up together to the temple at the hour of prayer, *the ninth hour*. And a certain man lame from his mother's womb was carried, whom they laid daily at the gate of the temple which is called Beautiful, to ask alms from those who entered the temple. . . . Then Peter said, 'Silver and gold I do not have, but what I do have I give you: In the name of Jesus Christ of Nazareth, rise up and walk'" (Acts 3:1–2, 6).

 "There was a certain man in Caesarea called Cornelius, a centurion of what was called the Italian Regiment, a devout man and one who feared God with all his household, who gave alms generously to the people, and prayed to God always. About *the ninth hour* of the day he saw clearly in a vision an angel of God coming in and saying to him, 'Cornelius!'" (Acts 10:1–3).

El Roi, the God who sees, turned his gaze upon Anna when she poured out her lament in a lonely garden. With great fervency, she prayed, "O God of our fathers, bless me and heed my prayer, just as you blessed the womb of Sarah and gave her a son, Isaac." And the Lord God did not remain silent. He heard the cry of his faithful servant. Why? Because El Roi isn't just the God of the high and mighty but the humble and lowly. When God's people pray, angels begin to move and things begin to change. Very soon, Anna would find this to be true.

Down in Egypt, Herod finally found refuge from his Parthian pursuers. Though the illegitimate king Antigonus held the Judean throne, at least Herod was safe and his family was secure on Masada's lofty heights. From the Egyptian port of Pelusium, Herod was transported along the coast as a dignified guest to the capital, Alexandria. Queen Cleopatra urged Herod to stay there and command an army in one of her wars, but Herod politely declined. He desired to press on to Italy and state his case before the Roman authorities.

He departed Egypt during the turbulent winter sailing season. Just like the apostle Paul experienced at a later time, so, too, Herod's ship ran into a storm and barely made landfall after the sailors threw their cargo overboard. From the island of Rhodes, Herod oversaw the construction of a new ship and crossed to the boot of Italy, where he switched to a carriage and hurried to the place where all roads eventually led.

Upon arriving in Rome, Herod gained an immediate audience with one of the city's most powerful leaders: Mark Antony, a figure noted in history as Cleopatra's tragic lover. Herod's sob story—how the Parthians drove him from his home, killed Phasael, mutilated and banished Hyrcanus, and illegally awarded Antigonus the Judean throne in exchange for the promise of money and a harem of aristocratic women—fell on sympathetic Roman ears. Herod also described how his relatives were forced to hide in Masada, while he himself had barely survived a storm at sea. Now he placed all his hopes in Antony's grace and mercy.

Mark Antony supported Herod for four reasons. First, Herod's father, Antipater, had been a strong ally of the Romans. Second, Antony was impressed by the vigor and virtue of the bold adventurer who stood before him. Third, Herod promised a large sum of money if he were given a political appointment in Judea. And fourth, Antony hated Antigonus, whom he viewed as disgustingly pro-Parthian, which therefore meant anti-Roman. Antony advocated vigorously for Herod with his new brother-in-law, Octavian, the future Caesar Augustus. Octavian, too, was inclined to support Herod because of Antipater's sterling Roman reputation.

Straightaway, the Senate convened, and things began to move at a rapid pace. Several prominent senators gave laudatory speeches in honor of Antipater and his good son Herod. Antigonus, in contrast, was declared an enemy of the Romans. And then came the decision that would change Herod's life forever. As Josephus put it, "When the Senate had been aroused by these charges, Antony came forward and informed them that it was also an advantage in their war with the Parthians that Herod should be king. And as this proposal was acceptable to all, they voted accordingly."

This unexpected turn of events astounded Herod. The royal appointment was beyond his wildest imaginations. Though he had come to Rome for political support, he certainly didn't think the Romans would make him king. At best, he had hoped that Princess Mariamne's handsome brother Aristobulus—a bona fide Hasmonean, though only about fourteen years old at the time—would be given the throne with Herod in an advisory role. Yet now, in only seven days on Italian soil, Herod's lifelong dream had come true.

When the Senate adjourned, Herod paraded with Mark Antony on one side of him and Octavian on the other, escorted by a host of magistrates and luminaries, to deposit the new decree in the Tabularium, Rome's official record-keeping house on the slope of the Capitoline Hill. Once this was done, the decree became law and Herod became king of the Jews—though only in theory, for Antigonus and his army still occupied the land of Judea.

But no matter. The Romans had declared Herod to be the rightful king. Their almighty will could not be thwarted. It was only a matter of time until Herod dislodged Antigonus and made Roman law the reality on the ground in Judea. Then he, and he alone, would reign over the Jewish people. No one could usurp that claim ever again. Herod would lock it down forever.

But unbeknownst to Herod, the angel that visited humble Anna had other plans. "Anna, Anna, the Lord has heard your prayer," the heavenly messenger announced to her. "You shall conceive and bear, and your offspring shall be spoken of in the whole world." Anna believed the angel's word and promised to devote her forthcoming child to God.

That child's name, of course, would be Mary.

CHAPTER 6

THE KING COMES TO ZION

No sooner had the angel of God left Anna with the encouraging promise of her future pregnancy than the news arrived of Joachim's return from the wilderness. An angel had visited him, too, announcing, "Joachim, Joachim, the Lord God has heard your prayer. Go down from here; behold, your wife, Anna, shall conceive." Overjoyed, Joachim ordered many of his lambs and goats to be sacrificed to God and distributed for a feast. When Anna went out to the gate and saw her husband coming with his flocks, she ran to him and hugged his neck, exclaiming, "Now I know that the Lord God has richly blessed me; for behold, the widow is no longer a widow, and I, who was childless, shall conceive." Then Joachim went inside and "rested" in his house with his wife.

Nine months later, the time of Anna's pregnancy was complete. Since the ancient world had no means to take away a woman's agony, the new mother's travail was accompanied by cries of deep pain. She sweated and grunted as she struggled to bring forth her firstborn child. At last, after much struggle, the baby was delivered. Anna asked the midwife, "What have I brought forth?" When the midwife declared, "A female," Anna responded, "My soul is magnified this day!" The new mother gave suck to the child and named her Mary.

Though Anna didn't yet know the messianic purpose God had in mind for this tiny baby, like all Jewish women of the time, she longed for God's deliverer to come soon into the world. *Messiah* is a Hebrew-based word that means "anointed one." The Hebrew verb *mashach* means "to rub or smear." In biblical times, physical objects destined for holy use were rubbed with oil to signal their consecrated status. So, too, God's special servants received an anointing upon their heads to show their dedication to divine service. The Greek equivalent of "Messiah" is *Christos*, or Christ. Both words describe someone who has been anointed with oil, that is, singled out in a visible, tangible way for a special, divine purpose.

That purpose, in particular, was to rule. The Messiah would necessarily be a royal figure—a king who would reign over Israel. He must descend from the Israelite tribe of Judah (Genesis 49:10) and come specifically from the lineage of King David (2 Samuel 7:12–16). This Davidic descent would ensure that the anticipated Messiah reigned with the piety and power of Israel's most famous ruler.

Yet the Messiah wouldn't just be an honored king but also a humble servant. The prophet Isaiah had made this especially clear. The messianic servant would carry out the will of God to perfection. He would bring justice to the nations (42:1) and restore Israel to the Lord (49:5–6). But his ultimate work would be to provide a substitutionary sacrifice to pay for Israel's sins. Isaiah 53 foretells a time when the people of Israel would recognize that they had gone astray, but "the LORD has laid on Him the iniquity of us all" (v. 6). Although the Messiah would be "cut off from the land of the living" (v. 8), God would not let this stand but would "prolong His days" (v. 10). The Messiah would "justify many" and "bear their iniquities" (v. 11) as God's promised redeemer and sin sacrifice.

Unlike human kings—who are at best foolish and flawed, and at worst cruel and tyrannical—the Messiah would rule over God's people with perfect wisdom and justice. Under his guiding hand, wickedness would be uprooted and righteousness would prevail. Everyone would find prosperity, harmony, and rest. The Messiah would bring God's true peace—his heavenly *shalom*—not only to Israel but to the whole earth.

As Anna gazed down at her newborn daughter and considered her future in Israel, did she understand these theological truths? Perhaps not with a scholar's insight, but Anna no doubt perceived them intuitively. All Jews felt the ever-present weight of foreign domination. They longed for a coming day when they would be treated with respect and dignity. Ancient women must have felt this longing even more acutely because they were so often treated as inferior to men. Anna surely hoped that her daughter, Mary, would live under the Messiah's glorious reign. Little did she know that the tiny body in her arms would one day house the body of the Messiah himself.

Far away from Anna, over in Rome, the newly appointed king of Judea wasted no time getting himself back from Italy to his homeland. Herod not only wanted to claim his rightful kingdom but to save his family at Masada. Although they were temporarily safe inside the fortress atop the plateau, the army of Antigonus was besieging them from below. Food remained plentiful but Masada's water cisterns had run dangerously low. When thirst began to threaten the family's survival, Herod's little brother, Joseph, decided to make a dash for Petra. But then God provided a miracle. The night before the planned escape, rain fell in abundance and replenished the cisterns. Joseph canceled the escape plan and resolved to hold tight until Herod arrived as his rescuer.

Herod's ship from Italy put in at the Greek port of Ptolemais, a city that much later would be one of the Crusaders' main landing points in their invasion of the Holy Land from the west. Today it is known as Acre, Israel. Since it is the natural point of entry into Galilee, Herod immediately began collecting troops from that region. Disenchanted with Parthian rule, the Galileans went over en masse to Herod, putting him in charge of a powerful army.

Unfortunately, his military aspirations received only half-hearted support from the two Roman commanders whom Mark Antony had ordered to help with the conquest. These men had taken bribes from Antigonus to lay low. Since they couldn't be counted on, the job of ousting the impostor king fell to Herod alone. He set about it with single-minded focus.

His first order of business was to break the siege at Masada and rescue his family. Like the Galileans, so also the Idumeans around Masada promptly went over to Herod's side. Some of them remembered his father, Antipater, with fond affection. Others were impressed by Herod's own capabilities. In any case, with his Roman appointment to be king of the Jews, it seemed only a matter of time until Herod was in charge. The locals figured it would be smart to win the favor of the future king.

Supported by these energized troops, Herod struck out into the desert, only to find that the enemy had set ambushes at the pinch points along the way. But those guerrilla tactics were no match for Herod's superior army, which brushed off the attacks like an ox swishing away horseflies with its tail. After overcoming the ambushes one by one, Herod routed the forces of Antigonus at Masada and joyfully rejoined his family. No doubt his mother (Cyprus), sister (Salome), fiancée (Mariamne), and future mother-in-law (Alexandra) were all relieved they wouldn't be served up to the Parthians as unwilling harem girls. The victorious Herod had become their strong and capable savior.

Yet Jerusalem still didn't belong to its legal king. Herod proceeded there at the head of his army. Instead of immediately attacking, he sent heralds to make an announcement before the walls. "The true king is here for the good of the city and to save the people," Herod's criers proclaimed. "Even his bitterest enemies will be given amnesty if you let him in." Inside the city, of course, Antigonus ordered no one to listen to Herod's lies. Now the only option was to duke it out with swords and bows, letting God determine who had the right to rule.

At this pivotal moment, one of the bribed Roman commanders showed his true colors as a double agent working against Herod. He ordered his troops to complain that they couldn't fight without suitable provisions and rations, since Antigonus had reduced the vicinity of Jerusalem to a wasteland. Undaunted by this cowardly response, Herod sallied forth into the countryside and rounded up an abundance of supplies. The Samaritans, who now supported Herod along with the Judeans, Galileans, and Idumeans, supplied ample grain, wine, oil, and cattle. The troops had all the rations they needed to fight.

But instead of pressing the attack, the Roman soldiers continued to be idle. They disbanded and withdrew to the countryside to live comfortably off the new supplies through the winter. Meanwhile, Antigonus and his defenders remained locked tight in Jerusalem with plenty of supplies. Although Herod was stymied for the moment, he refused to sit still. He safely lodged the women of his family in Samaria. Then, over the next few months, he set about securing his holdings in Idumea and expelling the last of Antigonus's supporters from Galilee.

One of the worst problems plaguing Galilee was a gang of bandits who used the chaos of the times to pillage the countryside. Like the bandits whom Herod had defeated before, these men resisted the Romans and their falsely appointed king, so neutralizing them was a priority. Their hideout was a series of caves high on Mount Arbel, a craggy peak that towered above the Sea of Galilee. Though Herod easily defeated the rebels in open combat, their remote caves proved more of a problem. The entrances gaped right in the middle of a sheer cliff that plunged into a ravine. The cave mouths could be reached only by a torturous and extremely narrow path that had to be traversed in single file. Soldiers couldn't ascend it during an assault because each man would be picked off as he approached.

Yet Herod refused to be thwarted. After considering the problem for some time, he ordered his troops to ascend to the mountain's summit above the caves. From there, they rigged wooden boxes on iron chains and lowered squads of soldiers from mechanical cranes to the cave openings. Like he had done before the walls of Jerusalem, Herod tried at first to be merciful. His heralds announced amnesty for anyone who would surrender. Fiercely loyal to their patriotic principles, many of the rebels refused the offer, preferring death to capitulation.

So Herod's attackers tossed firebrands inside the enemy hideout to torch the flammable supplies. They also carried grappling hooks with which they could snag the brigands and hurl them over the edge of the cliff. The daring assault enabled the soldiers to kill not only the rebels but their families, who had hidden with them in the caves.

The historian Josephus told the story of one old man who had seven children and a wife in the caves. They asked Herod to let them submit, and Herod agreed. But while Herod watched, the old man called his children one by one to the cave entrance and murdered each of them with his weapon, tossing their bodies onto the crags far below. Disturbed to his core by what he was seeing, Herod extended his hand and implored the man not to do this terrible thing. Full immunity would be granted if the killer would just give in.

But it was no use. Ignoring any words from the so-called king whom he despised—even mocking him as a "low-born upstart" who didn't deserve the Judean throne—the old man slaughtered his remaining children and wife, then flung himself over the precipice to his death. Such were the zealous passions of those times.

Meanwhile, on the larger scene, the Roman legions had successfully dislodged the eastern power, Parthia, from their lands. As soon as the Parthian leader Pacorus was slain and victory was assured, Mark Antony ordered his army to do a better job of assisting Herod. But in fact, it was Herod who assisted his master at this crucial moment. Hastening to where Antony was still assaulting a Parthian-allied city, Herod's troops made the difference and finished the task. The city surrendered to the besiegers. Herod's valor in combat—not to mention the heaps of booty he had captured on the way there—cemented Antony's high regard for his Judean friend.

Unfortunately, back in Judea, Herod's brother Joseph had tried to continue the war against Antigonus but met with defeat. After he fell gallantly in battle, Antigonus ordered the outrageous sacrilege of cutting off Joseph's head and mutilating the corpse. Though Herod was far from the action, he awoke from a nightmare that told him his brother had been slain just as the messengers arrived to convey the terrible news.

Once again, the killing of one of Herod's relatives spurred him to frenzied action. He quick-marched back to Jerusalem—"accelerated by the desire for speedy vengeance on his brother's murderers," Josephus said—and met Antigonus's general in battle. Herod's burning zeal for vengeance drove his troops to victory. He massacred a huge number of enemy soldiers, so many that the streets of the local villages became impassable due to the heaps of corpses.

Herod decided to take a hot bath after the exhausting battle. Unknown to him, several of the defeated soldiers had taken refuge in the bathhouse, fully armed and desperate. Yet even though they saw Herod naked and defenseless with no one to guard him, the enemy soldiers ran past him and fled the building rather than attack. Everyone recognized God's protection of the new king.

The next day, Herod decapitated the corpse of the general who had done the same to Joseph. No doubt this seemed like appropriate justice, fulfilling the Law's injunction, "An eye for an eye, a tooth for a tooth" (Exodus 21:24 NLT). Now Herod moved his army up to Jerusalem's walls, approaching the same vulnerable point that Pompey the Great had exploited several years earlier. Victory seemed imminent for the Herodians.

But then, unexpectedly, Herod did something that only a man like him would think to do. He left his lieutenants in charge of the siege and departed for Samaria, where he retrieved Princess Mariamne and married her in a glorious ceremony. Thus he made the royal wedding an interlude to the siege of Jerusalem.

With his new Hasmonean queen at his side and his Roman appointment as king in his hand, Herod was ready to assume his rightful place in the Holy City. His army consisted of eleven battalions of infantry and six thousand cavalry, plus a divison of Syrian auxiliaries. Everyone inside Jerusalem could see the mighty host encircling them. Some desperate citizenry concocted frenzied oracles that predicted their miraculous salvation. Other more practical men slipped past the besiegers and raided the nearby countryside for whatever provisions they could find. Still others built tunnels from which they could pop out and harass Herod's troops.

But it was no use. Though the defenders managed to rebuff their attackers for five months, in the end, twenty of Herod's most stalwart soldiers scaled the walls and leapt into the city. Several Roman centurions followed behind the brave commandos and secured an entry point. Now the streets of Jerusalem belonged to Herod, though not yet the lofty temple mount, where the last remaining defenders had taken refuge.

At first, it appeared that these lone holdouts were about to give in. Herod even allowed sacrificial animals to be sent to the defenders so the temple's worship could continue unabated. But when Herod determined that the loyalists of Antigonus were going to resist to the last drop of their blood, he ordered an all-out assault. This was too much for the defenders to withstand. The resistance broke and the victorious troops began to run rampant in the city.

Though Herod didn't allow the Most Holy Place to be violated by foreign eyes like Pompey had done, still, a great massacre ensued. The Romans were out for blood after so long a siege, while the Herodian troops wanted to leave no opponents alive among their countrymen. Herod dispatched messengers to order clemency, but his commands were widely disregarded. The invaders butchered the citizenry and heaped their bodies in the streets. No mercy was shown even to women, infants, or the elderly. "Like madmen, they wreaked their rage on all ages indiscriminately," said Josephus. The runaway looting continued until Herod finally convinced his Roman allies to accept payment from his own resources instead of plundering the citizenry. Begrudgingly, the troops pulled back.

As for Antigonus, he came out from his stronghold and begged for mercy before the victorious Roman general. Instead of granting it, the general laughed at Antigonus, mocked him with the female name Antigone, and locked him in chains to be dealt with later. Eventually, Antigonus was taken to Mark Antony, who ordered him scourged while bound to a cross—a penalty the Romans didn't usually apply to a royal captive—then beheaded by an axe. Such would be the fate, Antony declared, for any man who dared to ally himself with the Parthians!

And so, at last, the Romans withdrew from Jerusalem and left Herod in charge of a ravaged and defeated city. After two brutal years of constant blood-letting from Galilee to Masada, the legal king had won his appointed kingdom. Beautiful Mariamne stood at Herod's side, lending supposed Hasmonean dignity to what was in reality a scene of ugliness and despair. Herod had achieved his lifelong dream to become the king of the Jews. But was this the kind of Messiah that Israel had been expecting?

We do not know if all this fighting affected Anna and Joachim. Perhaps their livelihood was damaged or perhaps they escaped unscathed. Yet as they considered the future they hoped to experience in Israel, they would have longed for Messiah's advent to put an end to bloodshed and establish an age of peace. We can imagine godly Joachim reading Scripture with his wife after she delivered their firstborn child, encouraging her with the prophet Zechariah's description of the true king's arrival in Jerusalem:

> Rejoice greatly, O daughter of Zion!
> Shout, O daughter of Jerusalem!
> Behold, your King is coming to you;
> He is just and having salvation,
> Lowly and riding on a donkey,
> A colt, the foal of a donkey. . . .
> He shall speak peace to the nations;
> His dominion shall be from "sea to sea,
> And from the River to the ends of the earth." (9:9–10)

CHAPTER 7

MURDER IN THE PALACE

When Herod became king of the Jews, the people begrudgingly went along with the Roman decision despite his Idumean lineage. At least, they reasoned, the new king was married to a good Hasmonean girl, so the throne hadn't completely left the royal house. And in any case, Herod's army had defeated all challengers, so there wasn't much anyone could do about the matter. For good or ill, Herod was the king.

Yet there was one office Herod couldn't occupy, a prestigious position that his Hasmonean predecessors had often held: the high priesthood. Though the notion of "King Herod" met with begrudging acceptance among the Jews, if he had tried to become the high priest as well, chaos would have ensued. Even Herod, with all of his megalomania, knew better than to claim priestly prerogatives for himself.

Traditionally, ancient Israel received divine guidance from three main offices. First, Israel's *prophets* gave direct messages from God. The prophet Samuel was one of the earliest of these inspired figures, and many others came after him, such as Elijah, Elisha, Isaiah, Jeremiah, and the twelve "minor prophets" whose books are found in the Old Testament. Later, John the Baptist would be viewed as a prophetic figure who revived the inspired line.

The second important office was *king*. Israel's first king was Saul—a choice that displeased God, yet one he allowed because his people demanded it. Though Saul disobeyed God, King David took his place as a "man after His [God's] own heart" (1 Samuel 13:14). The Hebrew monarchy eventually split into two lines—Israel and Judah—and each came to an end when foreign nations conquered them. But when the Maccabees overthrew their Greek masters, a royal line was reestablished in Jerusalem.

Israel's third spiritual office was its *priesthood*. The original line of priests went back to the time of Levi, the great-grandson of Abraham. This man's descendants were known as the Levites. Instead of giving them a portion of the promised land, God gave the Levites divine service as their special allotment. Moses and his brother, Aaron, were both Levites. A few centuries later, in the time of King Solomon, Aaron's descendant Zadok founded an order of priests who would serve in the glorious Solomonic temple. Though the Maccabees (later called the Hasmoneans) weren't Zadokites, they were still Levites, so everyone accepted that this heroic family, and it alone, should provide the temple's high priest.

King Herod, however, couldn't claim Hasmonean lineage, so his newly acquired temple in Jerusalem needed someone else to serve as its high priest. The most obvious candidate was the man who had held the position before: John Hyrcanus. Herod sent for him to come home from Babylonia, where he had been living a life of honor among the local Jews. Yet Hyrcanus's mutilated ears, the work of the now-dead Antigonus, meant he could serve only in an advisory role instead of a sacerdotal one.

The ever-wily Herod now attempted a move that seemed like a good idea at the time but quickly turned sour. He nominated a minor figure from the Babylonian Jewish community, a fellow named Ananel, to emigrate to Judea as the new high priest. No doubt this foreigner would be easily controlled by Herod, to whom he owed his unexpected position with all of its wealth and prestige. The strategy also had the advantage of reappointing a Zadokite as the Jewish high priest, for Ananel was from that ancient line while the Hasmoneans were not. Didn't the book of Ezekiel declare that the Zadokites were "the only Levites who may draw near to the LORD to minister before him" (40:46 NIV)? Who could complain about Herod's restoration of this biblical priestly line?

Herod's mother-in-law, that's who. The sharp-tongued Alexandra blew up when she learned that her teenaged son, Aristobulus, the brother of Mariamne, had been passed over. And as it turned out, the move enraged Mariamne as well. Mother and daughter agreed that only the Hasmonean clan should run Judea. If the royal power had to go over to an Idumean interloper, at least the high priesthood should stay in the family. But now Herod had broken precedent by giving the prestigious job to some no-name from Babylonia. Hasmonean prestige ought to trump Zadokite lineage. At least, that's what Alexandra and Mariamne believed.

The pressing question was, Who could force Herod to change his mind? It would take someone with incredible political power. Fortunately, Alexandra knew just who to ask: Cleopatra, queen of Egypt, who was not only a fellow woman but a rival to Herod with a burning desire to increase her power at Judea's expense. To make matters worse for Herod, Cleopatra had Mark Antony wrapped around her little finger. The infatuated Roman ruler would do just about anything his sexy mistress would ask, even if it came at a cost to allies like Herod. Alexandra quickly dispatched a complaint to Cleopatra on behalf of her son. Cleopatra received the missive with outrage. Then the wily queen whispered her friend's complaint into Antony's love-tickled ear.

Though Mark Antony didn't act quickly enough for the women's liking, another Roman official began to move things along: Quintus Dellius, one of Antony's closest friends. And a strange friendship it was. The man often played the role of a pimp, securing bisexual pleasures for Antony's nighttime enjoyment. When Dellius showed up in Judea on other business, he took one look at Alexandra's two beautiful teenagers, Mariamne and Aristobulus, and immediately started scheming how to get them into Antony's bed. He flattered Alexandra by suggesting her children must have been sired by a god instead of a human. Like many a mother of attractive children, Alexandra agreed to have portraits painted of her offspring. Dellius told Alexandra that as soon as Antony saw their beauty, he would do whatever she wanted. Little did she know that Dellius had devious sexual intentions in mind.

When Mark Antony saw the portraits, he agreed that Mariamne's beauty was astounding. Fortunately, even the most profligate Roman rulers had their limits. Antony was unwilling to violate the newlywed wife of his Idumean friend. Nor did he want to arouse Cleopatra's jealousy by pursuing a dalliance with a gorgeous young princess. However, Aristobulus was another story. Mark Antony immediately summoned the handsome youth to Syria so he could exploit him sexually. (Homosexual behavior with boys wasn't frowned upon for Roman aristocrats as long as the adult man was in the dominant role.)

Upon learning of the terrible summons, Herod sprang into action. He had no intention of letting Aristobulus—who was popular, good-looking, and a legitimate heir to the Judean throne—find his way into Mark Antony's orbit. In an age when kingdoms rose and fell on a ruler's whim, Herod wanted to retain Antony's favor and prevent anyone else's star from rising. He stalled Antony with the warning that if the boy were to leave Judea, the people would protest, or maybe even rise up in rebellion since many hoped he might someday be king. Antony begrudgingly accepted the advice and forgot about pursuing a liaison with the boy.

Though Alexandra and Mariamne were relieved to keep Aristobulus nearby, their resentment of Herod's snub for the high priesthood still simmered beneath the surface. It was time for a family discussion—and in Herod's family, that was often a life-or-death affair. Mariamne used her wifely powers to impress upon her husband how bad a mistake it was to appoint a Babylonian interloper as high priest. "But your mother plotted against me," the king countered. "She tried to use Cleopatra to get me dethroned!" Herod directly accused Alexandra of disloyalty, pointing out how foolish that strategy was. "Your daughter is the queen of Judea," he reminded her. "If I'm gone, so is she. Do you want her to lose that honor?" But when Alexandra dug in her heels, Herod finally relented. "Fine! I'll get rid of Ananel," he told his mother-in-law. "I'll appoint your son as high priest."

The news elated Alexandra and Mariamne. Alexandra was even reduced to tears, not only of joy but relief that Herod wasn't going to put her to death for treason. "I only did this for my son's honor," she explained. "I never wanted the throne! I wouldn't take it if it came my way. Things are best with you in charge." Humbly, Alexandra promised to accept the status quo and remain loyal to Herod. She expressed gratitude for his generous benefactions. Herod, for his part, kissed and made up as well. "They gave each other assurances of good faith," said the historian Josephus, "and broke up their meeting, all suspicion, as it seemed, having been removed."

But in reality, it wasn't. Despite these promises of loyalty, Herod doubted that Alexandra—a hard-core Hasmonean snob—was truly on his side. He put a watch on his mother-in-law so he could keep tabs on all her doings, including the details of her private life. Soon this snooping became so intrusive that Alexandra's bitter spirit returned. "I only appear to have royal honor," she complained to Aristobulus. "But in truth, we are no more free than slaves." Once again, Alexandra wrote to Cleopatra, who suggested that the beleaguered mother and son flee the oppressive Judean palace and take up residence in Egypt. Alexandra agreed, so she hatched a devious plan.

She ordered two coffins to be made as if for a burial outside the city. The would-be emigrants hid in the conveyances and escaped Jerusalem. From there, the road to the coast lay open and a ship bound for Egypt awaited in the port. But one of the servants who knew about the plan incautiously mentioned it to another fellow named Sabbion. This man was under a cloud of suspicion because earlier rumors had connected him to the poisoning of Herod's father. Seizing the chance to get back into Herod's good graces, Sabbion reported Alexandra's escape plan to the king. Herod let it go far enough that he could seize the mother and son in the very act of flight. Flustered and ashamed, the two fugitives were hauled back to the city. Although their trickery infuriated Herod, he could do little to punish Alexandra, for he feared antagonizing Cleopatra. Though Herod made a big show of forgiving his mother-in-law, secretly, he waited for an opportunity to strike.

The opportunity came later that year, and it was none too soon, for Aristobulus's popularity had soared. As the people saw him making the holy sacrifices in the distinguished robes of the high priest, he seemed like God's man for the hour. His tall stature and natural good looks combined with his humble piety and Hasmonean ancestry to give him illustrious status among the citizens. They began to call out good wishes and prayers for his success as he officiated at the temple. Herod had every reason to worry that eighteen-year-old Aristobulus might someday supplant him on the Judean throne.

After the Feast of Tabernacles ended in early October, the royal family adjourned from Jerusalem and headed down to Jericho in the desert. There, at the local palace that served as a kind of aristocratic resort, Herod wined and dined his young brother-in-law. Yet at night as he lay in his bed, troubling thoughts kept Herod awake. Could the delicate balance of power in Judea handle two handsome and wealthy men, one serving as priest, the other as king? And more importantly, could Herod's own mind handle such a scenario?

I must remove him somehow, Herod mused.

But he is no outsider, replied another inner voice. *He is family! To kill him would be fratricide, a heinous crime. That line cannot be crossed.*

Or can it?

The next morning dawned as yet another blue-sky day in the desert. By noontime, the sun burned hot over the lowest city on earth. The family sat under an awning, lounging on sofas in the shade. A slave came by with a silver tray. "Have another drink," Herod urged Aristobulus. "Then everyone is going to take a dip in the pool."

"That sounds delightful," the handsome youth agreed.

A group of young friends—including some royal bodyguards—began to swim under Herod's approving eye. After Aristobulus watched them for a bit, Herod approached him with a gentle exhortation. "You should jump in with them, my brother! The water is cool and refreshing. Go on! Join the fun." Aristobulus could resist no longer. He stripped off his robe and took the plunge.

All afternoon, the friends cavorted in the pool, playing games and rough-housing. But as darkness began to approach and the family dispersed, Herod gave a prearranged signal to some of the guards in the water. Their play became rougher as they wrestled with Aristobulus—holding him down, letting him snatch only a quick gulp of air before dunking him again. Then strong fingers seized the back of his neck and forced him under. Desperately, the youth thrashed beneath the surface. Yet he was no match for the three or four swimmers who seemed to be playing but were under orders to kill. It took only a few moments before Aristobulus's body went limp. The guardsmen released him and slipped away. Herod, too, departed the scene of the crime, leaving the high priest's corpse floating face down in the pool.

The deed is done, Herod told himself as he returned to his bedroom and closed the door behind him. *Aristobulus will plague me no more!*

But alongside the satisfaction of eliminating a dangerous rival, guilty thoughts gnawed at the king's mind. For the first time, he had murdered not just an enemy but a close family member. The crime of fratricide was as old as humanity itself. Cain's murder of Abel was the original act of violence recorded in the Hebrew Scriptures. God's angry response to Cain's heinous crime applied equally to Herod: "What have you done? The voice of your brother's blood cries out to Me from the ground. So now you are cursed from the earth, which has opened its mouth to receive your brother's blood from your hand" (Genesis 4:10–11).

Whether Herod recalled those divine words of judgment on the night of the murder, we do not know. What is certain, however, is that only the true High Priest could atone for so great a stain upon Herod's soul.

CHAPTER 8

HELL HATH NO FURY

When Alexandra and Mariamne learned that Aristobulus had drowned in the Jericho swimming pool, both of them fell to pieces. They wailed inconsolably over the dead body that lay before them on a funeral bier. Mariamne immediately withdrew from Herod, shunning his presence as she would a leper. *I can't even stand the sight of him*, she thought as she retired to a private chamber. For a wife to share a bed with a murderer would be immoral and repugnant. But to share one with the killer of her own brother made Mariamne's skin crawl. A shiver ran through her as she contemplated his sexual touch. That sort of thing wasn't going to happen ever again.

Back in Jerusalem, the news of the high priest's "accident" hit the populace almost as hard as the royal family. The streets echoed with weeping and lamentation. Each person grieved as if one of their own relatives had died. All of Judea was in mourning. But soon enough, Alexandra realized she would have to accept—outwardly, at least—the new status quo. To mourn overmuch would be to put herself in danger. Alexandra had to act as if she didn't suspect foul play. She couldn't afford to seem disloyal to Herod when he was in a murderous state of mind.

Though Alexandra often came close to committing suicide during these times, one thing compelled the bereaved mother to press on: the hope that someday she could avenge her son's death. She pretended not to know the drowning was premeditated so she could avert Herod's suspicions that she was out for vengeance. Herod playacted his role, too, mourning Aristobulus with effusive tears and giving the boy a lavish funeral and magnificent tomb. Strangely, Herod's tears might not have been entirely fake. When he saw Aristobulus's beautiful body lying cold and inert on the burial slab, a deep sadness struck him. In the complicated family dynamics of the Herodian household, a necessary murder could also be viewed as a terrible tragedy, even by the murderer himself.

Though Alexandra was undercover, she wasn't inert. Like before, she decided to inform her most powerful ally about the devious doings in Jerusalem. When Cleopatra received another complaint letter from her friend, she once again wanted to help. Alexandra's previous overtures had fallen flat, and the women's maneuvering had failed to change the Judean political status quo. *This time*, Cleopatra vowed, *Herod is going to get his comeuppance! It's time to get a proper noble back on the Jewish throne.*

Cleopatra's conniving wasn't motivated simply by friendship or female solidarity; she also had Egyptian expansion in mind. The pharaohs of her distinguished lineage had possessed far more territory than she, including all of Herod's lands. Cleopatra wanted it back—and if she had to take down Herod to do it, well, that was no more than she had already done to several other kings in the eastern Mediterranean.

In 35 BC, Cleopatra and Mark Antony were in Egypt, where Antony had retreated after a failed attempt to invade Parthia. His bruised ego was particularly susceptible to Cleopatra's smooth tongue. The sly queen "did not cease urging Antony to avenge the murder of Alexandra's son, for, she said, it was not right that Herod, who had been appointed by [Antony] as king of a country which he had no claim to rule, should have exhibited such lawlessness toward those who were the real kings." So when Antony and his lover embarked for the Syrian city of Laodicea, he commanded Herod to meet him there. The king of the Jews was going to have to explain the mysterious death of Aristobulus.

The terrified Herod could do nothing but obey. Capital punishment for the crime of fratricide wasn't out of the question. Before Herod departed Jerusalem, he gave careful instructions to his uncle Joseph, who was also the husband of his sister, Salome. "If anything happens to me," Herod told Joseph, "I want you to kill Mariamne." The ghastly command must have shocked Joseph, but Herod explained that he was so in love with his beautiful wife, he couldn't stand the thought of another man possessing her after he was gone. The truth of the matter was, Herod feared Mark Antony would bed Mariamne, so he resolved that if he were going to be executed, at least he would deny that pleasure to his executioner.

After Herod departed, Joseph found himself in frequent talks with Mariamne about government business. Though he wanted to patch things up between the two star-crossed lovers, his incautious words had the opposite effect. "Your husband loves you above all others," he told Mariamne, but she could only scoff at the idea. "It's true!" Joseph insisted. "If things go bad with Mark Antony, he told me to kill you rather than let you be with another man. That's how much he loves you!" Understandably, instead of sparking warm affection in Mariamne, the revelation only served to heighten her impression of Herod's egomania and cruelty. Her already expansive hatred of him inflated even more.

But then some stunning news arrived in Jerusalem: Herod had been tortured and executed by Mark Antony! The palace buzzed with speculations, especially among the partisans of Mariamne and Alexandra. *Someone new was going to claim the Judean throne!* Although this was a happy prospect, the savvy Hasmoneans understood that danger always accompanied political transitions. Alexandra immediately urged Joseph to let the royal family leave the palace and take refuge among the Roman legions encamped outside the city. Not only did she want their protection from any potential mob actions; she also hoped the move would somehow get Mariamne into Mark Antony's presence. The proud mother was convinced that if Antony could catch just one glimpse of her daughter's beauty, he would restore the family's fortunes and put a Hasmonean back in power.

Alas for the women, the rumor turned out to be untrue. The arrival of a personal letter from Herod proved that, in fact, just the opposite had happened. Herod had showered Antony with lavish gifts, which, along with his own personal charm, quickly won over the Roman ruler. So convinced was Antony of Herod's innocence that he even went as far as upbraiding his beloved Egyptian consort. He told Cleopatra it would be best if she didn't meddle in his affairs. Herod ate at Antony's table every night and retained his favor despite Cleopatra's constant slander. The old boys' network had proved too strong to break. Herod announced in his letter that he would be arriving home soon, strengthened by the knowledge that Mark Antony supported him now more than ever.

But while Herod had scored a great political victory, his domestic troubles were far from over. No sooner did he arrive in Jerusalem than his mother, Cyprus, and his sister, Salome, rushed into his presence to reveal the true feelings of the Hasmonean women. "They're both plotting against you," Herod's female relatives reported, "and they despise you with an undying hatred. They rejoiced at the thought of your death." Salome even went so far as to betray her husband, Joseph, whom she accused of having frequent sexual relations with Mariamne. Salome said this because she resented Mariamne for constantly asserting her Hasmonean superiority and mocking Salome's low birth.

The bombshell accusation had its intended effect. As the historian Josephus put it, "Herod, who had always felt a burning love for Mariamne, was at once violently disturbed and was scarcely able to bear his jealousy, but he had enough control of himself all this time not to do anything rash because of his love." Though he didn't hurt his wife, he fiercely interrogated Mariamne, who denied the terrible accusations under oath. Only after many vehement protestations of innocence did Herod's anger begin to cool. Eventually, he even apologized to Mariamne for believing such shameful things about her.

The couple began to weep and embrace as they made up. Holding his beloved wife in his arms, Herod tenderly expressed his affection and begged Mariamne to feel the same for him. But she looked back into his eyes and countered, "It isn't the action of true love to command that if something bad happens to you, I should be put to death as well."

If Mariamne hoped this statement would lead her husband to further repentance, she was sorely mistaken. Herod exploded into a new rage and shoved Mariamne away. At first, he couldn't even speak but only gripped his hair so hard that tufts of it came out in his hands. When words finally came to him, he leveled a finger at Mariamne and snarled that he now had irrefutable and damning proof of her liaisons with Joseph; for a man would only reveal such a secret within the confidence of lovers.

Herod stormed toward the wide-eyed Mariamne with murder on his mind. His grip on her shoulders was fierce as she tearfully protested her innocence. Only with great difficulty was Herod able to restrain his violent urge to choke the life out of her. At last, he released Mariamne, who fled the room. Yet Herod's uncontrollable rage had to be vented somewhere, so he ordered the immediate execution of his uncle Joseph—a man who was actually his faithful friend—without even hearing his side of the story. Herod also slapped Alexandra in chains and kept her under guard for her role in stirring up so much domestic strife.

Meanwhile, up in Syria, Cleopatra was still trying to bring down Herod. By nature, she was ruthless and greedy. She had already poisoned her teenaged brother and convinced Mark Antony to execute her sister. She also had slandered numerous eastern rulers and snatched their lands when Antony agreed to prosecute them. No prize was beyond her desire and no means of getting it was beneath her scruples. Nor could any extravagance sate her extraordinary appetite. Now her covetous eye turned once again to the best of Herod's lands.

A famous story recounts how Cleopatra bet Mark Antony she could throw him the most lavish banquet ever—one that cost 10 million sesterces. Since one of the wealthiest men in Roman times was said to have owned estates worth 200 million sesterces, we can see that the sum Cleopatra proposed to spend on a single banquet was astronomical. It represented 5 percent of the total wealth held by that society's richest man, all consumed in a matter of hours. Today's equivalent would be a banquet costing $11.7 billion.

Mark Antony gladly took the wager, for he doubted his lover could win it. The next day, Cleopatra offered a typical banquet of the kind served every day, a meal that made Antony laugh at its modest cost. He believed he had won the bet. But Cleopatra only smiled and reached to her earlobe, from which she plucked an enormous pearl, one of the two largest in the world. Antony watched with curious eyes to see what she would do. Dropping the pearl into her cup of vinegar, she waited a few moments for it to dissolve, then proceeded to drink away the priceless gem. Antony's jaw dropped at the colossal expenditure. Calmly, and with a cocky smile, Cleopatra reached to her other ear for the second giant pearl. Only the intervention of another diner at the table, the referee of the wager, stayed her hand. "Antony has already lost," he declared.

In light of Cleopatra's rapacious greed, Herod rightly feared her designs on his kingdom, especially when she showed up unannounced in Judea. Though Mark Antony had departed on a war campaign, he had empowered Cleopatra to make yet another land grab. The powerful Roman ruler was so besotted by his consort—there is even evidence that she had him under the control of a drug addiction—that he had authorized her to steal some of the most precious territories in Judea and Arabia. Cleopatra had decided to lay claim to her new territories in person. "Hand them over," she demanded of Herod, and he was forced to comply.

Among Herod's losses was a region around Jericho famed for two natural sources of lucrative exports: palm trees, whose dates possessed honey-like sweetness, and rare, highly valued balsam trees. So precious was the aromatic sap of this plant that it was worth twice its weight in gold. Called "balm of Gilead" in the Hebrew Scriptures, the balsam tree extract served as an ingredient in many ancient medicines to cure various maladies. Herod had been reaping a hefty income from the trade in balsam, as well as dried palm dates and sweet date wine. When Cleopatra seized his lucrative orchards and gardens, he was obliged to pay two hundred gold talents to rent the properties back from their new owner just to keep the exports going.

Yet land-grabbing wasn't Cleopatra's only form of trickery during her Judean visit. She actually attempted to seduce Herod to her bed. Such lascivious behavior had become second nature to her. Sexual debauchery was her daily habit, and due to her immense power, she had no need to hide it. Nothing hindered the queen's indulgence in whatever fantasy pleased her. Herod was a trim, good-looking king in his late thirties. His charming tongue, obvious wealth, and aura of power made him even more alluring. To have sex with such a man would be a delight. Yet Cleopatra knew that once the deed was done, she could use it to her advantage. It would be easy to portray the tryst as a rape and thereby enrage Mark Antony. In that state of mind, an order of execution would be no problem to obtain.

Cleopatra immediately began flirting with Herod as they traveled around Judea and investigated her new landholdings. "I want you," she whispered to him when they were alone in the exotic palm groves of Jericho, backing up her words with the undulating movements of a temptress. "My body aches with desire! I cannot hold back any longer."

To Herod's credit, he resisted Cleopatra's repeated invitations, convinced that a fling with Antony's consort would surely lead to terrible accusations later. It wasn't divine law or devoted love for Mariamne that deterred Herod; it was fear of the repercussions. Knowing the power of his own jealousy, Herod had no intention of arousing it in his powerful Roman ally.

Instead, Herod contemplated a secret assassination of the troublesome Egyptian queen. Only the vigorous protests of his advisers, who scared him with visions of an enraged Mark Antony marching against him, convinced Herod to relent. Wisely, he took a gallant and respectable approach, showering Cleopatra with gifts and escorting her to the edge of Egypt before parting ways.

All of these dreadful conspiracies and betrayals in the royal household stand in sharp contrast to the simple marriage of Joachim and Anna. Far from the tumultuous Jerusalem palace, in a more peaceful and pastoral setting, this husband and wife lived out their humble lives in a God-fearing way.

It is worth considering one ancient account of Joachim's character, a description that comes from a later era yet reflects the traditions that the early Christians believed about this man. The account goes like this:

> In those days there was a man in Israel, Joachim by name, of the tribe of Judah. He was the shepherd of his own sheep, fearing the Lord in integrity and singleness of heart. He had no other care than that of his herds, from the produce of which he supplied with food all who feared God. . . . Therefore his lambs, and his sheep, and his wool, and all the things he possessed, he used to divide into three portions: one he gave to the orphans, the widows, the pilgrims, and the poor; the second to those who worshipped God; and the third he kept for himself and his entire house. And as he did so, the Lord multiplied to him his herds, so that there was no man like him in the people of Israel.[1]

These words depict a man of piety and virtue. Though Herod might have wished for such honorable things to be recorded about him, they were written instead about Joachim. He was a God-fearer and a giver of lambs for holy sacrifice. Little did Joachim know that his future grandson was destined to be the greatest sacrificial lamb of all.

---

1. J. K. Elliott, A Synopsis of the Apocryphal Nativity and Infancy Narratives, 2nd ed. (Leiden: Brill, 2016), 15.

CHAPTER 9

HEROD ON THE FIELD OF WAR

Though Mark Antony ruled the eastern half of the Roman Republic and waged wars of expansion with the Parthians and other eastern enemies, he wasn't the sole executive of Rome's incredible military might. During the early part of Herod's life, Rome was still a *res publica*—a "public thing." In other words, the government of the world's greatest city was held in common by the citizenry (which didn't include *all* the people in those days of slavery and strict class gradations, but still, a large number of elite people governed via the Senate). A *republic* can be distinguished from an *empire*, in which authority is vested in a single person. Mark Antony was no emperor, nor was his powerful colleague who ruled the West, Octavian. Yet due to the rivalry between these men, the Roman Republic was headed in an imperial direction. And as Rome went, so did the fate of one of its most loyal subjects: Herod, the client king who ruled Judea on Rome's behalf.

In the political division between Mark Antony and Octavian, Herod stood firmly on the side of his longtime patron. In fact, one of Herod's first deeds when he captured Jerusalem and established his kingship was to build a sturdy fortress, which he named the Antonia. This citadel loomed over the Jewish temple and gave the civic authorities a great deal of control over religious affairs. Troops could easily be deployed from the fortress if trouble arose in the temple precincts. Some Christian traditions identify the Antonia as the site of Jesus' trial, though that is historically questionable. Yet we do know that the apostle Paul visited this fortress, for Acts 21:34–37 describes how he was whisked into its confines when his gospel preaching evoked a violent response. Acts 22 then records Paul's evangelistic speech from the Antonia's front steps. Of course, back in Herod's day, the fortress's purpose was to enforce the king's will, not to proclaim the Prince of Peace.

In the late 30s BC, Mark Antony's relationship with his brother-in-law Octavian soured. A personal affront occurred when Antony divorced Octavian's sister so he could more freely run around with Cleopatra (whom he had illegally married under Egyptian rites). The insatiable political ambitions of these two Roman noblemen were bound to collide, leaving only one of them standing in the end. To every watching eye, a civil war seemed imminent. Battle preparations began to be made. This meant all the eastern subkings were expected to supply their patron with troops and matériel. Herod quickly mustered a good-sized army and began to march to Antony's aid, equipping his soldiers with top-notch weapons and gear. He was partway there when a message arrived instructing him to hold off. Antony wanted Herod to attack the Nabateans instead. How come?

When Cleopatra had grabbed a portion of Herod's prized lands, she had seized some Nabatean territories as well. Those Arabian holdings now owed her a fixed annual sum from their produce. To maintain control over the money flow, Herod had promised to serve as surety for the Nabatean king, guaranteeing the payment of two hundred gold talents in addition to his own debt of the same amount. But the Nabatean king, Malchus by name, had been remiss in sending his dues, forcing Herod to cover the obligation out of his own pocket. Mark Antony wanted that income more than he wanted Herod's troops, so he ordered his Judean proxy to go collect the debt. Since Malchus was the very king who had spurned Herod at Petra when he was fleeing the Parthian invasion, Herod had a triple reason to attack the Nabateans: revenge for the rebuff, obedience to Antony, and alleviation of the debts he had been covering.

Herod's nimble force of infantry and cavalry crossed the Jordan River and met the Nabateans head-on. The Jewish troops, full of esprit de corps, met with resounding success and put the Arabs to flight. But their spirited morale would soon be their undoing. They urged Herod to let them continue the assault even though a more careful approach would have been advisable. Herod allowed his men's zeal to prevail. They pressed forward and won the day—but then were ambushed on the way home by one of Cleopatra's generals who was hiding in the area. Herod's troops, flush with the exhilaration of victory and unprepared for more fighting, fell like wheat before the scythe.

This sudden turnabout revived the confidence of the Arabs, who returned to renew their own attack. Since the ground there was stony, Herod's horsemen couldn't operate well and the united armies overpowered them. A great victory had suddenly turned into a drubbing. Later, Herod would attribute the crushing defeat to insubordinate lieutenants who pressed the attack against his will. But the truth was, the combination of his too-aggressive strategy and an unexpected ambush had dealt Herod one of his worst losses ever.

As if the military setback weren't bad enough, the hand of almighty God suddenly seemed to be against the Jews. A terrible earthquake rocked the region, a tremor greater than any to strike Judea in living memory. Thirty thousand people were killed, not to mention untold numbers of cattle and sheep.

When the Nabateans caught wind of the calamity—its effects inflated by mouth-to-mouth retellings to the point that Judea was rumored to be empty and defenseless—King Malchus decided it was time to invade the neighboring kingdom. He slit the throats of the Jewish envoys who had sought a truce and crossed the Jordan in a swift offensive. Herod's demoralized troops caved before the assault and ran for the hills. Many more were slaughtered in battle. Herod's army never had been at such a low point. And that was when Herod did something remarkable and worthy of acclaim. He issued a rallying cry that deserves to stand alongside the greatest orations in all of military history.

The king's fiery speech has come down to us in two different works of Josephus. Combining them gives us a full picture of what Herod actually said. The setting was a military camp out in an open plain, a fortunate location that had preserved the army intact when the earthquake brought down shaky buildings on others' heads. Standing tall and handsome before his troops, with a sword on his hip and his cloak blowing in the wind, Herod began:

> I am not unaware, men, that during this time we have met many obstacles in our undertakings, and in such circumstances it is not likely that even men of superior prowess will keep up their courage. But since we are pressed to fight and nothing that has happened is so bad that it cannot be made good by one action well performed, I propose to encourage you and at the same time show you how you can keep your proper spirit.

The king then launched a broadside attack on the Nabateans, whom he called "a barbarous people without any conception of God." Not only had the

Arabs abandoned their obligations with respect to Cleopatra's tribute, they had gone so far as to slay the Jewish envoys—a group that in warfare was supposed to be held inviolable. Herod characterized the ambassadors as sacrificial victims—indeed, as crowned martyrs whose sacred memory must energize and revitalize the troops. "What greater impiety could there be," he asked his troops, "than to kill envoys who have come to discuss a just settlement? And how can [the Nabateans] possibly lead tranquil lives or have good fortune in war when such acts have been committed by them?"

Upon hearing these inflammatory words, Herod's men grew indignant. Their outraged shouts coursed through the camp as bright blades were raised to the sky. But Herod intended to do more than just infuriate his troops. He wanted to give them theological confidence in a coming triumph. Boldly, he reminded them that they alone "have God with them, and where God is, there too are both numbers and courage." Divine assistance had given the Jews the victory in the initial conflict. Although Cleopatra's general dealt them a treacherous blow, the fact remained that the original victory had been theirs, obviously reflecting the justice of their cause.

The subsequent earthquake, far from being an omen of God's wrath, actually signaled his special favor. "I regard that catastrophe as a snare which God has laid to decoy the Arabs and deliver them up to our vengeance," Herod declared. The news of the earthquake caused the enemy to be unwise, to rush into a battle they couldn't win. Whereas the Nabateans had to put their hopes in accidental calamities, the Jews would fight with courage and a sense of divine dependence. Herod looked his men in their eyes and urged, "You must teach these scoundrels that no disaster, whether inflicted by God or man, will ever reduce the valor of the Jews, so long as they have breath in their bodies!"

Herod described the slaughtered envoys as a source of inspiration and even of heavenly assistance, then concluded his speech with a rousing call to action:

> Bearing in mind these things, and—what is more important—that you have God as your protector at all times, go out with justice and manliness to attack men who are unjust to friendship, truce-violators in battle, sacrilegious toward envoys, and always unequal to your prowess. . . . Contrary to the universal law of mankind they have brutally murdered our ambassadors; such are the garlanded victims which they have offered to God to

obtain success! But they will not escape his mighty eye, his invincible right hand; and to us they will soon answer for their crimes if, with some vestige of the spirit of our fathers, we now arise to avenge this violation of treaties. Let us each go into action not to defend wife or children or country, but to avenge our envoys. They will conduct the campaign better than we who are alive.

Clearly, Herod's speech worked, for the men's zest for battle rushed back into their veins. After asking the Jerusalem priests to offer the appropriate sacrifices, Herod personally led his troops into the fray, promising them, "I myself will bear the brunt of the battle, if I have you obedient at my back." Courage had returned to the king's men, the confidence that they were on the Lord's side. Somehow, Herod could portray himself as God's chosen instrument even when he often did the things that God had expressly forbidden.

With his troops rallied and revitalized, Herod marched into Arabia and encamped near modern-day Amman, the capital of Jordan. Immediately, his forces began to harass the enemy and goad them into battle. Fear seized the Nabateans; dread even paralyzed their general. Though superior in numbers, the Arabian troops had no stomach for the fight. Five thousand men fell on the field of war; then their city was surrounded and besieged. When the Nabateans began to run out of water, many of them, parched with thirst, came out and surrendered.

Nevertheless, seven thousand diehards decided to make a final stand. But no sooner did they engage Herod's spirited soldiers than they were crushed and Nabatean resistance evaporated. The Arabian army was no more. The surviving leadership went into hiding. Since the common people admired Herod's prestige and prowess, they gladly came under Judean authority and named Herod as their protector.

After winning such a monumental victory after his initial setbacks, Herod should have been in the mood to celebrate. But instead he was "instantly plunged into anxiety about the security of his position." What could cause Herod's terror after such a magnificent triumph in service to his patron, Mark Antony?

Only a momentous event on the stage of world politics could have brought Herod to his knees like this. And as it turned out, such an event had just occurred: the Battle of Actium in 31 BC, one of the most pivotal moments in all of history. Herod understood that not just his throne but his very life was hanging by a thread that could break at any moment.

CHAPTER 10

A CHANGE OF ALLEGIANCE

During the years that Mark Antony went gallivanting about the eastern Mediterranean with Cleopatra, flaunting his extravagant love and even taking her as a pseudo-queen while he was still married to Octavian's sister, the Roman people watched it unfold with a skepticism that eventually turned to revulsion. When Antony divorced his Roman wife—who was admired by everyone as a paragon of feminine virtue—many senators finally called it quits. They defected to Octavian's side in disgust.

As a master propagandist, Octavian had been actively cultivating this widespread resentment of Antony. Octavian portrayed his rival as a lovestruck philanderer enslaved to a dynamic queen who was hell-bent on expansion. The prospect of an Egyptian conquest of Rome, though far-fetched, still managed to lodge in the popular imagination. Everyone remembered the ancient glories that the civilization on the Nile had achieved. Who was to say it couldn't happen again? All of this fear and disgust gave Octavian a sufficient pretext to declare war on Cleopatra. But of course, this was also a declaration of war on Mark Antony, who had cast his lot with the Egyptian queen and seemed poised to gain sole control of Rome.

The subsequent political maneuvering and military strategizing culminated in the famous Battle of Actium, a naval engagement off the western coast of Greece. Each side gathered an armada of warships in hopes of destroying the enemy once and for all. In addition to the galley oarsmen and combat-ready marines, land-based troops were stationed around the bay where the ships would, in theory, fight a winner-take-all confrontation.

However, it didn't turn out that way. A stalemate developed between the two adversaries, one that was far more destructive for Mark Antony than for Octavian. Antony's foolish war planning, so pitifully influenced by Cleopatra's goals, caused a rash of desertions from his camp. His provisions began to run low and disease hit the camp hard. Soon he didn't have enough rowers to man all his warships. Octavian also cut off Antony's rearward communication and supply lines. What had seemed as if it would be a great naval battle turned into a desperate hope for escape into the open seas. When Antony's galleys were furnished with sails—used for crossing large expanses of water, not for coastline fighting—the crew members knew what was coming. "Those sails are for chasing the enemy ships once we defeat them," Antony insisted. But the experienced seamen knew better.

The morning of September 2, 31 BC, started out with a storm but later became bright and calm. Mark Antony led out his 230 warships to face Octavian's 400. Though Antony was outnumbered, his vessels were larger and heavier, outfitted with bronze bands to prevent damage from ramming. Behind him was Cleopatra in her flagship, the *Antonia*, which commanded a squadron of sixty ships and was loaded to the brim with the Egyptian treasury. Each navy presented a formidable combat force, manned by marines who were itching to fight.

Throughout the morning hours the two sides didn't engage, remaining content to test one another's courage and wait for an advantage. Only when the regular afternoon breeze arose did Antony attack. For a time, the ships fought at close quarters, not using a ramming technique but instead exchanging a barrage of catapult stones, arrows, and sling bullets. Octavian's smaller ships surrounded and swarmed Antony's heavily fortified ones. The combat was more like a hard-fought siege on land than a naval battle with deft sea maneuvers.

The match appeared to be even and capable of going in either direction until Cleopatra suddenly joined the action. Her sixty ships threw the battle into confusion as she punched through the blockade to make a run for Egypt. Then, to everyone's great surprise, Antony abandoned his troops in the heat of battle and joined his queen in flight. Moved not by the instincts of a commander nor of a hero, Antony sacrificed his mighty warship and fled the scene on a speedier craft. Cleopatra took him on board when his vessel caught up to hers. The ancient historian Plutarch said Antony was "dragged along by the woman" as if his soul dwelt in her body and he must go wherever she did.

With their commander gone, Antony's remaining naval men lost their nerve. Their ships were assailed with firebombs and terribly burned. Though the lovestruck pair did manage to escape, Antony carried the burden of a crushing defeat. For three days, he sat alone in the prow of the *Antonia* and brooded over his loss of personnel, power, and prestige. Further news from Actium only confirmed the extent of the disaster. Antony's land army hadn't fought Octavian, nor even attempted a march around the eastern Mediterranean to rejoin him. Instead, they had defected en masse to his rival once they learned of their commander's cowardice. Utterly defeated and virtually alone in the Roman world, Mark Antony landed in Egypt where, like Pompey the Great before him, he and Cleopatra would meet their fateful ends.

Historians debate exactly how those ends were met. For a while, grim despair took hold of Antony. He lived alone in a little hut at the foot of Alexandria's famous lighthouse. But eventually, he decided to go out in grand style. He engaged in banquets and heavy drinking, renaming his previous party club from "The Order of Inimitable Livers" (that is, those who live so large that no one can imitate them) to "The Order of Comrades in Death." As for Cleopatra, she locked herself inside a huge mausoleum, surrounded by heaps of treasure—gold, silver, gems, precious woods, spices—along with enough tinder and firewood to burn it all to ashes. If Octavian wanted that treasure intact and unburnt, he would have to negotiate with the wily Egyptian monarch.

When Mark Antony heard of Cleopatra's refuge in a mausoleum, he seems to have misunderstood what had happened and took her for dead. Possibly she even sent him a message saying so, for she feared he might turn on her. Distraught and despairing, Antony ordered his most faithful servant to slay him, but the servant chose to kill himself instead of his revered master. With admiration, Antony cried, "Well done! Though you were unable to do what you were commanded, you have taught me what I must do," then rammed a sword into his own gut.

Although the wound was fatal, Antony hadn't yet died when some other servants found him writhing in pain and crying out. Upon learning that Cleopatra still lived, Antony demanded to be carried on a stretcher to her mausoleum. Since the queen couldn't open the massive doors, she lowered ropes from a window to haul up her wounded lover, assisted only by two hand-maidens. Plutarch described the piteous scene:

> Smeared with blood and struggling with death he was drawn up, stretching out his hands to her even as he dangled in the air. For the task was not an easy one for women, and scarcely could Cleopatra, with clinging hands and strained face, pull up the rope, while those below called out encouragement to her and shared her agony. And when she had thus got him in and laid him down, she rent her garments over him, beat and tore her breasts with her hands, wiped off some of his blood upon her face, and called him master, husband, and emperor; indeed, she almost forgot her own ills in her pity for his. But Antony stopped her lamentations and asked for a drink of wine, either because he was thirsty, or in the hope of a speedier release.

As the great Mark Antony breathed his last, he reached up to touch Cleopatra's face, urging her "to count him happy for the good things that had been his, since he had become the most illustrious of men [and] had won greatest power." And with that, Antony let his drooping eyelids close, content in the knowledge that he hadn't been defeated by some uncouth barbarian, but was still a nobleman conquered by a fellow Roman.

What about Cleopatra? During the months between the Battle of Actium and Octavian's invasion of Egypt, she had started conducting detailed research on poisons. The cruel queen had even hauled condemned criminals into her presence to observe what happened when various formulas were administered to them. She discovered that the poisons that led to the quickest deaths also caused the greatest pain. She then experimented with the bites of venomous animals. Cleopatra found that the bite of the asp, and it alone, induced a sleepy stupor from which a person could not be roused. The victim seemed to feel no distress beyond a light perspiration on the face.

Armed with this knowledge, Cleopatra prepared for her own death. Desperate to avoid the humiliation of being displayed in the streets of Rome for Octavian's victory parade, she refused to be dislodged from her mausoleum.

Only when one of Octavian's henchmen secretly climbed through the same window by which Antony had entered was Cleopatra captured. She attempted suicide with a knife but her captors prevented it and took her to their commander. Her worst fear had come true: she had fallen into Octavian's hands.

Yet at least he did not throw her in a dungeon. Octavian wanted her to recuperate so she would look good for his later triumphal display. For several days, Cleopatra lingered in sickness and pain. The fierce clawing she had given to her breasts tormented her. Even so, she found the strength to visit Mark Antony's tomb where his ashes were interred. Clinging to his urn, she vowed not to be made part of any parade that celebrated a victory over her beloved husband. When Octavian came to visit Cleopatra in her sickroom, he promised to be merciful and let her live comfortably after all was said and done. But the haughty queen knew better, and she had other plans.

Plutarch recorded that a basket was delivered to her private rooms as part of the evening meal. When the guards stopped the delivery man, he opened the lid to reveal a dish of huge, delicious-looking figs. "Have some," the delivery man invited. The guards grinned and took some of the fruit, then waved the man into Cleopatra's quarters. There, accompanied only by her two handmaidens, she wrote a final request upon a tablet, sealed it, and dispatched it to Octavian after the meal. Then she reached beneath the harmless figs and removed a poisonous asp.

When Octavian received the note, he knew instantly what had happened. Swift messengers were sent to investigate. Arriving breathlessly, they discovered that the guards didn't suspect a thing. But when the door to the private rooms was opened, a scene of death confronted the men. The asp had delivered three fatal bites. Cleopatra lay dead on a golden couch, arrayed like a queen upon her bier. One of her two handmaidens had already swooned from the powerful venom, while the other was arranging a diadem on Cleopatra's head when the guards burst in.

"What a fine deed this is!" shouted one of the outraged guards.

"Indeed it is fine," the second handmaiden replied, "for it befits the descendant of so many kings." And with those last words, she, too, fell to the floor in the throes of death.

Despite Octavian's frustration at Cleopatra's suicide, which thwarted his desire to display her in a victory parade, he honored her written request.

Cleopatra had begged to be entombed next to Mark Antony. At Octavian's command, the two of them were placed side by side—ardent lovers in this life now conjoined forever in whatever afterlife awaited them.

After so many years of fighting, Octavian had finally achieved sole possession of the Roman Empire. When he eventually held his triumphant parade through the streets of Rome, an image of thirty-nine-year-old Cleopatra was carried along in the procession. Everyone remarked on her stately appearance. Yet even more noteworthy was an unexpected addition to the portrait. Octavian had depicted Cleopatra with an asp entwining her body and two puncture marks upon her arm. That image would echo down through the ages to our own day. Whether it portrayed events that really happened or was just another bit of propaganda to cover up a murder is one of the many mysteries that surround Egypt's greatest queen.

What did all of this mean for King Herod? Obviously, the rug had been pulled out from under him. His mighty patron was now gone. The victor in a civil war didn't usually look kindly on those who had supported his opponent. Indeed, Octavian had already executed many of Mark Antony's partisans and he was on the lookout for others to eliminate. It was in this dangerous context that Herod pulled off the biggest U-turn of his life, perhaps one of the greatest political maneuvers of all time. He decided to meet Octavian head-on and cast his lot with the new Roman emperor. In this monumental endeavor, Herod was helped along by his personal charisma, smooth tongue, and the seemingly infinite resources of the Judean treasury.

When the news of Actium reached Judea, Herod's friends saw where things were headed and abandoned him. His opponents feigned sympathy but secretly took delight in his looming downfall. No one thought he could escape severe punishment, much less retain his hold on power. Everyone knew about his association—indeed, his deep friendship—with Mark Antony. It was said that Octavian didn't consider Antony fully defeated until his Judean ally was conquered as well. Though Herod could have cowered in Jerusalem awaiting his fate, that wasn't his style. When he learned that Octavian had come to the nearby island of Rhodes, Herod rushed to the coast, jumped in a ship, and sailed off to plead his case—though not before stationing his mother and sister at Masada and his wife and mother-in-law at another remote fortress, lest they stir up strife in his absence.

Standing before the victorious new emperor, Herod resolved neither to beg for mercy nor to proudly antagonize him. He would simply take a middle course of truthful directness. Herod wore no diadem or royal robes, yet he kept a dignified bearing worthy of a king. In plain terms, he explained that Mark Antony had indeed been his friend. Loyalty to a friend, Herod explained, was a virtue from which Octavian could benefit as well. Though Herod had done everything to advance Antony's cause during the time of their friendship, he gently reminded Octavian that he hadn't borne arms against him in the civil war. He had been engaged with the Nabateans instead.

Nevertheless, Herod admitted to sending money and grain to his colleague to help him in war, which is what any true friend should do. Herod also declared that he had served as a wise counselor to Antony, urging him to execute Cleopatra and make peace with Octavian (advice that not only would have benefitted Herod but no doubt sounded good to Octavian's ears). "I share in Antony's defeat, and with his downfall I lay down my crown," Herod concluded. "I have come to you with a plea for safety that rests upon my integrity. I can only hope that what matters most will not be whose friend I have been but how loyal I was to that friend."

After a moment of tense silence, Octavian chuckled and asked Herod to draw near. The Arab campaign that Herod had been forced to wage turned out to be his salvation. Octavian didn't view Herod as an enemy who had fought against him but as someone who had faithfully carried out his superior's orders. Octavian's astounding response to Herod's speech was:

Nay, be assured of your safety, and reign henceforth more securely than before. So staunch a champion of the claims of friendship deserves to be ruler over many subjects. . . . I therefore now confirm your kingdom to you by decree; and hereafter I shall endeavor to confer on you some further benefit, that you may not feel the loss of Antony.

After offering these gracious words, Octavian—soon to go by the title of Caesar Augustus—brought forth a royal diadem and placed it with his own hands on Herod's grateful brow. He also published the official decree of Herod's confirmation so everyone would accept it without a doubt. And Octavian later made good on his promise of further benefits by not only returning the palm orchards and balsam groves that Cleopatra had stolen but putting several new territories and tax-rich cities under Herod's dominion. The historian Josephus summed up Herod's triumphant homecoming from Rhodes with the understated observation, "Then he returned to Judea with even greater honor and freedom of action, thereby causing consternation among those who had expected the contrary, for it seemed as if he were one who by the kindness of God always achieved more brilliant success in the midst of danger."

And who would have (as Josephus so mildly put it) "expected the contrary"? Obviously, Alexandra and Mariamne had the most to gain from Herod's hoped-for downfall. These two co-conspirators boiled with resentment at Herod's apparent invincibility. Earlier, he had managed to get away with the drowning of Aristobulus in the swimming pool, convincing Mark Antony it was an accident while everyone else knew what had really happened. Now, another powerful Roman ruler had been duped by Herod's personal charm. *How did this lowborn Idumean keep managing to fool the whole world?*

As if Herod hadn't done enough to antagonize his wife and mother-in-law by the drowning of Aristobulus, the trip to Rhodes also served as the basis for putting to death another Hasmonean luminary: the former high priest, John Hyrcanus, who was directly descended from the founder of the Maccabean clan. As Herod headed off to his risky meeting in Rhodes, he had no intention of leaving behind such a prominent ruler, whom Octavian might replace him with. Better to take that option off the table. So after charging the elderly patriarch with sedition, Herod had him executed.

If the old man with the mutilated ears had remained among the distant Babylonian Jews, he could have lived out his life in honor. But his love for his homeland tempted him to return when Herod had summoned him back to Jerusalem in more peaceful times. That decision ultimately resulted in his death, which inflamed the anger already raging within his daughter, Alexandra, and his granddaughter, Mariamne. We cannot simply describe them as "enraged," "livid," "incensed," or "infuriated." Those puny words fail to describe the volcanic anger boiling within them. They loathed Herod with a visceral, daggerlike hatred that could have only one remedy: his immediate death—preferably painful and bloody—and the restoration of a true Hasmonean to the Judean throne.

What makes this family dynamic all the more complex is a fascinating and counterintuitive truth about Herod: he absolutely adored Mariamne. One might think this would have prevented the execution of her brother and, a few years later, her grandfather. But in the crazy Herodian clan, bloodshed, hatred, devotion, and obsession comingled in a toxic brew. Josephus described the king's feelings toward his queen this way: "Herod's passion for Mariamne, the consuming ardor of which increased from day to day, [made him] insensible to the trouble of which his beloved was the cause; for Mariamne's hatred of him was as great as was his love for her."

Blinded by love—if we can call it that—Herod couldn't discern his wife's true feelings for him. He mentally denied her disloyalty and continued to fawn over her like an infatuated teenager. The marriage that began with the betrayal of Doris was fated for future treachery. Both Aristobulus and Hyrcanus had fallen victim to Herod's murderous hand. To Alexandra's and Mariamne's way of thinking, that hand had done enough damage to last a lifetime. It was time for someone else's ruthless hand to take revenge upon Herod once and for all.

CHAPTER 11

BETRAYAL AND BLOODSHED

Out in the desert fortress of Masada, scorched by the unrelenting sun, Queen Mariamne seethed with an unquenchable fury. The intense heat overhead was tepid compared to the inferno within her soul. So bitter was Mariamne's world that she could scarcely abide it. *I am a Hasmonean*, she told herself. *I am the daughter of ancient kings! I should have the power to enforce my will . . . control my fate . . . inspire fear in all those around me. Instead, I am trapped under an appointed guardian, monitored like a little girl with a babysitter!* The feeling of being hemmed in—controlled by men, unable to leave the few acres of empty sand atop Masada's plateau—nearly drove Mariamne mad. Her only consolation was that Herod had gone to Rhodes to grovel before Octavian. Surely his throne would be taken from him. Even better would be his death at the emperor's command. Then things could get back to the way they ought to be.

During the enforced exile at Masada, both Mariamne and Alexandra had been using their feminine charms on Soemus, the man whom Herod had put in charge of them. At first, Soemus had been a stickler for Herod's rules. But over time—with the careful application of a compliment, a flirtatious bat of the eye, a little gift here or there—Soemus had softened. There were no sexual invitations, of course, for that would be far too dangerous. Yet adultery wasn't required here. All that was needed was the slow but steady manipulation of the male ego. "You know, Soemus, after Herod is gone, Mother and I are going to be left in charge," Mariamne suggested in a sly voice. "You'd be wise to be on our side. We could use a man of your impressive abilities."

Soemus took the advice to heart and eventually began to divulge information. "Herod commanded me to kill you both if Octavian does him in," he confessed. The news infuriated and terrified Mariamne at the same time. Once again, the two women would be victims of Herod's political miscalculations.

They would have to die for his foolish blunders. *Will there ever be an end to these threats against my life? Almighty God, please stretch forth your hand and destroy this man! Let Octavian's full rage be vented on Herod!*

Unfortunately for Mariamne, almighty God had other plans. When the news arrived that the exact opposite of her prayers had happened, the young queen couldn't believe what she was hearing. For weeks, all her hopes had ridden on the expectation that Herod would be dethroned, demoted, debilitated, maybe even decapitated. *But no! Octavian actually honored him? Crowned his head with a diadem? Promised the return of his lands, plus many more? Showered him with compliments? Confirmed his right to rule by imperial decree?* The shocking turn of events was too much to bear. As Mariamne rode back to Jerusalem with her mother in the royal carriage, she felt as if she were traveling to her own grave. "My life is intolerable," she muttered as she stared out the window. Alexandra could only nod her head in agreement.

The two women arrived at the Jerusalem palace around the same time as Herod. The triumphant king, revitalized by his trip to Rhodes, stepped down from his carriage and rushed to embrace his queen. Though various courtiers and Herodian relatives stood about, it was Mariamne whom Herod most wanted to see. "His Majesty honored me!" Herod exclaimed, though Mariamne already knew it full well. "Octavian blessed me beyond measure. He retained me as king. Now my rule is secure!"

Mariamne didn't even bother to conceal her revulsion at Herod's embrace. To be caressed by this lowborn Idumean felt like being defiled by a rapist. "That's wonderful," she managed to say as she squirmed out of his arms and backed away. She didn't care whether the palace officials noticed how fake her smile was. Though the churning in her stomach made her want to vomit, Mariamne held herself together long enough to go through the motions of celebrating Herod's good news.

The king, however, wasn't fooled. He could sense Mariamne's displeasure—indeed, her abhorrence of his very touch—and it bothered him greatly. When he had hugged her, she literally groaned aloud. Clearly, something was bothering her. Herod resolved to find out what it was. Yet once those tender feelings passed, anger rushed in to replace them. *How dare she reject me in front of my own courtiers? A king has the right to demand the affection of his queen. If she won't provide it, I'll find one who will!*

No, Herod reminded himself. *You mustn't hurt her. You'll regret it later. You can't live without her. That fate would be worse for you than for her!*

Herod's turbulent state of mind persisted for many weeks as he and Mariamne experienced a whirlwind of emotions. They kept repeating the same accusations against each other without ever getting close to forgiveness and resolution. Eventually, the couple's relations grew strained to the breaking point. The fractured state of their marriage presented a perfect opportunity for Cyprus and Salome to pursue their grievances against the Hasmonean women.

Ever since Herod's mother and sister had come into the Judean orbit, they had been fighting undisguised prejudice against their foreign birth. Shamed again and again by relentless mockery or aloof snobbery, the two women were in no mood to help Herod patch things up with his wife. They believed they were defending Herod's best interests when they slandered Mariamne and accused her (falsely) of numerous infidelities. But this only put the baffled king in a worse predicament. The historian Josephus remarked that Herod "was neither unwilling to listen to such statements nor courageous enough to take any action against his wife [despite his] belief in them." Herod and Mariamne were locked in a death spiral of mutual suspicion, hatred, codependence, and hostility.

A reprieve came in the marital infighting when the arrival of important news turned Herod's focus elsewhere. Octavian had officially ended the Roman civil war after Mark Antony and Cleopatra had committed suicide in Egypt. Herod knew Octavian would be traveling up the sea road along Judea's western coast. Previously, after the two of them had patched things up at Rhodes, Herod had gone to excessive lengths to provide food, water, and a friendly escort to Octavian as he marched his army down to Egypt to finish off the doomed lovebirds. Now Herod wanted to show the same loyalty on the emperor's return trip. He met Octavian in Egypt and supplied all his needs—plus many extra luxuries—on the way up to Antioch.

Octavian deeply appreciated the assistance, especially since he knew the lavish generosity Herod was bestowing on him exceeded his small kingdom's budgetary means. It was at this time that the grateful Octavian restored Herod's palms and balsam at Jericho, just as he had promised, as well as adding many other territories to Judea's dominion. Since these were lands that earlier Hasmonean kings had once possessed, the territorial expansion strengthened

Herod's claim to be a ruler on par with prior Jewish luminaries. Octavian even gave him a bodyguard of four hundred Gauls who had once served the mighty Cleopatra. The move signaled that Herod was just as important as the famed Egyptian queen.

Nevertheless, despite these wins, Herod's household troubles persisted. Josephus wrote that "the more he believed himself to be increasingly successful in external affairs, so much the more did he fail in domestic affairs, especially in his marriage, in which he had formerly seemed so fortunate." Herod and Mariamne endured the kind of tragic relationship that epic sagas and Shakespearean romances often chronicle—a toxic obsession that typically ends, just as with Antony and Cleopatra, in violent death.

Josephus described Mariamne as respectably chaste, never unfaithful to Herod in the sexual realm. Her physical beauty, of course, could be rivaled by no one. Nevertheless, "She had in her nature something that was at once womanly and cruel, and she took full advantage of [Herod's] enslavement to passion." Never did she treat him with proper wifely submission, nor with the obedience due to a king, but only with arrogant disdain. Although Herod laughed at this and pretended to take it lightheartedly, the disrespect ate away at his soul. He seethed internally when she dishonored him in front of others or reviled Cyprus and Salome as ignoble commoners.

For a full year, this terrible situation continued to simmer and bubble like magma beneath the surface of the earth. And then one fateful day, the volcano's top blew off and spewed deadly lava onto everyone in the palace, scorching everything it touched and leaving no one unharmed. Herod had retired on that particular day to his bedroom for an afternoon siesta; but first he called Mariamne to his bed. He spoke affectionately to her, inviting her to lie down with him. Clearly, he wanted to have sex with his wife. But instead of complying with a sweet spirit, Mariamne once again upbraided him for killing Aristobulus and Hyrcanus. Furious at the rebuff, Herod rebuked Mariamne for her constant arrogance and verbal contempt. Though Herod sent her away, those closest to him sensed he was about to lash out in a violent fashion.

At this highly charged moment, Salome recognized an opportunity to put in motion a prearranged plan. She sent Herod's butler to his master with a bit of disturbing information. The butler revealed that Mariamne had urged him with bribery to slip a love-potion into Herod's cup. (Ancient people believed that such potions would put the male recipient under the spell of the female who administered it, making men easy to control.) Salome had told the butler to gauge Herod's response to the news. If he reacted negatively, the butler was supposed to say that he didn't know the potion's formula, only that Mariamne had prepared it. But if the king's response was indifferent, the butler could simply let the matter drop.

Herod, of course, flew into a rage when he heard the butler's revelation. He asked what the drug was, but the butler denied knowing any details; his only purpose in speaking up had been to help the king. Desperate to know more about the drug, Herod put Mariamne's most trusted slave under torture. Since the whole story was made up, the poor fellow, despite being in extreme agony, couldn't reveal anything about the love-potion that didn't actually exist. Yet as the hot irons were mercilessly applied to his skin, the slave did admit that Mariamne's hatred had been stirred up by Soemus's revelation of Herod's order to kill his wife if things went sour at Rhodes.

Now the anger that Herod had earlier felt toward his uncle Joseph resurfaced, this time directed toward Soemus. Only if that man were in an intimate relationship with Mariamne would he have revealed such a closely guarded secret. Instantly, and without any formal inquiry, Herod ordered the death of a man whom he had once viewed as a faithful friend.

But while Soemus was summarily executed, Herod granted a trial to Mariamne. Convening his closest advisers and counselors, the furious king put his wife under hard questioning. Not only did he grill her about the love-potion; he accused her of infidelities with Soemus. Though Mariamne tearfully protested her innocence, Herod's advisers could see his insane jealousy. They had no wish to cross him in such a foul mood, so they ignored Mariamne's desperate pleas as they contemplated whether to sentence her to capital punishment.

At this moment, another voice spoke up at the trial, one that sealed Mariamne's fate. Her mother, who had always been faithfully on her side, now turned against her. The desperate Alexandra, fearing the reprisals that might fall on her own head in this toxic situation, threw Mariamne to the dogs to save her own skin. "You wicked girl!" she shouted at her daughter, jabbing her finger in fierce accusation. "You have always disrespected your honorable husband! Constantly you slander him, despite all he's done for us! Now your punishment is just." Then Alexandra ran forward and seized Mariamne by the hair, shaking her violently as she sought to prove her own innocence. "What an ungrateful wretch you are! You deserve to die for your crimes!" Once this terrible scene had played out, the counselors could no longer deny where things were headed. Lest any of them seem to be on Mariamne's side, they unanimously sentenced her to death. Herod immediately accepted the decree.

Yet after this heated moment had passed, cooler heads began to prevail. Some of the counselors advised Herod—in concord with his own wishes as he began to regret his rash decision—that Mariamne should only be exiled to some remote fortress. But while the men dithered, Salome jumped into the fray again. "Don't hold back from your decision, my brother!" she urged him. "If you let this woman live, the people will rise up in protest. They love you too much to allow your queen to treat you like this. They don't want to see her exiled. They want to see her *dead*."

"You are right," Herod agreed. "I will do it."

And with that, Mariamne had reached the end of her line. She was executed on Herod's direct orders in 29 BC. Josephus reported that she went to her death with grace and decorum. Even when her mother had shaken her by the hair in the courtroom, Mariamne didn't dignify such unworthy behavior with a reply. Though everyone could see she was in great distress, somehow, the princess had managed to maintain her aristocratic composure.

As she was led out to the execution grounds to be decapitated, Mariamne's face wasn't pale nor was her step faltering. Instead, her noble bearing proved to the onlookers that she was worthy of her Hasmonean bloodline. According to Josephus, Mariamne's only flaw was her inability to curb her tongue. She couldn't help but berate her husband—whether for his treacherous crimes, his low birth, or his twisted expressions of love—in the mistaken view that he would never hurt her. But in this life-or-death calculation about King Herod, his beloved queen found out the hard way that she was sorely wrong.

The death of Mariamne immediately began to drive Herod mad. From the beginning, his love for her had been what Josephus called "enthusiastic"—a Greek-based word that described a frenzied madness caused by demonic possession. Now those dark forces seized Herod and held him in their fierce and unrelenting grip. "What have I done? Oh God, what have I done?" he asked himself over and over, then asked it again. Yet no solace came to him. Herod never had been able to control his intense desire for Mariamne. Even when he supposedly possessed her in marriage, his drive to conquer her had only increased. Now, with Mariamne executed, Herod's quest to possess her could never be fulfilled. She was dead and gone forever. Though he knew this on a rational level, his mind began to deny reality as his world spun out of control.

To maintain his tenuous hold on sanity, Herod tried to distract himself with parties and entertainments. Of course, the day-to-day governance of Judea was thrust to the side as Herod struggled to cope with his mind-twisting grief. Yet everyone in the palace knew he was losing the mental battle. Often, he would call out his wife's name or burst into inconsolable groans. "Bring Mariamne to me," he would sometimes order his servants as if she were still alive. But she never came to see the heartbroken king. One ancient Jewish source, the Babylonian Talmud, claims that Herod preserved Mariamne's corpse in honey for seven years and he would sometimes even copulate with it. While those legends cannot be verified, such behavior wouldn't have been out of character for Herod in the extremity of his insane grief.

To make matters worse, a deadly plague struck Judea at this time. Everyone interpreted the disaster as God's judgment upon their king. The pestilence claimed some of Herod's wisest advisers and closest friends. All of this plunged him into deeper depression. Though he went away on a hunting trip to escape the threat of sickness and the travails of palace life, the disease caught up with him in the wilderness, tormenting him with headaches and mad raving. No remedy could heal the despondent king. The doctors feared for his life.

When Alexandra learned of Herod's seemingly fatal illness, she sprang into action. She demanded that the troop commanders hand over Jerusalem's two strongest points: the Antonia fortress at the temple and Herod's fortified palace near the present-day Tower of David (where one of the three Herodian-age towers still stands). Whoever controlled these twin citadels in Jerusalem would control the whole Jewish nation, for they safeguarded the daily temple sacrifices without which the Jews could not survive. Alexandra argued that these strategic military sites should be held in her possession so no illegitimate claimant could seize them if Herod were to die. "Of course, I will give them back if he happens to live," Alexandra promised.

But the commanders didn't believe her. They were old friends of Herod's. In fact, one of them was Achiabus, the loyal cousin who later prevented Herod from stabbing himself in the gut. These military men immediately dispatched a messenger to Herod at his hunting retreat where he was struggling to recover from the plague. Whether he was in his right mind when he received the message is hard to say. What Herod did realize was that he'd finally had enough of Alexandra's incessant scheming. "Execute that woman," he ordered.

The command was swiftly carried out. Alexandra the Hasmonean, who had betrayed Mariamne in the courtroom, now joined her daughter in death as yet another victim of Herod the Great. The line that was crossed when the jealous king ordered Aristobulus to be drowned had led directly to the slaughter of Herod's beloved wife, her grandfather, and her mother. Where would the bloodshed end? Clearly, the violence in Herod's household reflected the growing mayhem within his own soul.

CHAPTER 12

PAGAN JERUSALEM?

The turbulence in the Herodian household stood at the opposite end of the spectrum from the godly peace within Joachim and Anna's home. Their generosity toward God with their resources had been blessed by him in return. Their marriage rested on a solid foundation because it was based on mutual worship of the Lord, not an obsessive worship of the self that led to using each other for selfish gain.

Despite their marital harmony, the one trial that came to Joachim and Anna was their barrenness. Though God eventually answered their prayers and sent an angel with good tidings, for twenty years the couple lived without conceiving a child. Their long struggle is worth considering, especially in the way that Anna's experience mirrors the archetypal narrative of infertility in Scripture: the story of Hannah, the mother of the prophet Samuel. Through the parallel accounts of these two Jewish heroines, we gain four key insights about the proper way for a devout woman to conduct herself before God.

The first thing we notice when we compare Anna with her biblical namesake, Hannah, is that *life's trials call for authentic lamentation.* The opening chapter of 1 Samuel describes how Hannah's childlessness terribly afflicted her soul, especially when her rival (who was her husband's other wife) mocked her infertility. Assailed by such profound anguish, Hannah "wept and did not eat" (1:7). So total was her sorrow—involving not just her inner thoughts but her outer body—that even her husband could not understand her desolation.

In the same way, Anna deeply grieved her inability to conceive. She laid her sorrow before God with many tears and sang a dirge to the heavens. Anna's song expressed her sadness at being mocked when her husband's sacrifices were rejected at the temple. Mournfully, she compared herself to a nest of sparrows, bubbling waters, and the fertile earth—all of which brought forth life while she could not. Both Hannah and Anna expressed authentic lamentation to the God who sees.

The second thing we learn from these two heroines is that *life's trials must be taken into the presence of the Lord.* The families of Hannah and Anna were known for attending the temple worship of Israel—both husband and wife alike. Only in a house of prayer can life's deepest problems find resolution. When Hannah brought her petitions before God at the temple, the high priest, Eli, mistook her silent utterances for a sign of inebriation. "No, my lord," she replied. "I am a woman of sorrowful spirit. I have drunk neither wine nor intoxicating drink, but have poured out my soul before the LORD" (1:15). This response elicited a blessing from Eli.

In the same way, Anna took refuge in God's presence by finding a quiet place in her garden; for prayers can ascend from any holy sanctuary, not just the formal temple. In that peaceful, natural place, Anna prayed for deliverance from the infertility that troubled her soul. Like Hannah, she had the wisdom to seek God's presence in a time of need.

Our third lesson is that *open hands lead to blessed hearts.* Both Hannah and Anna relinquished to God what they desired most. Their stories parallel each other in perfect harmony: Hannah gave her son, Samuel, to serve in the temple, while many centuries later, Anna did the same with Mary. Neither of these mothers clung to what they so deeply desired. Instead, they devoted their offspring to the Lord's service, trusting that he would know what was best for their children. While Anna was still caught in the struggle of her infertility, she prayed with great faith, "For you, O God, know my heart, that from the beginning of my married life I have vowed that if you, O God, should give me a son or daughter, I would offer them to you in your holy Temple." At the very moment when Anna uttered these words an angel appeared to announce God's pleasure to grant conception. Anna's open hands had led to a blessed heart.

Finally, these two godly women teach us that *divine blessing must receive a voice of thankful response.* It is not enough to praise God in the quietness of one's inner thoughts. When God's power shows up in a big way, a public acclamation of his holy name is required. According to one ancient account, the angelic news of Anna's pregnancy led her to Jerusalem's Golden Gate— the very gate through which the Messiah will someday return to claim his kingdom. There, Anna awaited her husband's return from the wilderness. When Joachim arrived, Anna testified publicly about what God had done for her. "And when this was heard of, there was great joy among all their neighbors and acquaintances, so that the whole land of Israel congratulated them." Then Joachim threw a banquet at which everyone ate, drank, and made merry. The great deeds of the Lord always require a public celebration and thanksgiving.

Anna's grateful attitude finds a precedent in the famous Song of Hannah (1 Samuel 2:1–10). Long before Anna's lifetime, Hannah exalted the Lord for his wonderful work on her behalf. Her glorious song let everyone know who deserved the praise and who did not. The wealthy, the powerful, the arrogant, the self-sufficient—each of these is brought low before almighty God. In his own good timing, the Lord raises up the humble and brings down the proud.

The new mother rejoiced that she had found favor with God. Hannah also longed for the day when God would "give strength to His king, and exalt the horn of His anointed" (2:10). That future hope was why Hannah began her song with the exultant cry, "My heart rejoices in the LORD! The LORD has made me strong. Now I have an answer for my enemies; I rejoice because you rescued me" (2:1 NLT). The opening words of that prayer remind us of another godly woman—still unborn in Hannah's day—whose soul would likewise magnify the Lord at the annunciation of angelic good news.

For King Herod, it wasn't the Lord's name that needed to be magnified; it was his own. His reputation, once synonymous with glory and prestige, had taken a hit in recent times. Herod had backed the loser in a colossal civil war, then only barely managed to switch sides after his foremost ally was vanquished. Closer to home, his bloodstained hands had started the rumor mill turning in Judea. Two high priests, Aristobulus and Hyrcanus, had died under mysterious circumstances. So had a royal matriarch. Even Herod's own wife had been killed—a beautiful princess from the revered Hasmonean lineage. No amount of fake legal charges could erase the fact that Herod was starting to look like a ruthless tyrant, a persecutor of friends and enemies alike. Perhaps he was even a madman? The troubled king realized he needed to change the narrative and clean up the Herodian name.

But as Herod considered how to execute the plan, a puzzling conundrum confronted him. The two constituencies he needed to please most, the

Jews and the Romans, wanted to see exactly the opposite outcomes. Herod had convinced the Senate, and even Caesar Augustus himself, that he was a proud Roman with the kind of values that would make Jupiter smile from up on Mount Olympus. But Herod's Jewish subjects hated Rome and anything that smacked of *Romanitas*. Worst of all were the pagan gods. So if Herod tried to show himself a good Roman, the Jews would balk. On the other hand, if Herod placated his Jewish subjects, he would look like a worshiper of the crude, backwater god that the Romans believed Yahweh to be. *How do I solve this dilemma?* Herod wondered. *Could I split the difference and win both sides?*

True to his bold and undaunted nature, Herod didn't opt for a fifty-fifty approach but one hundred–one hundred. Starting in the year 28 BC and continuing for the better part of the next two decades, he embarked on a building campaign the likes of which the world has rarely seen. Indeed, Herodian architecture was one of the king's most lavish gifts to his people. The ruins of his edifices can still be seen all over the Holy Land and even as far away as Greece. Every modern photo of Jerusalem's skyline centers on the massive Temple Mount that Herod constructed. Though the temple itself is gone, no one can miss the monumental stone blocks called *ashlars* for which he became famous. But Herod was playing both sides. In addition to honoring the God of the Jews, he also funded the construction of temples for the pagan gods and for emperor worship.

Though Herod's temple architecture remains one of his lasting legacies, putting up religious buildings wasn't the only way the energetic king tried to restore the luster of his tarnished reputation. He also demonstrated his Romanitas through the ever-so-Roman practice of staging games, hunts, and gladiatorial combats. When modern people think of Rome, the image of the Colosseum immediately springs to mind. There's good reason for that. The ancient Romans perfected the art of turning brutal slaughter into glitzy entertainment. Though today's sports can sometimes turn rough, they pale in comparison to what went on in every major city of the Roman Empire. Beheadings and bloodshed, not bumps and bruises, resulted from those life-and-death contests. It was Herod who decided that even the Holy City shouldn't miss out on the gory fun.

The precise location of Herod's Jerusalem coliseum—more properly called an amphitheater—is something of an archaeological mystery today. Nobody has been able to locate it beneath the modern city.[1] Nevertheless, the ancient historian Josephus clearly referred to a new building used for sporting events, along with a new theater for staging plays. He reported that Herod's games and spectacles were especially noteworthy for their lavish scale. The bountiful prizes awarded to the winners lured all types of famous contestants to the various competitions: athletes in footraces and gymnastic games, chariot drivers, horse racers, even actors and musicians. As if a good chariot smashup wasn't bloody enough, Herod imported lions and other exotic African beasts to put on display in his amphitheater. These unfortunate animals were pitted against one another or else trained hunters were matched against them. Condemned criminals were also thrown in the ring to be slaughtered by the beasts.

To make sure nobody missed the intended PR message, Herod erected inscriptions in honor of Caesar Augustus around these public venues. But what irked the Jews even more than all the imperial flattery, bloodshed, bawdy plays, or naked sporting competitions were the victory monuments that Herod installed in plain sight of every pious eye. These so-called trophies were great heaps of weapons—forged out of gold or silver for extra glory—that symbolized the enemy weapons captured in Caesar's battles. The Jews believed these memorials weren't just empty symbols but served as hidden idols to worship Rome's military gods.

All of these actions got Herod in hot water with the local religious authorities as well as the more scrupulous observers of the Jewish faith. On the other hand, we begin to find Greek inscriptions from this time that use interesting new terms to describe Herod. One was *philokaisaros*, "friend of Caesar." Even more total in scope was *philoromaios*, "friend of the Romans." Herod's reputation with his distant overlords was well on its way to repair, even if the local Jewry didn't like it.

In order to placate the offended Jews, Herod adorned Jerusalem with some

---

1. Several modern scholars believe an amphitheater for gladiator combat was combined with a horse racing track into a single multipurpose entertainment venue (which is similar to how Rome's Circus Maximus was sometimes used). Certain archaeological remains in Jerusalem have been identified as the possible ruins of such a structure. Other scholars believe these buildings were originally made of wood and later decayed, which is why we haven't found any remains of them beneath the modern city of Jerusalem.

nice touches that could make the citizens proud. He erected three magnificent towers above his palace, the tallest of which was equal to a fifteen-story building—a true skyscraper by the standards of antiquity. Indeed, these three towers pleased the Jerusalemites in the same way that New Yorkers take pride in the Empire State Building or Parisians delight in the Eiffel Tower. One of the pinnacles contained a deep cistern to supply the water needs of the palace residents. All three of them were made of finely crafted stones, so perfectly joined that they looked like natural rock rising from the earth rather than a man-made construction.

Herod named the two tallest and stoutest towers for his deceased brother, Phasael, and his dear friend Hippicus, who had fallen in battle. The third tower, more slender and beautiful than the others, was named Mariamne. Its upper portions contained gorgeously decorated apartments that served as fitting tribute for Herod's beloved former queen. Today, the base of one of these towers—either the Phasael or the Hippicus—survives at the Citadel in Jerusalem's Old City. Later generations mistook it for an earlier structure and renamed it the Tower of David. But it wasn't King David who built this structure; it was a successor of his who wished to possess the mantle of David but often fell short of the kingly ideal.

Of course, not all Jews in those days lived in Jerusalem. The central area of ancient Israel, formerly known as the Northern Kingdom, had come to be called Samaria and was inhabited by quasi-Jews whom the Judeans looked down upon. As a quasi-Jew himself—that is, an Idumean whose people had only lately come into the true faith—Herod felt sympathy for the Samaritans. He honored their territory by building a huge new city called Sebaste, which is the Greek form of Caesar's Latin title of Augustus. The rebuilt city thus served to honor Herod's new master while at the same time giving the Samaritans a point of pride to rival Jerusalem. But instead of housing a temple for Yahweh, Herod crowned the highest point in Sebaste with a temple to Caesar Augustus, thereby endorsing the emerging practice of emperor worship. Though this didn't please the Judean Jews, the local Samaritans couldn't help but take pride in the impressive architectural achievement that had been set up in their midst. Sebaste's premium location in the middle of a fertile agricultural area also made the locals feel that God cared even for their form of the Jewish religion.

Yet agriculture could always fail; and it did, terribly so, in 25 BC. A widespread and persistent drought robbed the whole region of productivity for two straight years, not only decimating the cultivated crops but preventing the growth of any plants at all. Soon the storehouses were depleted and the people began to starve. Their weakened condition led to rampant disease that claimed those whom starvation did not. The grieving survivors couldn't muster the will to do anything about their horrific fate. Everyone sat around, waiting to die. Despair reigned in Israel.

Since the famine was juxtaposed against Herod's expansive building campaign, the people began to hate him for his selfish constructions that seemed to come at their expense. Under duress from this rising tide of disrepute, and thus moved more by self-preservation than by pity, Herod melted down all the gold and silver ornaments from his numerous palaces, including many items that had sentimental or artistic value. With a treasury full of newly minted coins, Herod was able to purchase a rare commodity: Egyptian grain from the government storehouses that normally wouldn't be allowed for export. But since Egypt's current ruler was a personal friend of Herod's, an exception was made and the beleaguered king obtained the precious foodstuffs that put him in the role of savior to his people.

And Herod doled out the rations wisely. To those capable of preparing it for themselves, he gave careful measures of raw grain, while the aged and infirm received already-baked bread from government bakeries. He also distributed woolen clothing to keep the people warm during the winter, since any wool-bearing sheep had long since been consumed as food. Herod even made himself a friend to the surrounding nations. To any neighboring country that sought his aid he gave precious seed, saving those people and enhancing his reputation for generosity at the same time. When the rains returned at last, Herod dispatched fifty thousand workers on his own payroll to help with the harvest, taking the place of the many farmers who had perished. The crops came in and the people were saved.

All in all, the crisis of the famine turned out to be a huge victory for Herod. Josephus remarked: "Now Herod's solicitude and the timeliness of his generosity made such a powerful impression on the Jews and were so much talked about by other nations, that the old hatreds which had been aroused by his altering some of the customs and royal practices were completely eradicated throughout the entire nation, and the munificence shown by him in helping them in their very grave difficulties was regarded as full compensation." In other words, Herod went from being viewed as a Romanizing supporter of foreign customs to a generous and resourceful king who had the welfare of God's people at heart.

To cement this newfound affection, Herod contracted a new marriage as a replacement for Mariamne. He took a Samaritan wife, Malthace—a choice that further pleased the already giddy people of Sebaste. Clearly, their new city was on the rise. Yet in order to win the approval of the Judeans as well, Herod married another woman, ironically named Cleopatra but called Cleopatra of Jerusalem to distinguish her from Herod's former nemesis.

Soon after this, a third woman—again, one with an ironic name—came to Herod's household and bed: Mariamne II, the daughter of a minor priest. One thing about her was similar to the original Mariamne: she was "considered to be the most beautiful woman of her time." When Herod caught wind of the rumors about this Jerusalem belle of the moment, he took one look at her and was "greatly smitten by the girl's loveliness." At first, he considered raping her, but he quickly decided that would bring shame on him so he opted for marriage instead. Yet since the prospective bride's station in life wasn't high enough to deserve the status of being a queen, Herod deposed the current high priest and gave the job to Mariamne's father. Now her family had the necessary prestige to allow a marriage to Herod. Needless to say, Herod's intemperate lusts and wanton polygamy stood in sharp contrast to the biblical marriage of Joachim and Anna, who embodied God's original design that two faithful spouses should become "one flesh" (Genesis 2:24).

With peace now established in his kingdom, the famine alleviated, and a house full of wives to please every constituency, Herod finally felt he was in a good place again. He was fifty years old and at the top of his game. To what great project could he turn his attention?

Herod's answer would become a marvel of ancient engineering and lavish magnificence. He decided to build something that his kingdom sorely lacked: a gateway he could call his own, a point of entry from the Mediterranean Sea that would serve Judea and Samaria without foreign interference. The new port city of Caesarea—named, like Sebaste, in honor of Caesar Augustus—would rise from a bare stretch of coastline that God had not endowed with the natural necessities of a harbor. But that didn't matter to Herod. He would bend the very fabric of land and sea to his will. In so doing, he would establish a direct line to Rome itself. The future Caesarea by the Sea would become a wide-open portal to the Roman world and all that it had to offer. But by lifting the lid of this Pandora's box, would Herod lose his Jewish soul?

CHAPTER 13

GATEWAY TO ROME

The eighty miles of coastline between the Roman province of Syria to the north and Herod's southern port city of Ascalon formed a gentle arc of windswept beaches without a significant break anywhere along its length. The long, flat plain up and down the coast made for a natural trading route, one that ancient caravans had been using to travel between Egypt's delta and Anatolia or Mesopotamia since time immemorial. This corridor was a natural land bridge between continents, aptly called the *via maris* or "way of the sea." The prophet Isaiah predicted the Messiah's arrival with the words, "The people who walked in darkness have seen a great light; those who dwelt in the land of the shadow of death, upon them a light has shined" (9:2). And where would God's holy deliverer arise, according to Isaiah? "By *the way of the sea*, beyond the Jordan, in Galilee of the Gentiles" (9:1).

King Herod, however, was thinking less about messianic implications and more about economic ones when he considered the geography of his domain. The coastline that was so perfect for a north-to-south highway—with road branches running into Galilee, Samaria, and Judea—also made for a lousy place to moor a ship. No natural landforms jutted into the sea to stand between anchored vessels and the fierce Mediterranean winds. For that reason, the captains of large merchant ships passed along Israel's coastline but rarely stopped. No great sea traffic brought the wares of the world directly into the central part of Herod's kingdom. He was determined to change that, the natural landscape notwithstanding.

Several centuries earlier, the Phoenician king Straton I had built a seaside fortress that came to be called Straton's Tower. Eventually, a community grew nearby that included some naval commerce. But by Herod's day, previous attempts at creating a harbor there had fallen into disrepair. The southwest winds constantly dredged up sand, backfilling whatever attempts had been made to create a port. To make matters worse, the incoming waves crashed against the rocky cliffs and rebounded out to sea, creating turbulent water that no sailor wanted to navigate. Yet it was here, at this dilapidated village along a dangerous stretch of coastline, that Herod decided to build his grand new city. Caesar Augustus had awarded him control over the little community, and by God—or by the gods?—Herod was determined to make something of it.

The first order of business was a new harbor, for merchant vessels wouldn't come calling if they couldn't find safe moorages. At great expense, Herod's workmen created floating wooden frameworks that could be towed into position and filled with a special underwater concrete made from Italian volcanic ash. These huge chunks of concrete were clamped together and submerged to a depth of 120 feet. Many individual blocks were fifty feet long, eighteen feet wide, and nine feet high—some even larger. Alternatively, a large wooden box with stakes could be pounded into the ocean floor and filled with concrete to set hard, then the box was removed. On top of this concrete wall, a mole made of stone and rubble was raised above sea level to create the harbor's basic shape.

When the whole thing was complete, the ingenious construction formed two long, curving jetties that served as protective arms into which ships could be welcomed. The above-water surface of each jetty was up to two hundred feet wide, equal to two-thirds of a modern football field. Half of this width served as a breakwater to hold back the pounding waves, while the other half was surmounted by a seawall to provide shelter from the wind and spray. Lofty towers lined the harbor's wall, the highest of which was named for Augustus's stepson, Drusus, whose premature death was commemorated in this magnificent way.

Now that the ships had a safe place to dock, it was time to beautify the wharf. Herod created a lovely promenade all the way around the inside of the harbor, "a very pleasant place to walk for those who wished to do so," according to Josephus. The mouth of the harbor was oriented toward the north so only the gentlest of breezes would caress the cheeks of the pedestrians on a hot summer's day. Gorgeous mansions of polished white stone adorned the seafront, inhabited by wealthy traders and other important townsmen. Spacious avenues separated the palatial homes from one another. All the streets were laid out according to the meticulous city planning for which the Romans were famous.

But inside the harbor's embrace, right where the city met the waterfront, one resplendent sight surpassed all the mansions, walkways, boulevards, and towers combined. Herod ordered the construction of a broad terrace that rose four stories above sea level to form an artificial hill. Its main axis was set on an angle, aligned directly with the mouth of the harbor so incoming ships would see it as they approached. Expensive homes flanked three sides of the terrace, while its fourth side faced directly onto the waterfront promenade.

On top of this smooth-paved terrace, which was accessed by a marble staircase coming up from the quay, Herod erected a magnificent temple whose colonnaded porch gazed out upon the western sea toward Rome. This was no temple for Yahweh, nor for any other local god. Two colossal idols sat enthroned within the inner sanctum. One depicted the deified Caesar Augustus, modeled after the statue of Zeus at Olympus, while the other was the goddess Roma, who personified the capital city and appeared as Caesar's royal queen. Clearly, Herod intended his new port of Caesarea by the Sea to forge an unbreakable tie with his imperial patron and the divine glory of Rome itself.

Unfortunately, the surrounding area lacked a sufficient water supply for a large population, but that didn't deter Herod from raising a city at his chosen site. His workmen instead constructed an aqueduct that piped in fresh water from natural springs in the foothills of Mount Carmel, six miles to the northeast. When the pipeline hit a ridge of stone, the diggers simply tunneled through it and kept going. The aqueduct terminated at a civic holding tank from which ceramic or lead plumbing conducted the water to beautiful fountains where the women of the city could fill their jars. Other lines carried the water to neighborhood spas where the citizenry could refresh themselves in heated baths or socialize in swimming pools and saunas. Once all this water was used up, the complex underground sewer system—no less expensive than the aboveground constructions—carried away the city's effluent and sent it out to sea. Clever engineers constructed the system so that incoming pulses of seawater would regularly flush the hidden pipes.

To provide civic entertainment at Caesarea, Herod included all the standard accoutrements of a Roman town, including a theater and hippodrome. The first was used for plays and musical recitals while the second housed chariot races, footraces, wrestling, and gladiator bouts. At the city's inauguration after a decade of construction, the king instituted magnificent games to be repeated every five years. The victors won the most extravagant prizes. Yet Herod also awarded substantial prizes to the second- and third-place finishers, providing an incentive for all the best athletes and combatants to compete in the Caesarean games. Over four thousand spectators could attend the theater, while the stadium held around thirteen thousand bloodthirsty souls.

A king as wealthy and grandiose as Herod required, of course, a residential and governmental palace worthy of his name. This he constructed on a natural promontory that jutted into the sea, providing views on three sides from the second-story windows. All the rooms of the residential complex faced inward upon a sunny courtyard with a lovely swimming pool in the center. A reception hall and grand dining room served to welcome Herod's most esteemed guests. Mosaics, marble columns, and painted frescoes adorned the palace at every turn. Down at the tip of the peninsula, a covered porch offered shade from the Mediterranean glare and caught the passing sea breezes. Couches on the porch would allow the king to watch trading ships arrive from distant ports or enjoy a sunset on the horizon.

Where the palace promontory met the mainland, Herod also constructed a governmental complex that housed a giant audience hall, numerous guest rooms, baths, and even a heated floor for brisk winter days. Yet this opulent praetorium also included a stout military guard so no one would think the king's lavish lifestyle meant he had gone soft. Herod was always a ruler first and an epicure second. A good supply of soldiers had to be kept nearby at all times. If the necessary barracks and forts could be adorned with sumptuous luxuries, so much the better.

After the days of Herod, the city of Caesarea went on to have important biblical and church historical significance. The book of Acts attests that the two foremost apostles, Peter and Paul, both spent time there. One of the city's military leaders, a centurion named Cornelius from the Italian Regiment, gave generously to the poor and worshiped the true God. When he received a divine vision, he sent messengers to Peter, who came to his house and shared the good news of Jesus. "I perceive that God shows no partiality," the apostle announced to the centurion's household. "But in every nation whoever fears Him and works righteousness is accepted by Him" (Acts 10:34–35). To back up this bold claim of a universal gospel, the Holy Spirit came down upon the new Gentile believers. Thus Cornelius became the first non-Jewish convert to the Christian faith.

Likewise, the apostle Paul made evangelistic forays into Caesarea. He was also remanded in chains to this city after he was accused of crimes and appealed his case to Rome. So great was the local antagonism toward Paul that he had to be guarded by two hundred soldiers, seventy horsemen, and two hundred spearmen—a troop that traveled in the middle of the night to avoid conflict. Upon arrival in Caesarea, Paul was jailed in the very praetorium that Herod had constructed eighty years earlier (Acts 23:35). Despite all this opposition, Paul was undaunted. He proclaimed the gospel to three high-ranking officials with holy boldness. After a two-year imprisonment, Paul was shipped from Caesarea to state his case before Nero.

Yet it wasn't just friends of the gospel who lived at Caesarea. Ironically, the grandson of Herod the Great, known as Herod Agrippa, resided at the family palace and eventually met his end there. This later Herod was a persecutor of the church, killing the apostle James (the brother of John, not Jesus) and ravaging many of the early believers. The New Testament records how God responded to his pride and arrogance: "So on a set day Herod, arrayed in royal apparel, sat on his throne and gave an oration. . . . And the people kept shouting, 'The voice of a god and not of a man!' Then immediately an angel of the Lord struck him, because he did not give glory to God. And he was eaten by worms and died. But the word of God grew and multiplied" (Acts 12:21–24).

The Jesus-hating evil of Herod Agrippa was rivaled only by another resident of Caesarea, a fact we know because of an astounding archaeological discovery in 1961. In that year, a stone was uncovered whose inscription recorded that a temple for emperor worship was erected at Caesarea by none other than Pontius Pilate, the prefect who condemned Jesus Christ to death. A government official of his status and rank would have lived and worked in the Herodian praetorium. The characters of the New Testament, whether good or evil, couldn't help but interact with the important city that King Herod built.

In the later centuries of church history, Caesarea continued to be a prominent location. It became home to the most significant Christian library of the ancient church. The brilliant scholar Origen took up residence there in the third century AD. Origen's wealthy patron provided him with numerous scribes for the copying of Christian books. The rapidly growing collection made Caesarea the preeminent place for studying theology, Bible translations, and church history. In the fourth century, the famous bishop Eusebius of

Caesarea presided over the library. His ten-volume *Church History* is still a vital source for reconstructing the activities of the ancient Christians. Much later, after Caesarea had fallen to Arab conquerors, the medieval Crusaders arrived on its shores and made the city a central location for their invasion of the Holy Land. Today, the archaeological site of Caesarea by the Sea is administered by the national park service of Israel.

Back when Caesarea was newly carved out of the rocky coastline, it displayed in grand fashion King Herod's attachment to the ruler of the Roman Empire. Every architectural detail conveyed a message of imperial reverence that was really a form of emperor worship. Yet for Herod, this fawning adoration wasn't limited to one city on the sea. He dotted his entire domain with reminders of his unwavering devotion to his patron. Josephus remarked, "One can mention no suitable spot within his realm which he left destitute of some mark of homage to Caesar. And then, after filling his own territory with temples, he let the memorials of his esteem overflow into the provinces and erected in numerous cities [many other] monuments to Caesar." With such a widespread propaganda campaign like this, no one could miss Herod's allegiance to the divine Augustus. But how did all this Romanophilia sit with Herod's Jewish subjects?

Obviously, they didn't like it. Yet the true depth of their hatred for Herod's friendship with the Romans can be seen in an incident that nearly claimed Herod's life. Although he tried to explain to the Jews that he was forced to build pagan temples and monuments by the expectations of Gentile rulership, many of them weren't buying it. A secret group of conspirators decided that the changes Herod had wrought would be only a precursor to more apostasy. It was their sacred duty to Yahweh, the plotters decided, to eliminate their irreverent king. And so they decided to assassinate him. Ten men—including a blind fellow who could only offer moral support—swore an oath to kill Herod as a holy offering to God. They began to carry daggers under their cloaks and seek an opportunity to use them.

The day came when Herod was headed to Jerusalem's theater for the day's entertainment. No doubt he was glad to enjoy some of the fruits, if not of his physical labors, then at least of his expenditures to build so many venues for public amusement. But as Herod arrived at the theater and started toward his personal box, one of his spies rushed to his side. "There's a plot against you!" the man exclaimed. "We've found an informant who told us everything!"

Knowing the hatred that his recent actions had aroused, Herod didn't consider the report improbable. *It seems every time I do something for the Gentiles, the Jews rise up in protest!* Instead of entering the theater, the king retreated to his palace under armed guard. Using the knowledge obtained from the informant, Herod summoned the ten conspirators by name. To their credit, they didn't deny their deadly desire but displayed their daggers and proclaimed their purpose was pious. "All Jews have a duty to preserve God's customs or die for them," the men declared.

"Then die you shall," Herod replied.

The king's troops led away the men in chains. After exposing them to every kind of torment, Herod had them publicly executed. As for the informant who had snitched to Herod's spies, some locals found out who this traitor was and seized him. The enraged men not only killed him but "cut him apart, limb from limb, and threw him to the dogs." Though many people witnessed the revenge killing, no one wanted to convey the news to Herod, whose life had been saved by the now-dismembered man. Eventually, however, Herod made an inquiry into the disturbance. He learned the true facts only after torturing some women who had witnessed what had happened. Then Herod punished not only the men who had killed the informant but their families as well.

Though Herod had emerged from the conflict unscathed, the close brush with death left him concerned. The religious passions of his subjects could too easily lead to conspiracies, perhaps even to open rebellions. To deal with this constant danger, Herod decided it was time to surround Judea with fortresses that would remind everyone of the repercussions they would encounter if treason crossed their minds. *The sight of nearby dungeons will be a good deterrent,* Herod reasoned.

And so he embarked on another kind of building campaign, not one of civic munificence but of military prowess. His ring of fortresses would be constructed in a manner worthy of his reputation: powerful beyond assault, luxuriously appointed, and defiant of nature's limitations. Herod would build many such redoubts in the coming decade, foremost among them the splendid palace-fortress at inhospitable Masada. Though Herod didn't know it at the time, he was creating a lofty stage where many great events in Israel's future were destined to play out. It is to that famous desert fortress of Masada that we must now turn our attention.

CHAPTER 14

GREATNESS ACHIEVED

In the year 23 BC, Herod was a fifty-year-old man at the height of his wealth, fame, and power. During the decade of his fifties, the energetic king initiated many of the building projects that would define his legacy and leave a lasting mark on the world. We have already seen how he turned a decrepit coastal village into a thriving harbor city that bustled with international trade and served as a gateway for Rome's elite. Forever afterward, the city would be called Caesarea in honor of the Roman Empire's founder. We have also seen how Herod turned the Jewish capital of Jerusalem into a true Roman city, endowing it with the necessary features of modern life in the imperial age. Yet it wasn't only in a civic context that Herod displayed his architectural brilliance. He also adorned remote desert crags with lavish palaces. The most amazing of these lofty retreats was Masada.

Herod wasn't the first military tactician to recognize Masada's strategic value as a natural fortress.[1] Earlier Hasmonean rulers had built fortifications on top of the plateau, providing a good place for Herod to hide his family when he had to flee Jerusalem because of the Parthian invasion. Later, he was forced to fight a battle at the plateau's base to rescue his besieged family. Apparently

---

1. Nor was he the last. Long after Herod was gone, an army of Roman soldiers assembled beneath the plateau to set a siege against the Jewish freedom fighters encamped on top. These patriots (often referred to as Zealots) had rebelled against Rome, sparking an immediate war. After piling up a massive amount of rubble to form an assault ramp, the legionaries rolled up a siege tower with a battering ram and began to smash Masada's walls. Battle cries filled the air as the final confrontation approached. But upon breaking through the defenses, the attackers weren't greeted by fierce shouts or the slashing swords of resistance. Instead, an eerie silence pervaded the plateau. Finally, two old women emerged from their hiding place along with five children. One of these seven survivors told the Romans what had happened. With many tears of lamentation, the males among the rebels had killed their beloved wives and children. Then they drew lots to determine which ten men would kill the rest. After their necks were slashed, the ten executioners again drew lots to determine who would slay the other nine. The last man alive lit Masada's palace on fire, turning the plateau into a vast altar for a holocaust offering, then ran himself through with a sword. Rather than be captured and enslaved by the Romans, the adamant resistors had committed mass suicide. They performed this renowned act, so Josephus informs us, on the evening of the Passover in the year AD 73.

these events—and their dramatic location—made a deep impression on Herod. After he secured his power, he immediately improved the plateau's top by adding a royal residence, some barracks for the troops, and more storehouses and cisterns.

However, a decade later, such basic accommodations were no longer enough for a great king like Herod. Sometime in the 20s BC, he embarked on a project that would adorn the plateau's surface with a palace that still astounds visitors today. We can imagine that on a blazing summer day, with the pale blue expanse of the Dead Sea shimmering nearby, Herod approached the north end of the plateau and peered over the edge. The plateau's top was oval-shaped with a point at either end, making it reminiscent of a ship. Herod stood at the north-facing prow of the ship. Below him were two broad ledges, one above the other. Perpetual shade guarded these terraces from the sun's fierce glare. A delightful coolness met Herod as he descended a short way over the rim, giving him a sheltered eagle's aerie from which to survey the stark desert landscape. "I must have a palace here," he decided. And soon enough, it was so. Herod's builders wasted no time fulfilling their master's architectural vision.

The main plateau level of the Northern Palace was approached by a footpath from the water cisterns. A wide-open space served as a kind of plaza before entering the palace itself. Herod's guests would be met in a grand reception hall, off which branched bedroom suites decorated with floor mosaics and wall frescoes. The great hall led out to a semicircular balcony under a protective colonnade. The view from here was grand. Yet a staircase beckoned the visitor to descend to the middle terrace.

Upon arriving at the first of the ledges beneath the rim, Herod's guests discovered a round building with open spaces between the columns, to again offer expansive views in three directions. A cistern and ritual bath on this level provided for the visitors' religious needs. Since this terrace was below the top of the plateau, its constant shade and the passing breezes served as natural air-conditioning to keep the guests cool.

Descending to the lowest terrace, the visitors came to yet another hall, this one in a square shape with a covered porch. An intricate stucco coating decorated all the columns, walls, and ceilings. Now the guests were shown to their private bedrooms in a sheltered nook. The view from their windows overlooked the sheer drop down the side of the plateau. It was a perfect place to relax and enjoy the magnificent vista. And of course, after the rigors of desert travel, a bath would be most welcome. The small yet sufficient bathing facility offered the triple pleasure of a warm lounge, a cold plunge, and a hot tub—no doubt a delightful indulgence on crisp desert nights. Surely the bathers must have marveled at the audacity of the man who had installed such luxury in the crags of a remote precipice. As for Herod, he just viewed it as yet another aspect of his inborn greatness.

———————

At the age of fifty-eight, Herod received some news that sent him into a frenzy of preparations. Marcus Agrippa, the second most powerful Roman after the emperor himself, was coming to Judea. Herod determined that Agrippa's welcome would be a grand one—the kind of reception that only a fabulously wealthy king could provide.

When Agrippa arrived in Caesarea, what he found there astounded him. The harbor with its waterfront temple to the emperor impressed even a man who had seen all the glory that Rome had to offer. Herod wined and dined his guest every day, omitting no luxury in his lavish entertainment. The two men traveled around Samaria and Judea as close friends. At each stop—whether at Sebaste, the desert fortresses, or Jerusalem itself—Agrippa found himself awestruck by his host's architectural ingenuity and high style.

The sacrifices at the Jerusalem temple especially caught Agrippa's eye. The great Jewish philosopher, Philo of Alexandria, told us that

> when [Agrippa] had beheld the temple, and the decorations of the priests, and the piety and holiness of the people of the country, he marveled, looking upon the whole matter as one of great solemnity and entitled to great respect, and thinking that he had beheld what was too magnificent to be described. And he could talk of nothing else to his companions but the magnificence of the temple and everything connected with it.

Day by day, Agrippa kept going back to the temple to behold the spectacle there. He gave many gifts to the Jews, including a hundred oxen to be sacrificed. Agrippa paid Herod many public compliments, and Herod returned them in abundance. It has been said that in those days, Agrippa loved Herod second only to Caesar Augustus, while Augustus loved Herod second only to Agrippa. Somehow, the king of the Jews had become the third greatest man in the Roman Empire!

Eventually, Agrippa returned to Caesarea with the whole Jewish nation escorting him along the road, scattering palm branches in front of him to honor his royal dignity. He sailed away from the sparkling new harbor before the winter storms could close the seas.

The following spring, Herod received word that his friend intended to attack a breakaway kingdom on the Black Sea. Since Herod had been building a navy at Caesarea, he decided to rush to Agrippa's aid with a fleet of warships. Due to bad weather, Herod missed Agrippa at Lesbos, then again at Byzantium. By the time he finally caught up to his friend on the shores of the Black Sea, the enemy kingdom had surrendered without a fight.

But no matter. The expedition gave Herod the chance to journey back through Asia Minor with Agrippa, enjoying each other's company as they returned home. Herod's easygoing demeanor made him fun to be around. Though he was a peer and equal, Herod always displayed humble loyalty to Agrippa. Together they entertained many local officials along their route, giving extravagant gifts at each stop and resolving petitions with efficient briskness. Everyone loved these two leading men of Roman politics.

Herod is known to history as Herod "the Great." If ever he deserved that description, it was during this phase of his life. Though he doesn't appear to have claimed the Greek title *ho megas* during his lifetime, his descendants did put that language on their coins, even though they were all inferior to their forefather. Josephus called Herod "the Great" only in one brief passage, where the term probably refers to his seniority within his clan more than his greatness as a king.

Yet "great" this man certainly was, despite his many flaws. According to Josephus, he had "pre-eminent gifts of soul and body, [and] he was blessed by good fortune." Herod was a skilled horseman and hunter who in a single day killed forty boars and stags in the chase. "As a fighter, he was irresistible," Josephus gushed. Whether with the bow or the javelin, his aim was unerring. In war, he rarely lost; and if he did lose, it was because his troops failed instead of their commander. Herod was rich beyond words, powerful beyond opposition, charming beyond resistance. His subjects viewed him as generous, capable, and wise—though not immune to occasional fits of rage or murderous revenge. Yet such vices were common to ancient kings. They could be overlooked.

I truly am a great king, Herod told himself on a daily basis. *There can be no question about it! Nothing more can be done to prove my greatness beyond what I have already achieved.*

Unless . . .

What if I rebuilt the temple of God into the greatest marvel the world has ever seen?

━━━━━━━━━━

Though Herod didn't know it, the great temple he was about to erect would serve as the home of an unknown Jewish girl whose honor would eventually eclipse even his own worldwide fame. This girl, Mary of Nazareth, wouldn't bear a title such as "the Great." She was no mighty ruler, no commander of armies, no wealthy aristocrat. Instead, the word that Scripture applies to Mary is *blessed*. She herself prophesied that "all generations will call me blessed" (Luke 1:48); and her relative Elizabeth declared, "Blessed is she who believed" the word of the Lord (v. 45). In fact, even Mary's womb and breasts would be blessed because of the Savior whom she would one day bear and suckle (Luke 11:27).

When was Mary born? Though we don't know the date for sure, it was probably sometime during this period of greatness in Herod's life. Scholarly estimates suggest that Jesus was born in the autumn of 5 BC, just before the death of Herod. Since Jewish girls in those times usually married in their mid-teens, we can conjecture that Mary was about fifteen when she was betrothed to Joseph. Fifteen years before 5 BC would be 20 BC, give or take a few years.

The ancient Christian document *The Original Gospel of James* may contain some accurate remembrances about Mary's birth and early life, interspersed with pious legends. According to this text, Mary's mother, Anna, realized that her daughter had a special destiny when she was only six months old. Anna set Mary on the ground, where she promptly toddled ahead for seven steps and fell into her mother's arms. Then Anna swore an oath to God that Mary would walk no more in the secular world until she had been brought to the temple for divine service. Anna made a sanctuary out of Mary's bedroom, allowing no unclean thing to pass inside. Holy Jewish girls from nearby in the village helped to take care of little Mary.

On her first birthday, Joachim celebrated a great feast. He invited the chief priests and scribes to attend, along with many commoners. The proud father asked the Jewish elders to bless the girl. They did so with the words, "O God of the heavenly heights, look upon this child and bless her with a supreme blessing which cannot be superseded." Then Anna took her baby into the bedroom and nursed her, singing a hymn of praise to the God who had opened her womb and granted conception.

When Mary turned two, Joachim suggested to Anna that the time had come to take Mary to the temple and dedicate her to holy service. But the mother's heart was still tender toward her tiny daughter. "Let us wait until the third year," she advised, "[so] that the child may then no more long for her father and mother."

"Yes, let us wait," Joachim agreed.

On Mary's third birthday, Joachim called for the virgin daughters of Israel to assemble at his house. Each was to take a burning torch in hand and escort the family to Jerusalem. Arriving there, the high priest took the toddler in his arms, kissed her, and blessed her, saying, "The Lord has magnified your name among all generations; because of you, the Lord at the end of the days will reveal his redemption to the sons of Israel." Then the priest set Mary upon the third step of the great temple. And what did the little toddler do? *She danced!* The ancient text tells us that "the Lord God put grace upon [Mary] and she danced with her feet, and the whole house of Israel loved her."

Though Joachim and Anna felt sad about giving up their daughter to God's service, they knew it was the right thing to do. As they departed, they paused and looked back at the gleaming temple. Mary was standing there, delighted by her new home, not crying for her parents. This gave great comfort to the godly couple. They marveled and offered up many praises, rejoicing that Mary was now in God's gentle hands. Her heavenly Father would care for all her needs. From then on, Mary "was in the temple of the Lord, nurtured like a dove, and [she] received food from the hand of an angel." Confident in this, Joachim and Anna were at peace.

CHAPTER 15

THE TEMPLE OF THE LORD

Long before the days of Mary, and long before the days of Herod, an elderly shepherd climbed a lonely mountain in the wilderness. God had told him to go there, accompanied by a few servants and his beloved son. As he approached the lofty mountain, he told the servants to wait while he and his son ascended for worship. Then he laid beams of wood upon his son's shoulders, picked up a torch and a knife, and the two of them went up.

On the mountain's summit, the old shepherd prepared a fire for sacrifice. Yet there was no animal, and the intelligent boy noticed it. "Look," he said, "here is the fire and the wood. But where is the lamb for a burnt offering?"

"My son, God will provide for himself the lamb for a burnt offering."

Then the old shepherd did something strange. Instead of tying up an animal, he bound his son with cords and laid him on the altar, atop the very wood that the boy had carried to the summit. Obeying the command of God, the father took up the knife and raised his hand to slay his son.

At that moment, a heavenly voice intervened. It was the angel of the Lord—the Son of God himself. "Abraham! Abraham!" the voice cried.

"Here I am."

"Do not lay your hand on the lad," the angel commanded, "or do anything to him. For now I know that you fear God, since you have not withheld your son from me, your only son."

Just then, a rustling sound made Abraham lift his eyes to a nearby thicket. A ram was caught in the branches by its horns. Rushing over, Abraham seized the ram and laid it on the altar in place of his son. He sacrificed it to God as a burnt offering, overwhelmingly grateful to receive his son alive. Yet Abraham's faith had never wavered during this divine trial. He had been confident that even if his son, Isaac, had been slain, God could have raised him from the dead.

Abraham gave a special name to the holy mountain: *Jehovah Jireh*, "The LORD Will Provide." A later editor of this story in Genesis 22 added an explanatory comment about that place: "It is said to this day, 'In the Mount of the LORD it shall be provided'" (v. 14). What did that mean? Abraham's name foretold that there, one day in the distant future, God would make a way for his people to fellowship with him. Upon this mountaintop, what humanity needed would be provided.

Back in the time of Abraham and Isaac, the region was more commonly known as Moriah. Many centuries later, the First Temple of Solomon was built on that very spot. Then, after more centuries had passed, King Herod proposed to refashion the Second Temple into the most glorious house of worship the Jews had ever seen. It was also there that Jesus Christ taught God's people the true meaning of sacrifice. All of these things took place on Mount Moriah, the place of divine provision for the world.

How did it come about that King Solomon—Israel's wisest and wealthiest ruler—built a temple on Mount Moriah? The Old Testament book of 1 Chronicles recounts how Solomon's father, the warrior-king David, captured a city from the Jebusites and made it his capital (11:4–9). Soon, however, King David committed a sin that aroused God's wrath (ch. 21). To appease the Lord, David decided to build an altar on the mountain adjacent to his new city of Jerusalem. But the summit of Mount Moriah was already occupied by a threshing floor, a high place where cereal crops were beaten to separate the edible grains from the stalks, then steady winds caused the chaff to blow away. David paid the owner, Ornan, the full price of the threshing floor so he would be giving something valuable to God. There, the king built his altar and God's mercy appeared in the sacrificial fire. Like chaff being scattered by the wind, David's sins were removed. He decided to build a permanent temple on this spot, so he began to make the initial preparations.

However, David was a man of war, a man of bloodshed. Though God often strengthened him for battle, it also meant David wasn't the right man to build a house of prayer. This task fell to his son, King Solomon. Second Chronicles 3:1 tells us, "Now Solomon began to build the house of the LORD at Jerusalem on Mount Moriah, where the LORD had appeared to his father David, at the place that David had prepared on the threshing floor of Ornan the Jebusite." The biblical account goes on to describe the incredible magnificence of Solomon's temple: its gilded paneling, innumerable gems, soaring pillars, immense bronze altar, lampstands of solid gold, decorations of angels and pomegranates, and the multicolored veil of wool and linen that shielded the Most Holy Place from unworthy eyes.

But greatest of all was the sacred object that Solomon installed in the inner sanctum. It was the ark of the covenant, a gilded chest upon whose lid dwelled the glorious presence of the Lord God himself. Second Chronicles 5:13–14 describes the moment of the ark's arrival: "It came to pass . . . when [the musicians] lifted up their voice with the trumpets and cymbals and instruments of music, and praised the LORD, saying: 'For He is good, for His mercy endures forever,' that the house, the house of the LORD, was filled with a cloud, so that the priests could not continue ministering because of the cloud; for the glory of the LORD filled the house of God." From that moment on, God literally dwelled in the midst of his people at Jerusalem. And just outside the sanctuary, sacrifice upon the altar was the means by which the people were to reach him.

King Solomon's amazing prayer of dedication in 2 Chronicles 6 tells us the purpose of this great temple. "Will God indeed dwell with men on the earth?" Solomon asked. "Behold, heaven and the heaven of heavens cannot contain You. How much less this temple which I have built! Yet regard the prayer of Your servant and his supplication, O LORD my God, and listen to the cry and the prayer which Your servant is praying before you" (vv. 18–19). What specific thing did Solomon request of God? "May You hear the supplications of Your servant and of Your people Israel, when they pray toward this place. Hear from heaven Your dwelling place, and when You hear, *forgive*" (v. 21). In other words, Solomon affirmed that on Mount Moriah, and there alone, divine forgiveness could be found.

Yet Solomon's temple wasn't just a place for the Israelites to worship. All the world could find God there. The king went on to pray, "Concerning a foreigner, who is not of Your people Israel, but has come from a far country for the sake of Your great name and Your mighty hand and Your outstretched arm, when they come and pray in this temple; then hear from heaven Your dwelling place, and do according to all for which the foreigner calls to You, that *all peoples of the earth may know Your name and fear You*, as do Your people Israel" (6:32–33). From Mount Moriah a light would now shine forth, a mighty beacon to the nations, beckoning everyone to come and find the eternal love of Yahweh.

For almost four hundred years, Solomon's temple served as a prayer house for Israel and a lighthouse to distant nations. In the time of King Hezekiah, it was expanded to an even larger size. But in 586 BC, catastrophe struck. A powerful and ruthless empire, the Babylonians, invaded Judah and sacked the city of God. The evil king Nebuchadnezzar utterly destroyed the temple and plundered its great riches. Then the beacon of Mount Moriah was snuffed out. Many Jews were deported to Babylon in chains. Even so, God wasn't finished with his people as a means of salvation for the world.

———————————————

After seventy years of suffering in Babylon, the Jews were granted permission to return to their ancestral homeland. Then the Second Temple rose on the site of the original one when great Jewish leaders like Zerubbabel and Jeshua began to lead their people back from foreign exile. Yet the political winds had shifted during the decades of Babylonian captivity. The new masters who ruled the region weren't favorable to the rebuild. Many of the Jews themselves, especially those who had remained behind and never went into captivity, were either reluctant or unable to devote resources to the new construction. Times were tough, survival was difficult, and to many residents of the city, a gigantic temple seemed superfluous.

Nevertheless, the leaders pressed ahead. An altar was constructed and the foundations for the new building were laid. When some of the elderly men saw the dimensions of the planned temple, they wept aloud, for they had beheld the grandeur of the First Temple and they mourned that its replacement would be so small. Even so, shouts of joy and thanksgiving mingled with the laments of the elders (Ezra 3:12–13). At least a temple would stand on Mount Moriah again, even if it was less splendid than before. Surely this was a bittersweet moment for the hard-pressed people of God.

After some years of inactivity due to political opposition, the Second Temple finally arose upon its new foundations. The Persian king Darius, whose empire included Jerusalem in those days, turned a favorable eye toward the Jews and paid all the construction costs out of his royal treasury. The line of Levitical priests was reestablished to serve in the temple, and its golden implements were brought back to be used in worship once more.

Yet perhaps the most important event of that historic moment happened not inside the temple but just outside of it. Ezra 6:19–21 recounts,

> And the descendants of the captivity kept the Passover on the fourteenth day of the first month. For the priests and the Levites had purified themselves; all of them were ritually clean. And they slaughtered the Passover lambs for all the descendants of the captivity, for their brethren the priests, and for themselves. Then the children of Israel who had returned from the captivity ate together with all who had separated themselves from the filth of the nations of the land in order to seek the LORD God of Israel.

With this restored Passover celebration, the people of God had finally come home. Their time of exile was over. Sufficient atonement had been made for their sins. Once again, they could meet the Lord at a temple in their midst and commemorate his covenant faithfulness through the sacrifice of the Passover lamb.

———

This incredible saga helps us understand the magnitude of what King Herod was doing, five hundred years later, when he decided to update the Second Temple that the exilic returnees had built. Once Herod got the idea in his mind, he resolved to achieve it (like everything else he did) in the grandest fashion possible. Was he motivated by his typical pride and pomposity? Was this yet another monument erected by an egomaniac obsessed with his own reputation? Or was something spiritual happening here that made this project special to him?

As always with Herod, his motives were mixed. Sometimes, he seems to have displayed a genuine allegiance to the God of Israel. He thought of himself as a good Jew. Other times, his massive ego couldn't help but get in the way. Nothing was ever simple when it came to Herod the Great.

The perceptive king understood that his Jewish subjects would have concerns about a difficult construction project that could disrupt temple worship for many years. That didn't mean the work shouldn't be done, only that the people needed to be placated first. *I shall give them a reassuring speech*, Herod decided. *This rebuild will be the greatest accomplishment of my life. If I can pull it off, my name will be remembered forever!*

On an appointed day, Herod gathered the citizens of Jerusalem in a public place where he could address them directly. He surely felt nervous about his speech, though perhaps no more than his audience, who were in the dark about what their king was going to say. When the people were quiet and attentive, Herod began to deliver his oration. He first reminded them of the great construction projects he had already completed—the many buildings he had commissioned not for his own benefit but for theirs. Israel had become world-famous for its architectural wonders. "I have, by the will of God, brought the Jewish nation to such a state of prosperity as it has never known before," Herod bragged.

Yet Israel still lacked one great thing. "The enterprise which I now propose to undertake is the most pious and beautiful one of our time," Herod told the crowd, pausing to heighten the tension as every eye stared back at him. He gestured dramatically toward the Second Temple that the exiles had erected after coming back to Jerusalem. "This was the temple which our fathers built to the Most Great God after their return from Babylon. But it lacks sixty cubits in height." (Sixty cubits was the amount by which Solomon's temple had exceeded the current smaller version.) Herod warned the crowd not to blame the forefathers for making such a small temple since their construction plans had been limited by the decree of Darius. However, the times had changed since then. A new regime was in charge. "The Romans, who are, so to speak, the masters of the world, are my loyal friends," Herod reminded the people. "So I will try to remedy the oversight caused by the subjection of that earlier time. By this act of piety, I will make full return to God for the gift of this kingdom to me!"

Upon hearing Herod's plan for a new and bigger temple, the astonished crowd broke into a frenzy. Though they hadn't known what their king would say, a reworking of the nation's most cherished monument was the last thing they had expected. What if Herod tore down the five-hundred-year-old temple but didn't have the means to rebuild a new one? What if this project was too big for him? What if his plans changed or his energy stalled and the Jewish people found themselves without a place to access the Lord God?

But the clever Herod had anticipated these anxious responses. "Never fear!" he told his listeners. "I will not demolish the old temple until I have totally prepared for the new." And then he backed up his promise. He had already mobilized a thousand wagons to carry stones from the nearby quarry; selected ten thousand of the best carpenters and stonemasons to be ready to start work; and would even train a thousand priests in construction skills so they could build the Most Holy Place on the sacred ground where only priests were allowed to stand. The announcement of these extensive preparations placated the nervous Jews, and they allowed the king to proceed.

As it turned out, the work was completed in record time, an outcome that greatly pleased the people. Herod insisted on vastly expanding the boundaries of the old temple precinct. The new Temple Mount required hauling in huge blocks of Herodian stone, distinctively beveled around their edges and gleaming white, to create a retaining wall topped by a plaza of 1.5 million square feet. Amazingly, this flat platform took up one-sixth of the city's total area.

In the middle of this wide-open space, Herod built a brand-new temple whose facade was covered in solid gold. It faced east so it would reflect the fiery splendor of the rising sun. Courtyards and porticoes surrounded the central sanctuary. Josephus marveled that Herod "surpassed his predecessors in spending money, so that it was thought that no one else had adorned the temple so splendidly."

When all was said and done, the new temple wasn't the disaster many had feared it would be. Quite the contrary, it was a national marvel, a source of patriotic pride as well as spiritual salvation. What would this grand building have looked like to ancient eyes?

———————————

Let us imagine that Mary, at twelve years old, was living in the temple area. Perhaps she would occasionally journey home to visit her parents. After one such visit, it was time for her to head back to Jerusalem with her traveling companions. As she approached the Holy City, the Temple Mount appeared on the horizon like a gleaming mountain of snow, its white stones standing out against the dusky brown color of the hillsides. When the morning rays reflected off the temple's golden front, it gleamed like a beacon calling her home.

Mary entered the gates of Jerusalem. After climbing a staircase from the city streets, she emerged onto the wide plaza that surrounded the temple. A military tower loomed to one side—the Antonia fortress that Herod had named after his former colleague, Mark Antony. A long colonnade called the Porch of Solomon ran along one side of the plaza. Adjoining it at the corner was the Royal Stoa, a three-aisled hall formed by four rows of massive columns.

As Mary proceeded toward the temple itself, she mingled with Gentiles who were allowed to be in the outer plaza. But then she passed a low wall beyond which Gentiles couldn't go upon penalty of death. Even Marcus Agrippa, the empire's second man, hadn't dared to cross this sacred threshold. Now Mary proceeded through an imposing gate in a high wall. She entered the Court of the Women, the closest she could get to the Most Holy Place.

Taking leave of her companions for a time of spiritual reflection, Mary walked across the courtyard and ascended a staircase of fifteen semicircular steps. From there she peered through the Nicanor Gate into the Court of Israel where purified Jewish men could enter but she could not. Beyond that was the Court of the Priests. Mary could see the enormous altar where the priests were sacrificing animals as burnt offerings to God. Beside it was an immense bronze basin to provide water for ritual washings. And behind all of this was the brilliant facade of the temple, completely covered by golden plates. Its massive doors were flanked by pillars wreathed in vines. Huge grape clusters made from gold, each as large as a man, dangled over the doorway and signaled the fruitful abundance that could be found through those doors.

Though Mary had never entered the temple building itself, she knew well what was inside. The Holy Place, also called the Sanctuary, contained a lampstand and a table for the Bread of Presence, as well as a small altar for burning incense. A heavy veil of multicolored fabric hung at the rear of the room, screening the Most Holy Place where only the high priest could enter once a year on the Day of Atonement. In earlier times, the ark of the covenant had been situated in there, but now the space was empty and the ark's foundation stone was unoccupied. Yet Mary wasn't disturbed by the absence of any objects in the inner sanctum. She knew what all other Jews understood as well: that Yahweh wasn't represented by idols like the false gods of the Gentiles. He was the Lord of heaven and earth, so no man-made image could capture or contain him.

As Mary stood in the Court of the Women and contemplated the sacrifices that gave access to God's presence, a sadness came to her heart. She had recently been told by the priests that because she was now twelve years old, the imminent onset of her menstrual flow would make her ritually unclean. It was time for her to leave the temple precincts and eventually be united to a husband. The thought saddened her, for the glorious temple of God was the only home she could remember.

Yet as Mary considered the impurity that her emerging womanhood would soon bring, as well as the religious restrictions that barred women from full entry to the temple, an even deeper sadness descended upon her. *Will this ever change?* she wondered. *Will there ever come a time when I can be one with God, and he with me?*

Though Mary didn't know it then, the baby she would one day bear would bring these changes to the human race. As an adult man, he would promise his disciples, "I will pray the Father, and He will give you another Helper, that He may abide with you forever—the Spirit of truth, whom the world cannot receive . . . but you know Him, for *He dwells with you and will be in you*" (John 14:16–17).

Not long after Jesus spoke those words, Mary got to see her Son's glorious promise come to pass. She was in the upper room when the Holy Spirit made the human heart—not the golden constructions of men like Herod—his new temple of spiritual residence. The book of Acts describes how the eleven faithful disciples gathered for worship after Jesus ascended to heaven. "These all continued with one accord in prayer and supplication," the Scripture says, "with the women and Mary the mother of Jesus, and with His brothers" (1:14).

What happened next? The Bible goes on to say, "When the Day of Pentecost had fully come, they were all with one accord in one place. And suddenly there came a sound from heaven, as of a rushing mighty wind, and it filled the whole house where they were sitting. Then there appeared to them divided tongues, as of fire, and one sat upon each of them. And they were all filled with the Holy Spirit and began to speak with other tongues, as the Spirit gave them utterance" (2:1–4).

From that moment on, everything would be different. No longer would God have to be accessed through repeated sacrifices in front of a restricted temple. No longer would a veil obscure the dwelling place of God. No longer would Mount Moriah, and it alone, be the lighthouse of the world. After the descent of the Spirit, each believer in Jesus—whether a woman or a man—would serve as a temple of God's presence. The once-for-all sacrifice had been made. Although Mary's twelve-year-old mind couldn't have comprehended such ideas, all of these wonders lay ahead in her future. Her only job was to be faithful and say, "Yes, Lord. Let it be done to me according to your will."

CHAPTER 16

THE BEGINNING OF THE END

When King Herod turned sixty, the greatness of his former years began to take a turn for the worse. He was still immensely rich and powerful, make no mistake. Yet his subjects began to wonder about the obvious questions: *What will happen after Herod dies? Who will take his place?* And it wasn't just the citizenry who speculated about such things. Herod looked at his own aging face in the mirror and began to consider the same problem. *After I go . . . who will inherit my glorious kingdom?*

Questions of succession were especially complex for a man like Herod, who had multiple wives. Roman aristocrats tended not to pursue such polygamy, preferring one noble matron whose children were legitimate along with many courtesans and concubines whose children might be loved but certainly wouldn't be expected to inherit. In eastern lands, however, polygamy was more acceptable. Even the great patriarch Abraham, the forefather of the Jews, had multiple wives. So did King Solomon. Herod was likewise a practitioner of polygamy, so establishing his rightful heir was no easy matter.

How many wives did Herod have? We can enumerate five primary women whose offspring would have been considered legitimate contenders for the Judean throne. (Herod had five other wives, totaling ten, but their children weren't viewed as potential heirs.) The main five wives and their respective sons were:

- Doris and her son, Antipater, both of whom Herod cast aside once Mariamne had caught his eye
- Mariamne I, whom Herod adored yet executed for treason, and her two sons, Alexander and Aristobulus (the latter having the same name as Mariamne's brother whom Herod drowned)

- Malthace and her two sons, Herod Archelaus and Herod Antipas, who were destined to be important rulers in New Testament times
- Mariamne II, a Jerusalem beauty from a nonroyal family, and her son, Herod II, who eventually married his niece, Herodias, but she divorced him to marry Herod Antipas, which John the Baptist sharply criticized
- Cleopatra of Jerusalem and her son, Philip the Tetrarch, who also became a ruler in the New Testament era

Over time, Herod realized that none of these fractious boys would make a desirable successor. Yet somebody had to inherit the throne, so Herod became obsessed during his final years with writing wills and establishing the best possible replacement for himself.

At the beginning of this convoluted process, two of his sons stood out as the most likely options: the ones he had fathered with the first Mariamne. Since Herod's guiding political principle had always been to stay on good terms with the Romans, he believed the right way to groom a young man for the future responsibilities of kingship was to provide him a prestigious education in Rome. Therefore, he sent Mariamne's two boys, Alexander and Aristobulus, to the capital city around the time that he turned his attention to rebuilding the Jewish temple. Only this pair, out of all his sons, had royal Hasmonean blood coursing through their veins. And besides, they were the offspring of the woman Herod had loved the most. It seemed likely that one of these two boys was destined to rule Judea someday.

In AD 17, Herod personally went to Rome to pick up the two princes when their education was finished. After bringing them home, his next step was to arrange marriages for them. Since the young men were descended from the beautiful Mariamne and the dashing Herod, both had the outward good looks to make them attractive mates. They were unquestionably blue-blooded through their mother's line. While Herod's lineage wasn't quite as distinguished as Mariamne's, he was still the king by Roman decree, and fabulously wealthy to boot. Any aristocratic girl would want to marry either of these princes.

The wife arranged for Alexander was Glaphyra, a princess from the neighboring state of Cappadocia. It was an eminent kingdom on par with Judea.

Glaphyra thought very highly of herself, believing she was descended from the god Hercules on one side and from the great Persian king Darius on the other. Anyone who didn't know about her exalted ancestry soon found out. Though she was beautiful and alluring, she was also a haughty snoot.

Aristobulus's wife came from much closer to home. King Herod's sister, Salome, had a daughter named Berenice who seemed like a suitable in-house match for the second son. But the problem was, these two sons of Mariamne had a full share of their mother's (and their grandmother's) incessant snobbery toward anyone not from a royal house. The same arrogant superiority that Mariamne and Alexandra had always displayed toward Herod's family reappeared in the two boys. The newcomer, Princess Glaphyra, wholeheartedly joined them. Poor Berenice, who was perceived to have come from lowly Idumean stock like Herod himself, received constant mockery from her new husband. Aristobulus often complained that while his brother had been awarded a glamorous princess, he had gotten stuck with a mere commoner. The dejected Berenice tearfully related these slurs to her mother, who seethed with resentment toward the two Hasmonean boys.

Though Alexander and Aristobulus weren't sure how everything would play out for them in the political realm, they shared one goal in common. As soon as their father died and they got hold of power, they were going to force all of Herod's other wives into servitude, making them weave cloth beside the slave girls in the factories. Likewise, the other Herodian sons would be reduced to village clerks as a mockery of their inferior education. All of this would be sweet revenge for Herod's execution of their beloved mother when they were small children. The boys agreed that if they ever saw one of their stepmothers wearing one of Mariamne's fine gowns, that impostor would be dressed in rags and locked in a dungeon where she couldn't see the sun. The boys openly reviled Herod and constantly celebrated their tragically murdered mother.

Of course, word of this disloyalty soon filtered back to Herod. He immediately began to reconsider whether these two ungrateful brothers ought to inherit his kingdom. But where to turn for an alternate? After racking his brain for a while, Herod decided to reach out to his first wife, Doris, and recall her son, Antipater, out of familial exile. Years ago, it had been convenient to dump them when Herod's eyes turned toward Mariamne. Now they were useful again, so Herod brought them back into his favor.

He decided to send Antipater, his firstborn son, to Rome for a respectable education. In fact, Herod sent the young man (who was in his early thirties by then) to the capital city in the company of Marcus Agrippa, Herod's chummy friend and the second-ranked man in the whole empire. Antipater went to Rome with a priceless document in his hand: Herod's will (the first of several he would make), which informed the emperor that Antipater should succeed to the Judean throne. Clearly, after a long period of obscurity, Antipater's star was back on the rise.

But was Antipater really a suitable heir, any better than Mariamne's boys? Far from it. During all the years that he and his mother had been sidelined, a tidal wave of resentment had built up in them both. Now it crashed onto the shores of the Judean palace. The embittered duo immediately began to scheme against Alexander and Aristobulus, the mother operating from within Herod's household while the son worked the halls of Roman imperial power. It was a powerful one-two punch against the Hasmonean princes.

Of course, the two snobby boys grew enraged at the promotion of a commoner like Antipater. Their furious outbursts only made them seem more suspicious to Herod. In contrast, Antipater was subtle and wily. He used slander, flattery, and carefully placed gossip to discredit the princes; while for her part, Doris began having sex with Herod again and used that opportunity to discredit her son's rivals. Herod even began to consider executing the two boys. When a rumor arose that Alexander intended to poison his father, Herod decided to haul the youth to Rome, put him on trial before Caesar Augustus, and let the emperor himself determine what should happen.

This move wasn't a smart one for Herod. It made him look weak and indecisive. All the emperor wanted in a client king was an efficient ruler who quietly handled his duties, guarded the frontier from incursions, and collected the required taxes. Adjudicating family squabbles wasn't part of the bargain. Yet because of Augustus's affection for Herod, he took on the role of referee in this messy domestic dispute.

The trial happened at the Italian town of Aquileia where the emperor had traveled on business. There Alexander's fine schooling revealed its value. The crowning aspect of a Roman education was oratory. Alexander had been well trained in rhetoric, and he possessed natural gifts for public speaking. His defense against the charges of treason reduced the whole court to tears. He not only proved his (and his brother's) complete innocence; he also laid grievous charges at Antipater's feet. Herod's two royal sons were cast as tragic victims, undermined by a lowborn upstart who was conniving for power. Caesar Augustus was so moved by the youth's eloquent speech that he immediately dismissed the charges and commanded all three sons to start respecting their father.

Though Herod still held private doubts about Mariamne's boys, he accepted the verdict and promptly sailed back to Jerusalem, where he set his three heirs before the people. "Thanks be to God and to our great emperor, my family is now at peace," Herod declared. He informed the assembly that all three sons would one day inherit power. Each of them deserved a share of the dynasty: one by right of being firstborn, the other two from their noble blood. "My kingdom is big enough for even more than three," Herod bragged.

The king then asked the people to ratify his decision in principle, yet not to elevate the young men prematurely. Until the time came for them to assume control, Herod would remain in charge and he wasn't going away anytime soon. He felt certain God would bless him with many years to come. "Consider, each one of you, my age, my manner of life, my piety," he said. "I have served the deity so faithfully that I may hope for the longest term of life." Herod then made an impassioned plea for peace and unity within his family, reminding everyone that since even the animals of nature could live in harmony, his own household ought to follow their example.

Unfortunately, Herod forgot that many wild beasts slaughter their young and fiercely compete for singular control of the pack. And human beings could be the most brutal animals of all. The truth was, savage infighting lay in store for Herod, no matter how many play-nice speeches he might give.

Though Herod had only mildly irritated Caesar Augustus by embroiling him in his ugly household strife, one of Herod's next actions did far more damage to his relationship with the most powerful man on earth. Herod managed to get the emperor on his bad side despite their long history of warm relations. Clearly, Herod's famous political acumen—which had always been so perfectly attuned to every nuance of statecraft and international intrigue—was beginning to slip in his old age.

The falling out was caused by Herod's excessive revenge for an offense committed by the Arabs. Some bandits whom Herod had previously subdued and reduced to peaceful farming rose up to resume their marauding while he was away in Rome. Though Herod's generals eliminated many of these raiders, a gaggle of the leaders fled across the border to Arabia. There, a political schemer named Syllaeus gave them a fortified base of operations from which they could continue to ransack the Judean countryside. When Herod learned about this criminal behavior upon his return home, he slaughtered the bandits' relatives, yet he could do nothing to the actual perpetrators because of their fortress across the border. The bandits only increased their forays of rapacious looting and brutal murder. To make matters worse, Syllaeus refused to repay a huge debt of five hundred talents that he owed to the Judean treasury. Syllaeus felt slighted because Herod had denied him permission to marry his sister, Salome.

The bad feeling between the two sides broke into open war in 9 BC. Although Herod had gained permission for a military strike from some nearby Roman officials, the war he waged seemed larger than necessary for the size of the problem. He acted with unwarranted ferocity, marching his army into Arabia at such a speed that the seven-day journey was covered in only three. The invaders immediately seized the bandits' fortress, demolished it, and executed or enslaved the malefactors. When one of Syllaeus's relatives, Nakebos, tried to put up resistance, Herod's crack troops killed him in battle and routed his army. Then Herod returned home with prisoners, booty, and best of all, the gratification of revenge.

However, unknown to Herod, the Arabian conniver Syllaeus had already gone to Rome, where he had managed to gain the emperor's ear. When word of the swift attack arrived via Arabian messengers, Syllaeus dressed himself in the black robes of mourning and appeared before Augustus. He greatly exaggerated Herod's actions, making it seem that his troops had run wild throughout the countryside, pillaging as they went. "The whole kingdom is devastated," Syllaeus tearfully protested. "My beloved relative Nakebos was slaughtered. Twenty-five hundred Arabian noblemen were murdered by Herod's rampaging army!"

For the first time, Caesar Augustus found himself furious with his longtime friend. It seemed outrageous that one of the emperor's dependent kingdoms would invade and despoil another, all without his permission. Augustus asked

Herod's allies and other eyewitnesses a single yes-or-no question: "Did King Herod march into Arabia for war?" The witnesses were forced to answer in the affirmative without being able to provide a more nuanced explanation of what actually had happened.

Now truly enraged, Augustus wrote Herod a scathing letter in which he said he would no longer consider him a friend but only a subject. Gleefully, Syllaeus also wrote home to his people, who were emboldened by the good news. The Arabs continued to give refuge to the bandits in their midst, refused to repay their loan from Herod, and quit paying rent on lands they had leased from Judea. They even went so far as to allow the raiders to invade and terrorize Herod's homeland of Idumea.

In one fell swoop, everything in Herod's world had fallen apart. He tried to send ambassadors to Augustus to explain his version of the story, but the emperor wouldn't even receive them. The historian Josephus put it bluntly when he wrote, "In view of these things, Herod was in despair and fear." Reduced to desperation, Herod sent another friend to Rome, a man called Nicolaus of Damascus. This distinguished fellow, an elegant and intellectual Jew, served as Herod's official court historian. In fact, much of the data recorded in Josephus's description of Herod came from Nicolaus's flattering biography of his master.

Though the first Herodian embassy to placate the emperor had failed, the suave Nicolaus managed to win back Augustus's favor. Knowing that Augustus didn't want to hear any words in support of Herod, Nicolaus instead accused Syllaeus of egregious mismanagement and double-dealing back in his homeland. Furthermore, Nicolaus claimed Syllaeus was guilty of adultery, not only with Arabian women but even with some noble ladies of Rome. These charges all stuck because everyone knew they were true.

But then Nicolaus dared to slip in a defense of his master. "In addition to all these crimes of Syllaeus," he said, "that treacherous rogue has unfairly slandered the faithful King Herod."

"Stop right there!" the emperor interjected, holding up his hand in protest. "Answer me one question only. Did your king invade Arabia, kill twenty-five hundred inhabitants, and take away captives and spoil?"

Nicolaus smiled coyly. "I do indeed have information about that, Your Highness, but it is not what you think. You have been severely misled."

Now Nicolaus had the emperor's full attention. Intrigued by the surprising statement, Augustus gave him permission to continue. Nicolaus proceeded to lay out the actual situation. Twenty-five hundred people certainly had not been killed. In truth, only twenty-five men had died in the battle for the bandits' fortress. Herod's captives weren't innocent peasants but worthless robbers who had been causing wanton destruction. Furthermore, Herod had been given legal permission by local Roman officials to invade Arabia. He wasn't making war on an adjacent kingdom but using justified force—which he was contractually allowed to do—to reclaim the five hundred talents that he had lent to the Arabs but Syllaeus refused to repay. To back up these assertions, Nicolaus had the loan documents and affidavits about the rampant Arabian banditry read aloud to the court.

Once the emperor learned all this new information, his view of the situation completely reversed. Syllaeus had been revealed not merely as an exaggerator but an outright liar. Augustus sent him back to Arabia under strict orders to repay the debt. A short time later, when he continued his double-dealing with the Romans, the emperor had him beheaded. In contrast, Herod was restored to Augustus's good graces. The emperor even expressed regret that he had written such a harsh letter, blaming Syllaeus for causing him to malign a true friend.

Somehow, Herod had managed to work his way back into imperial favor. Even so, it was clear to everyone who watched these events unfold that the king's aura of invincibility had been diminished. For the first time, his Roman shine had been tarnished. Everyone in the Herodian court—especially within his own household—took notice of the change. High overhead, the ever-vigilant vultures circled in the sky, waiting for the right moment to swoop down on the carcass of Herod and tear it apart.

Far from the halls of power in Rome or Jerusalem, twelve-year-old Mary had returned to her family household. Her new life of simplicity and obscurity stood in contrast to all the intrigues of the Herodian dynasty. We don't know exactly what Mary's role might have been at the temple, nor even for sure that she truly lived there. Certainly, she wouldn't have lived inside the temple complex itself but only in some house nearby.

If the early Christian traditions are correct about Mary's residence at the temple, we can imagine that she may have played a musical role in service to Israel. Mary wasn't a Levite, so she wouldn't have assisted with formal liturgical singing around the altar. Yet perhaps there was a role for non-Levites as choir singers or instrumentalists during parades and processions. Though we don't know the details of Second Temple musical worship, we do know from Scripture that such parades included female musicians. Psalm 68:24–25 says, "They have seen Your procession, O God, the procession of my God, my King, into the sanctuary. The singers went before, the players on instruments followed after; *among them were the maidens playing timbrels.*"[1]

If Mary had become familiar with public temple music during her girlhood, it would explain how she was later able to compose the lovely song known as the Magnificat (Luke 1:46–55). This Latin-based title comes from the song's opening couplet: "My soul *magnifies* the Lord, and my spirit has rejoiced in God my Savior." In contrast to the chest-thumping braggadocio of Herod, Mary emphasized her lowly estate before God's mighty power. She was but a "maidservant" who was humbly grateful (even a bit astonished) that "He who is mighty has done great things for me" (v. 49). Instead of glorifying herself, Mary focused on God's attributes: his holiness, mercy, strength, provision, and help. Israel was lifted up by God's grace alone, not by anything a mere man could do for the nation.

Mary's song celebrated God's topsy-turvy way of doing things. Those who were laid low would soon arise, while those who stood on the high places would find themselves cast down. "[God] has scattered the proud in the imagination of their hearts," Mary sang. "He has put down the mighty from their thrones, and exalted the lowly" (Luke 1:51–52). With those words, the humble virgin on the fringe of her society displayed more insight than all the rulers of Judea combined. They strove for power and riches, while she sought the face of the Lord. The blessed maidservant of God discerned what Herod and his devious family didn't have eyes to see: that the route to exaltation begins with humility of heart.

---

1. See also Exodus 15:20; Judges 11:34; and 1 Samuel 18:6.

CHAPTER 17

LIKE FATHER, LIKE SONS

"It's better to be Herod's pig than his prince."

So quipped Caesar Augustus when he caught wind of Herod's murderous domestic strife. The joke, of course, reflects the emperor's knowledge of Jewish food laws. A good Jew wouldn't eat pork, so Herod's pigs were safe. Not so his sons. Those could more easily be slaughtered by a desperate and paranoid Jew like Herod.

Despite the emperor's exhortations to settle the family disputes and start showing proper respect all the way around, things had only grown worse in Herod's household. The complaints of Mariamne's boys had reached the ear of their stepbrother, Antipater, who used the palace gossip to make his father fear that a coup was imminent. Everyone knew Herod was on edge and felt threatened by the traitorous princes. The younger of the two boys, Aristobulus, decided he could use some help from his mother-in-law, Salome, who was the king's sister. But Salome remembered how Aristobulus had mercilessly mocked her daughter, Berenice. So instead of helping the youth, she only inflamed Herod all the more. A double execution on the grounds of treason seemed imminent. Yet a bit of advice was needed first.

Again making a poorly calculated move, Herod wrote to the emperor for counsel. Though Augustus was no doubt irritated to be redrawn into Herod's domestic squabbles, he patiently replied that an authoritative and respectable trial should be convened. All of Herod's counselors should be present, along with several high-ranking Roman officials from Syria. Instead of holding the trial in Jerusalem, Augustus advised that the Romanized town of Berytus (modern Beirut, Lebanon) would make for a neutral site. Though Herod was given permission to inflict any penalty he saw fit, the emperor implied that a lenient and careful approach should be taken.

Herod felt relieved that he had been endowed with full capital authority. A murderous and savage paranoia had taken hold of his mind, so he wanted the freedom to inflict the death penalty on his sons. The trial would give him legal cover to eliminate the two ungrateful wretches. *But what if I let them speak? Then that smooth-tongued Alexander might sway the judges in his favor!* It had happened once before, so Herod resolved it mustn't happen again. He commanded that the two youths should be transported in chains to the trial but not be allowed to appear. Instead, they would be imprisoned in a nearby suburb without the chance to defend themselves.

The great trial assembled 150 leading men from Judea and the Roman province of Syria. Grotesquely, Herod served as the primary prosecutor for his sons. Though he knew he should have felt saddened to be making such harsh accusations against his own flesh and blood, Herod found himself overtaken by a fierceness that disturbed the sober judges. By their grimaces and shifting in their seats, he could see they disapproved of a father saying such terrible things about his sons. *No matter*, Herod told himself. *The youths must die. Keep going!* He forged ahead with his claims of filial treachery and disloyalty. "Behold!" he said to the packed courtroom, waving a packet of papers. "I present to you their own letters that give evidence against them."

A clerk passed the dossier to the leading council member. "There is no mention here of treachery or plotting," the judge remarked once the letters had been read aloud. "The youths just wanted to escape your fury to save their lives."

"They insulted me!" Herod cried. "They mocked and disrespected me!"

"No, they merely criticized you for unwarranted hostility. You should be less suspicious and more affectionate toward them, as befits a father."

But Herod would hear nothing of it. He was determined to see his sons die for their crimes. Pressing harder and louder, he denounced the two boys as traitors. Just like their mother, they should have loved him but did not. Then Herod forced the issue on legal grounds. He reminded the assembly that not only does a father naturally have capital authority over his sons—an ancient tradition going back to the earliest days of Rome—but the emperor had explicitly granted him the right to inflict the death penalty.

Furthermore, the law of Moses also gave a father this right. A "stubborn and rebellious son" could be presented to the elders for public execution

(Deuteronomy 21:18–21). "You aren't at this trial to decide the outcome!" Herod screeched at the assembly of great men. "That is my right alone! You're only here to share in the rightful anger of a father against his double-crossing sons!"

Although the judges weren't convinced by Herod's rantings, neither were they willing to oppose him. Obviously, a sweet family reconciliation wasn't about to happen. Rather than destabilize the political status quo in the region, the two boys would have to be sacrificed to their father's paranoid rage.

Yet one man, an eminent Roman governor named Saturninus, counseled restraint. "Though your boys are surely guilty, their penalty is excessive. I, too, have sons, and I would not dare to slaughter them for such crimes. My advice is to find a lesser punishment." Then Saturninus's three adult sons, each of whom was in attendance at the trial, spoke in favor of the more lenient approach.

Unfortunately for the two accused princes, the rest of the judges sided with Herod. Some did so out of political expediency, while others agreed because they were jealous of Herod and sensed that this travesty of justice would make him look bad. For whatever hidden reasons, a guilty verdict was promptly returned, and the sentence was death.

But before Herod could inflict the ultimate punishment, he traveled down to Tyre, where his counselor, Nicolaus of Damascus, had just returned from Rome. "What do my friends there think of this case?" Herod asked him.

"They all think the same thing," Nicolaus replied. "They believe your sons are disloyal but you shouldn't kill them. Instead, you should keep them in prison. Or maybe even reconcile with them. Whatever you do, try to appear reasonable and sober, not overtaken with a rage that is unworthy of a father."

"And what is your opinion of this case?"

"I believe you should delay judgment," Nicolaus answered briskly. "Do not make a rash decision about your own flesh and blood. Once you take that step, it cannot be undone."

The cautious comment made Herod lapse into silent contemplation. On the one hand, mercy had certain advantages. After several recent missteps, Herod couldn't afford to anger his Roman patrons again. *Yet those wicked boys deserve to die*, whispered another voice whose diabolical urgings couldn't be ignored. *Do not let them go free or they'll find a way to kill you!* Herod pondered the dilemma for a long time. Finally he turned back to Nicolaus. "Sail with me down to Caesarea. I will continue to consider this matter, and I want your advice."

In Herod's gleaming new capital of Caesarea, the people still loved their benefactor but didn't like what he was up to. The populace found his recent actions repugnant. Nevertheless, widespread fear of the revenge-hungry king draped a veil of silence over the city. No one dared to voice their sympathy for Alexander and Aristobulus. Everyone hoped the king wouldn't go through with the cruel sentence. Little did they know that Herod wasn't contemplating whether, but when, to execute the princes.

At the height of the civic tension, when everyone's nerves had been stretched to the breaking point, one man set a catastrophe in motion. An old and trusted army veteran named Tiro rose up to accuse Herod publicly. Tiro's son was friends with Alexander, the elder of the two accused princes. In Tiro's interpretation of things, Herod was acting monstrously toward two fine, upstanding young men. "Justice has been trampled underfoot!" Tiro shouted in the streets. "Truth is dead, the laws of nature have been overturned, and the world is full of lawlessness!" Many citizens in Caesarea agreed with Tiro and viewed him as courageous for speaking up. Though they were afraid to join him openly, they felt he was saying things that needed to be said.

Amazingly, Tiro presented himself to Herod, who granted him a hearing. "In my opinion, you seem demon possessed!" Tiro boldly told his king. "Where has your good sense gone? Where is that extraordinary intelligence with which you accomplished so many great deeds? You trust the words of scoundrels against your own children. Are you really going to execute those two youths who were borne to you by a queen and who exemplify every great virtue? Can't you see that although the people are silent, they abhor what you're doing? Be careful that killing those boys doesn't arouse the hatred of the army. Every one of the soldiers pities those lads. Many of the officers are freely saying so."

Those were inflammatory words. The suggestion of a potential army uprising grabbed Herod's attention. Yet before Herod could react, the situation grew even stranger. The royal barber rushed forward and turned himself in. "I, too, have something to say!" he cried. "This Tiro urged me to cut your throat while I was shaving you. He said I'd get a large reward from Alexander."

Bewildered by the accusations and counter-accusations, Herod imprisoned everyone—the supposedly disloyal army officers, Tiro and his son, and the barber—and put the latter three under torture. Despite their agony, Tiro and his son wouldn't admit anything, while the barber knew of nothing more to disclose. "Rack Tiro even harder!" Herod ordered the torturers. "Tear him apart!" The great wheels turned, the wooden rack creaked, and the hideous machine pulled Tiro's joints out of socket. His suffering went beyond human comprehension.

At last, anguished by his father's unbearable torment, the son cried, "Stop! I will tell you everything." He then confessed that Alexander had tried to get Tiro to slay the king. No one knew whether the charge was true or just a ploy to end his father's suffering since he was mortally wounded already. In any case, the men's fate was now sealed. Herod brought the accused army officers, along with the barber, the disjointed Tiro, and his son, before a public assembly. After accusing them all of treason, Herod turned the crowd loose on them. The frenzied mob snatched up sticks, rocks, and whatever else came to hand, then bludgeoned the condemned men to death.

With so much blood in the streets and demonic poison in the air, Alexander and Aristobulus had no chance of survival. Not only had Herod lost his mind; he had lost his soul. He gave the order—firmly, and without hesitation—to take the princes to Sebaste for immediate execution. No longer did anyone wish to debate their fate or defy Herod's order. The youths were strangled with a noosed rope and laid to rest in the tomb of their forefathers. Now Herod's last tie to his beloved Mariamne had been lost forever.

———

After recording all these horrors in Herod's house, Josephus paused his narrative to reflect on what had just happened. He asked philosophically, "Who was to blame here?" Was it the princes, whose continual disloyalty drove their father to hate them? Was it Herod, who had allowed himself to become so hard-hearted that he would stoop to anything to secure his kingdom? Or was it simply that the impersonal wheel of fortune had turned against Herod, allowing a terrible tragedy to strike him?

Josephus (or possibly a later editor who added this section) embarked on a brief consideration of fate versus free will in the case of Herod's household intrigues. Though the wicked deeds might have been fated to occur, even so, the two sons and their father bore some responsibility for the outcome. Alexander and Aristobulus impudently allowed their father to be slandered, often adding their own calumnies to those of others. Their incautious words enabled their enemies to build a case against them.

Yet who could hold a father innocent for executing his sons, even if they had committed serious crimes? Such a thing is despicable. The two Hasmonean princes were handsome specimens of manhood, admired by everyone. They were adept at hunting, the military arts, and public speaking. Without sufficient evidence, Herod had executed these youths for treason—the very men who might have ruled Judea well as his successors. Wouldn't it have been enough to keep them imprisoned instead of wringing their necks like pigs for the slaughter?

Herod had acted rashly, or one might even say, insanely. Josephus sharply criticized Herod's mental state: "For him to kill them so quickly to gratify the passion that overpowered him was a sign of an irreligious spirit that is beyond assessment, especially when he committed so great a crime in his old age." Life's wisdom should have tempered the king's actions instead of driving him to demented violence. The fact that Herod delayed his decision shouldn't win him any pardon, for that only meant it wasn't a crime of passion but a fully considered decision. "This is the act of a murderous mind that cannot be turned from evil," Josephus declared.

Modern observers can't help but agree about the maelstrom of violence that surrounded Herod. "A murderous mind" aptly describes his deranged psyche. Shocked by so many crimes and atrocities, we are driven to ask, "Were there no good men in the land? Was no one in Israel a follower of God?"

As it turns out, Scripture does identify a certain person of those times as "a just man" (Matthew 1:19). He was a servant of the Lord who resolved to do good for the woman under his care. This man was Joseph, the gentle husband who took the teenaged Mary as his beloved wife.

CHAPTER 18

A HOUSE DIVIDED

Who was Joseph? Modern people who have encountered nativity scenes all their lives tend to imagine Joseph and Mary as impoverished peasants who naturally made their abode among farm animals. They also imagine the couple as twentysomethings—young adults just starting out in life with little money to spend but plenty of love to console them in their poverty. Their penniless phase of young marriage is imagined as a time of challenging yet joyful deprivation. In reality, however, this wasn't at all how the ancient church remembered the man Joseph.

For starters, Joseph wasn't ever depicted as extremely poor. The Bible gives us a hint of Joseph's financial situation when it tells us that Mary's postpartum cleansing sacrifice at the temple was the lesser of two possible choices, "a pair of turtledoves or two young pigeons" instead of a more expensive lamb (Luke 2:24; Leviticus 12:8). From this, it is often deduced that Joseph was impoverished. But all that the lesser sacrifice implies is that the worshiper was of modest income, not extreme destitution.

The reality is that Joseph was a skilled worker whose expertise would have been in high demand. Scripture doesn't identify him as a "carpenter," as is so often assumed, but as a *tekton*, a Greek word that means a craftsman and builder who probably worked with stone more than wood. Israel at that time was more of a stone-shaping culture than a woodworking one. So we should picture Joseph (and Jesus after him) as a stonemason who probably made a good living from his trade. This recognition provides great insight into the later teachings of Jesus, who so often referred to stones and foundations!

Nor did the ancient church depict Joseph as young. In fact, he was actually described as elderly. The earliest record of Joseph's betrothal to Mary recounts how the temple authorities wanted to find a spouse for the young girl who had just come into her womanhood and could no longer serve in the sacred precincts due to ritual purity considerations. No doubt there is some legend mixed into the narrative, but even so, the ancient traditions about Joseph are instructive.

They tell us that the high priest, Zechariah, went into the Most Holy Place for prayer. There he was told by an angel to assemble all the widowers of the land so the Lord could reveal Mary's caretaker by a miraculous sign. When the heralds announced the edict in the surrounding villages and the trumpets were blown, the widowed men came running. Among them was Joseph, "who threw down his adze and went out to their meeting."

Each of the widowers carried with him a wooden rod like Aaron's rod that budded in Numbers 17. Though nothing happened to the other men's rods, a sign occurred to Joseph's: a dove flew out of it and landed on his head. Then the high priest announced, "You have been chosen by lot to receive the virgin of the Lord as your ward."

Perhaps we might imagine this caused Joseph to rejoice. But the ancient text *The Original Gospel of James* tells us exactly the opposite. "I have sons and am old," Joseph protested when he heard the announcement. "She is but a girl. I object lest I should become a laughing-stock to the sons of Israel." In other words, old Joseph didn't want to seem lecherous by taking a teenaged bride!

The high priest, however, didn't let Joseph off the hook. He cited an Old Testament incident when the earth split open and swallowed up some rebels against God's will. The priest's face grew stern: "Beware, Joseph, lest these things happen in your house too!" The chastened Joseph quickly relented and received Mary as his fiancée.

Although determining Joseph's exact age and financial situation is probably impossible today, these ancient traditions suggest that the marriage demanded a sacrifice from the stonemason of Bethlehem. Being appointed to care for Mary—by whatever means God led him to her, whether miraculous or not—wasn't something that brought Joseph a great benefit. He had a mature life of his own, a busy career with various obligations and opportunities, while Mary was young and inexperienced. By her own admission, she was humble and lowly. Her main attraction was her upright moral character, not her famed beauty or high social prestige. Even so, Joseph agreed to take Mary as his fiancée. His willingness to do so speaks to his high character, a trait worth emulating by every good man.

In Herod's palace, by contrast, the mistreatment of loved ones was an almost daily occurrence. The king of the Jews had just compounded his earlier murder of Mariamne—who was by no means innocent herself—by trumping up charges against their two boys and dooming them to strangulation in a gloomy dungeon. Everyone found Herod's action repulsive, a sure sign that the once glorious king was losing his mind. The boys had been popular and respected, so their loss stung hard. Only a few people celebrated the Hasmonean princes' demise. Foremost among them was the only legitimate heir left standing: Antipater, the son of Doris, Herod's first wife. Now the throne of Judea seemed tantalizingly close. Surely the fat, old Herod would die soon!

It wasn't long, though, before Antipater witnessed a scene that sent shivers running through him. Before an assembly of friends and high court officials, Herod brought in his most favored grandchildren—the offspring of Alexander and Aristobulus, and thus the descendants of Queen Mariamne. With tears in his eyes, Herod lamented that he had been deprived of the children's fathers "by some evil spirit," taking no personal responsibility for the executions that he himself had ordered. Herod woefully told the gathered officials that pity for the orphans' terrible plight compelled him to provide for their future. "If I have been the most unfortunate of fathers, I will try at any rate to prove myself a more considerate grandfather," he vowed.

Herod then proceeded to announce the carefully selected spouses for the grandchildren who would make their futures bright. (Ironically, the same thing was being arranged for the Virgin Mary, but with a much more blessed outcome.) Herod even had the audacity to seek divine favor for the marriages: "I pray God to bless these unions to the benefit of my realm and of my descendants." He then asked God to look more favorably on the grandchildren than he had on their fathers, as if the two princes had died by the Lord's decree rather than Herod's own deranged paranoia. With tears flowing down his cheeks, Herod made all the children join hands as a sign of family unity. After hugging each orphan to his bosom, he dismissed the assembly.

All of this Antipater watched with growing alarm. Just when he had eliminated his two primary rivals, up had sprung a horde of Hasmonean grandchildren to compete for the throne—each with a prestigious future marriage to enhance their aristocratic status! Everyone in the assembly could see the chagrin on Antipater's face. And it certainly didn't help that the whole nation hated him. The people suspected sibling rivalry was largely to blame for the deaths of the handsome youths. Eventually, when these orphans grew up, the memory of their noble fathers would loom large. The Jewish nation would want to see legitimate Hasmonean offspring back on the throne.

Antipater knew he had to unravel these misguided marriage plans. Instead of planting subtle seeds of doubt in his father's head as he normally did, Antipater decided to tackle the issue head-on—a strategy that worked in this case. He got himself in front of Herod and begged him not to do this thing. Antipater claimed these impressive marriages would make it impossible for him to ever rule in safety, for any direct descendant of Mariamne with aristocratic marital alliances would pose a constant threat to whoever occupied the Judean throne.

Though Herod was angered by the pleas of his firstborn son—*Did this lad's slanders have a hand in the princes' deaths?* he wondered—he finally gave in to Antipater's flattering words and canceled the plans for the grandchildren's impressive unions. (Even so, one of them would grow up to be a Judean ruler: Herod Agrippa, who imprisoned the apostle Peter and put the apostle James to death.)

Antipater then headed off to Rome with, for the second time, a priceless document in his hand: Herod's rewritten will that named Antipater as his royal heir. Yet the impatient Antipater, who was in his early forties by now, had no desire to wait for the glory of kingship until Herod expired from natural causes. Antipater and his mother, Doris, had struck up a friendship with Herod's brother, Pheroras. All three of them stood to benefit if Herod were off the scene. Yet these supposed friends, along with a host of female relatives who were part of the royal family, were plotting against each other even as they collectively plotted against Herod.

The tipping point came when Pheroras took ill and died. Though Herod had come to his brother's sickbed with tender worry, the doctors couldn't save the invalid from his deadly disease. Only after his funeral did the truth come out: Pheroras had been poisoned.

Herod now flew into a terrified rage in which no one—whether slave girl, royal clerk, or noble lady—was free from the interrogator's red-hot irons. Anyone in the palace who might know something was put to the test. Even the innocent were hauled into the torture chamber in case they had valuable information. Too often, they did not, so the frying of their flesh went in vain.

Amid all the agonized screams and desperate pleas for mercy, the interrogators determined that Antipater's mother was one of the conspirators. Herod immediately sent Doris into exile, dressed in rags and penniless once again. Yet the rampant torture of the palace staff continued, revealing new aspects of the plot. A deadly Egyptian poison intended for Herod had been delivered to Antipater's devious hand, but he had passed it to someone who could more easily administer it to the king: Herod's trusted brother Pheroras. Though Pheroras was now dead from poison too, he had relayed the deadly drug to his wife. Herod summoned the widow into his upstairs chamber and ordered her to produce the toxic substance. She agreed to go get it and started for the door—but then, terrified of the torture chamber, she flung herself over the railing onto the pavement below.

Unfortunately, the suicidal woman didn't land on her head, so she only managed to stun herself. Herod had her brought back to him and revived. "Why did you do that?" he demanded. "Tell me the truth and I'll exempt you from torment. But lie to me and I'll have you torn to pieces without a single limb for burial!"

The terrified widow promptly confessed. "Why should I guard any secrets now that my husband is dead? Should I save Antipater, who has been the ruin of us all? Listen to me, O king, and may God hear me too. He who cannot be deceived will bear witness to the truth of my words!"

Pheroras's widow then explained how her dying husband had called her to his deathbed. "I've been wrong about my brother," he confessed. "I plotted to kill the very one who loves me and came to my side as I died! Now I am receiving the just reward for my sins. As for you, bring that poison Antipater gave us and destroy it before my eyes, lest an avenging demon accompany me into the underworld." The widow then explained that she had emptied most of the poison into the fireplace while Pheroras watched, reserving only a little for herself because she feared Herod's wrath.

"Go get it!" Herod barked.

This time, the woman didn't attempt an evasive suicide. She went and fetched the box, which indeed had only a little bit of the poison left inside. The corroboration of her testimony sealed Herod's suspicions of his son.

A short time later, his suspicions were confirmed when one of Antipater's servants revealed under torture some more damning evidence among his master's possessions: a backup poison, this one extracted from asps and other reptilian secretions, along with a batch of falsified letters that terribly maligned Herod's other sons in case they started to display royal aspirations. To cover up the exorbitant fees paid to the poisoners and false witnesses, Antipater had let it be known that he had been splurging on expensive furnishings from Herod's generous allowance. Obviously, toxins and slander were Antipater's standard tools of the trade. Now Herod understood that getting rid of Mariamne's boys hadn't left him with a suitable heir. Quite the contrary, his firstborn son was even worse than them: a crafty conniver with lies on his lips and murder on his mind.

But far away in Rome, Antipater knew nothing of how his reputation had soured back home. He still assumed no one knew about his nefarious dealings behind the scenes. And since no one liked him in Judea, no one bothered to warn him of the thundercloud gathering over his head.

Then word arrived in Rome of Doris's dismissal from the royal house without her accustomed gowns and other finery. Worried about such a disconcerting development, Antipater announced an early return to Jerusalem, an idea that Herod warmly endorsed. In order to get Antipater back in his hands, Herod wrote his son cheerful letters that disguised his fury under an affectionate facade. The king promised to drop his charges against Doris as a minor matter that could easily be forgotten.

But when Antipater showed up in Caesarea's harbor, an eerie silence— "profound and ominous" in Josephus's words—pervaded the place. No civic officials stood on the wharf to welcome him as would befit the arrival of the king's son. Instead, the people ignored or even cursed him. Now Antipater knew something bad was afoot. He hastened to Jerusalem to see if he could make things right.

Arriving in the city wearing his royal purple robe, he rushed to the palace, where he was allowed inside, though not with his retinue, whom the doorkeepers wouldn't admit. When Antipater strode forward with open arms to embrace his father, Herod thrust him away. "To hell with you, impious scoundrel!" he cried. "Don't you dare touch me until you've cleared your name. At dawn tomorrow, I'm putting you on trial for your crimes. Prepare yourself! I'm giving you some time to cook up your usual devious tricks."

As with the trial of the Hasmonean boys, so Antipater's trial in Jerusalem was a major affair. A respected Roman official named Quintilius Varus presided as judge over the proceedings. Antipater immediately fell at his father's feet and begged him to be unprejudiced and open to hearing a fair defense. "I shall, if you permit, establish my innocence," the desperate man promised.

"Shut up!" Herod barked back, then turned to the judge. "That you, Varus, like any honest judge, will condemn Antipater as a lost cause, I am completely certain." Herod then began his prosecution. He excoriated Antipater as a "foul monster, gorged with the benefits of my forbearance," an ungrateful wretch who had spurned his father's countless affectionate gestures and grand provisions. Returning evil for good, Antipater had plotted to kill his half brothers and steal his father's throne, through violence if necessary.

Herod then warned Varus to be on his guard. "I know this creature and foresee the plausible pleading, the hypocritical lamentations that are to follow . . . . When I recall, Varus, his knavery and hypocrisy on each occasion, I can scarce believe I am alive and marvel how I escaped so deep a schemer. But since some evil demon is bent on desolating my house and raising up against me one after another those who are nearest to my heart, I may weep over my unjust destiny, I may groan in spirit over my forlorn state, but not one shall escape who thirsts for my blood, no, *not even if the conviction should extend to all my children!*"

Upon making this shocking threat, intense emotions took hold of Herod. His genuine belief in his own innocence and his corresponding outrage that his sons kept betraying him overwhelmed the king so that he could not continue. He signaled for his adviser, Nicolaus of Damascus, to take over the prosecution.

When Nicolaus finished entering the evidence, Antipater offered an impassioned defense. He proclaimed not only his absence of ill intent but, in fact, a deep love for his father that everyone could see. "All of Rome is a witness to my filial devotion," Antipater cried with puppy-dog eyes. "And so is Caesar, the lord of the universe, who often called me Philopator—'lover of my father.' Here, behold his own words!" Antipater showed the court a supportive letter from Augustus, then begged Herod to regard it higher than the warped testimony gained under torture. "Let the fire be applied to me instead!" Antipater suggested. "Let the instruments of torment course through my very guts! Do not spare my bloodstained body. For if I am to be judged as a father-killer, I ought not die without being tested for truth."

Herod glanced around the room. Clearly, Antipater's tearful pleas and gushing blandishments had had a powerful effect. Everyone had been moved to compassion, even the stoic Varus. But Herod remained resolute. No moisture gathered in his eyes; no spark of pity glimmered in his heart. *It doesn't matter what he says now. I know the evidence against him is true. He's trying to kill me!*

It was Nicolaus, a good and faithful servant, who turned the tribunal back to Herod's side. With the dispassionate tone of a careful prosecutor, avoiding irrational emotions and appealing instead to hard evidence, Nicolaus reminded the judge and his assembly about the facts of the case. The warm feeling toward Antipater, the sense that he was an innocent victim of a suspicious father, slowly drained from the room. Herod smiled as he saw the jury panelists come back to their right minds.

And what were the facts? The deaths of Alexander and Aristobulus were directly attributable to Antipater's secret schemes. He had also corrupted the king's brother Pheroras by convincing him to attempt fratricide. Each of Nicolaus's accusations was supported by proofs. Even the poison that Antipater had purchased was brought into the courtroom and given to a condemned criminal, who drank it and immediately keeled over dead. So devastating was the evidence against Antipater that when Varus called upon him to make a formal defense, all he would say was, "God is witness of my innocence."

No, he isn't, Herod thought. *God is a witness of your crimes!* Antipater had expended all his energy on his only line of defense: an emotional plea that tugged on his listeners' heartstrings. When it came to an actual rebuttal of hard evidence, Antipater had nothing to offer. His own actions condemned him. Everyone could see it clearly now.

In the days after the trial, more evidence came to light. Antipater had also schemed against Salome, Herod's sister, misrepresenting her to the point that the king had almost put her to death for imaginary crimes. *What a tragedy that would have been!* Herod felt relieved that he hadn't been so rash. To correct the matter, he called for his will and rewrote it a third time, assigning lavish bequests to Salome. He also changed his successor to Herod Antipas, his son by Malthace, instead of Antipater, who had proven to be a constant source of discord and mayhem.

But before Herod could determine what should happen to his imprisoned firstborn son, he took ill and delayed the decision to another day. Death was lurking everywhere in the royal palace. Who it would claim next was anyone's guess.

CHAPTER 19

HOPE IS ON THE WAY

The bad sons of a bad earthly father stood in stark contrast to Mary, the good daughter of her good Father in heaven. Mary behaved toward God the way all Israelite girls were expected to behave toward their fathers: with respect and obedience, leading to blessing. Mary knew that her God was worthy of devotion, no matter what he might ask of her.

Mary's faith was tested one day when she was alone in her house. Now that she was legally betrothed to Joseph, she had moved from the Jerusalem area to Galilee in the north, to a tiny Galilean village called Nazareth. Joseph was living there for a while even though his hometown was Bethlehem. As Joseph's fiancée, Mary was expected to live there too—though, of course, she hadn't yet consummated her union with her husband-to-be.

On the day of her testing during Hanukkah, the Jewish Festival of Lights in December, a man startled her by showing up in her house unannounced. Mary knew that as a young woman, she was expected to provide hospitality to all guests, which in that culture would have included expressions of esteem. But this man seemed more intent on honoring her than being honored. "Grace to you, highly graced one," the visitor said. "The Lord is with you; blessed are you among women!" (Luke 1:28, author's translation).[1] This greeting sounded strange to Mary's ear. *Why did he say I'm "graced"? And why did he single me out among all women? What is this stranger doing here in my house? Does he wish to do me harm?*

When Mary shrank back from the suspicious man—admittedly, he was

---

1. Bible versions give various translations of this verse, such as "Greetings, you who are highly favored!" (NIV). The Greek is, "*Chaire, kecharitomene!*" You can see that forms of the Greek word for grace, *charis*, are repeated in both words, then again in verse 30. Mary would have heard this graceful overtone when these words were spoken to her. Also note that many Greek manuscripts do not include the expression, "Blessed are you among women," though the NKJV does include it here.

also an extraordinarily handsome man—the visitor stepped forward with comforting yet authoritative words: "Do not be afraid, Mary, for you have found grace with God" (v. 30, author's translation). *There's that word* grace *again! How does this outsider know my name? Who is this strange man?*

As if these words and this behavior weren't troubling enough, the man now made a stunning announcement that shook Mary to her core. "Behold," he said, "you will conceive in your womb and bring forth a Son, and shall call His name JESUS. He will be great, and will be called the Son of the Highest; and the Lord God will give Him the throne of His father David. And He will reign over the house of Jacob forever, and of His kingdom there will be no end" (vv. 31–33).

Shocked, Mary gripped her garment in her fists and staggered backward. Her marriage to Joseph was at least a year away, but Mary realized the strange visitor was talking about events in the near future. The "grace" he had spoken of was coming soon—but it was no grace at all! To conceive a child out of wedlock would result in terrible shame, possibly even death by communal stoning. Certainly, Joseph would call off the marriage, resulting in a life of poverty and rejection as a tainted woman who couldn't keep herself chaste. Even if the illegitimate son went on to become a great king like the visitor said, Mary knew she would still have to contend with the immense cultural disgrace of an unwanted pregnancy. *Can such a thing really be from God?*

One fact of nature helped Mary cling to the hope that these things might not take place. Since the inspired visitor, whoever he was, had blessing in his mouth, not cursing, Mary knew the pregnancy wouldn't happen by human force. That meant as long as she kept herself chaste in her relationship with Joseph, a pregnancy could not occur. The realization prompted a question to the messenger. Using a euphemistic verb so as not to be too forward with her male guest, Mary asked, "How can this be, since I do not know a man?" (v. 34).

Unfortunately, the visitor—was he actually an angel of God?—had a ready answer. "The Holy Spirit will come upon you, and the power of the Highest will overshadow you; therefore, also, that Holy One who is to be born will be called the Son of God. Now indeed, Elizabeth your relative has also conceived a son in her old age; and this is now the sixth month for her who was called barren. For with God nothing will be impossible" (vv. 35–37).

The messenger's announcement sobered Mary. She realized a great mystery was taking place. The words from the synagogue readings sprang to her mind, the oracle of the prophet Isaiah: "Therefore the Lord Himself will give you a sign. Behold, the virgin shall conceive and bear a Son, and shall call His name Immanuel" (7:14).

Immanuel—"*God with us.*" *Jesus*—*the "Savior." The Holy One. The Son of the Most High. The Son of God. The heir of David. The true King of Israel!*

In a flash, Mary perceived why she was being hailed with the word *grace*. Her body was destined to be the vessel of grace for the entire world! The names that the angel had been using were messianic. They spoke of God's Anointed One who was promised to save his people. Now that very Savior was coming into the world, and according to the ancient prophecy, God was using Mary's virginal body as the instrument of salvation. By human means, this would have been impossible. But as the angel had said, "With God nothing will be impossible" (Luke 1:37). God had already put life into the barren womb of Elizabeth. Now he would bring forth life from her own immaculate womb.

Since God was clearly at work here, nothing remained to question or resist. With a deep sigh of determination, Mary resolved to take the plunge. She would allow this promised "Jesus" to enter the core of her being, to become one with her, to guide everything about her destiny. The festival of Hanukkah now had a new, more personal meaning: not just the rededication of the temple after the Greeks had profaned it but the dedication of her own body to become a temple in which the Divine Presence would dwell. Once Mary gave her assent to this heavenly commission, there would be no going back. Little Jesus, "God with us," was going to change everything—forever.

"Very well," Mary said meekly to the angelic visitor. "Behold the maidservant of the Lord! Let it be to me according to your word" (Luke 1:38). And upon hearing those words of humble assent, the angel departed from her.

A pious Jewish girl like Mary could sense that God was up to something big even if she couldn't yet see what it was. In this way, she was like all her people, who were constantly trying to discern the signs of the divine hand. Collectively, the Jews longed for deliverance. People under the thumb of a more dominant power like the Jews under the Romans (and before that, under the Hellenistic Greeks) have essentially four possible ways to relate to their overlords. The first is *collaboration*. Herod chose this path throughout his life, learning early from his father, Antipater I, that the best strategy was to get along with the Romans and grab as much peace and prosperity for the nation as possible. Herod was a pro-Roman collaborator par excellence.

The second route is *separation*, with two potential avenues for doing so. The dominated people can separate themselves within their society by going about their private business and rubbing shoulders as little as possible with the oppressors. Or, as a third option, they can remove themselves to remote areas and maintain their vigorous nationalistic hopes while prepping for an end-times restoration of the righteous ones.

The dominated nation, fourthly, can resort to *insurrection*. The Maccabees had chosen this path when the religious oppression of the Greeks had grown intolerable. Later, several decades after the time of Herod, the Jewish people would once again choose this route, rebelling against Rome only to lose badly and see their temple destroyed in AD 70. All four of these options were represented by leading sects of the Jews—collaboration by the Sadducees, internal separation by the Pharisees, external separation by the Essenes, and insurrection by the Zealots.

Herod, who was proclaimed king of the Jews by the Roman Senate and always curried the favor of whoever steered the ship of state, did find success through his strategy of getting along. In terms of achieving general well-being and peace for Israel, collaboration had its merits. Yet for those who hated Rome no matter how much national prosperity was bought in exchange for subservience, the collaborative option could never be a long-term solution. For most of Herod's reign, the advocates of separation from Rome's paganism quietly bided their time. But as Herod grew older, fatter, and weaker, the separatists saw their chance—and the steely eyed insurrectionists weren't far behind them.

The name "Pharisee" came from the Hebrew word for separation. Although they didn't advocate flight to the desert like more radical groups, they nonetheless achieved separation from contaminating Roman ways through rituals and purity regulations that added extra strictures to the Mosaic law. These, it was believed, would keep faithful Jews from violating God's command to be a distinct people. As the apostle Paul—himself an excellent Pharisee—would later put it, "Come out from among them and be separate, says the Lord. Do not touch what is unclean, and I will receive you" (2 Corinthians 6:17).

———————————

A terrible incident just a few months before Herod's eventual death galvanized the separatist Pharisees against Herod the Roman collaborator. It brought violence not just to the halls of the Herodian palace but to the public squares of Jerusalem.

Herod's sickness had continued to worsen and the prognosis didn't look good. His body had bloated up like a wineskin, his feet ached, his limbs convulsed, his skin itched, and the increased pressure on his lungs made breathing difficult. Herod's old age of seventy years didn't help matters either. *I might not make it past this one*, he realized, and the thought maddened him. People across the land would gloat at his demise. *Why do they hate me so unjustly?* he wondered bitterly. *After all I've done for them—the cities I built . . . the gifts I gave . . . the temple I set upon Zion!*

The king's severe illness, compounded by the distraction of his son's trial, gave the separatist-minded Pharisees the perfect opportunity to rectify a matter that had long bothered them. Good Jews weren't supposed to make graven images of any kind. For the most part, Herod had tried to comply with that ancient law. Yet here and there, he had crossed the line and allowed decorations to be made in the form of animals.

One image that particularly rankled the Pharisees adorned the temple itself: a shining golden eagle on a high pediment. Eagles could, of course, represent good things. "But those who wait on the LORD shall renew their strength; they shall mount up with wings like eagles," said the prophet Isaiah (40:31). And Moses, in a beautiful song, had even compared God to an eagle who "stirs up its nest, hovers over its young, spreading out its wings, taking them up, carrying them on its wings" (Deuteronomy 32:11). Yet the eagle was also the primary symbol of Rome, associated for centuries with its cruel army and the impostor god Jupiter. The Pharisees hated seeing the idolatrous Roman eagle adorning Yahweh's glorious temple.

With Herod on his sickbed, two eminent Pharisee scholars, Judas and Matthias, saw their chance. They used their high status among their disciples, who hung on their every word, to call for immediate removal of the eagle. Not only would anyone who achieved this glorious deed go down in history as a hero but the rabbis also promised that his soul would be welcomed into immortality for such pious faithfulness.

Then the rumor began to circulate that Herod had died. Now was the time to act! The riled-up students clambered onto the temple's roof, lowered themselves by ropes, and began to hack at the golden sacrilege. As soon as it hit the ground, other holy warriors smashed it to bits with axes. The exuberant students rejoiced in the greatness of God's victory—until the sound of hob-nailed boots on the pavement drained the color from their faces.

About forty of the rebellious students were arrested by the temple guards, along with the two Pharisee professors who had instigated the action. The rebels were taken down to Jericho for interrogation. "Why did you do it?" Herod demanded. Their smug, self-righteous answers about "God's will" infuriated him. Empowered by a rage that overcame his debilitating sickness, Herod appeared before a public assembly and denounced the youths and their teachers as sacrilegious temple-robbers, not national heroes. "How dare you disregard all I did for you in building the great temple!" Herod screeched. "How dare you ignore the vast sums I paid for it! For 125 years, the Hasmoneans ruled, and they gave you no temple like that. But I did! I gave you that glorious edifice! When you insult the temple and its decorations, you insult me!"

The crowd of onlookers in the public assembly began to grow nervous as they discerned the agitated state of their king. Fearing widespread reprisals and bloodshed, they asked Herod to relent. Begrudgingly, he decreed a lighter, more merciful penalty than what they had feared. The two professors and the students who had actually climbed onto the roof would be publicly burned alive. The rest of the captured students would be executed by normal means. Much to the relief of the crowd, no one else would be harmed. As if to signal God's approval—or maybe his disapproval?—of these executions, that night there was an ominous eclipse of the moon.

Exhausted by the affair of the eagle and the ungratefulness it represented, Herod sank back into the throes of his afflictions. With horror, he found beneath his robe that his genitals were rotting from within. His gangrenous groin was beginning to look like raw meat instead of the flesh of a man. Herod was also afflicted by terrible, burning pains in his gut. Food only made the stabbing agonies worse, so while he craved nourishment, he could take none lest it stir up the inner fires. Like the mythological figure of Tantalus in hell, Herod was always hungry and never able to satisfy his cravings. The decay inside his body also made his breath a repugnant vapor that no one could stand to be near. Yet Herod no longer cared about that. Just gasping for air was hard enough. Why should he worry about its stink?

Despite his many ailments, Herod clung to the hope of healing. Perhaps God would use a natural means? Herod ordered his attendants to transport him to Callirrhoe, a spa town not far from Jericho. Its mineral waters were reputed to be healthy, even sweet enough to drink until the moment they ran into the salty expanse of the Dead Sea. Surely here was a solution!

Unfortunately, the spa waters had no effect. The doctors even had Herod lowered into a bath of warmed olive oil. When the heat overcame him and he fainted, his eyes rolled back in their sockets and everyone took him for dead. The mournful wail that arose shook Herod back to awareness. But he had been revived from his stupor only to be returned to hopeless despair. Now that every natural means had failed him, no hope for a cure remained. Returning to Jericho, Herod's darkened mind began to brood over what kind of legacy he could leave after he died.

Soon, he hit upon a devious plan. He called for his faithful sister Salome to help him, along with her husband. Herod ordered all the leading men from every Judean village rounded up and brought to Jericho. He put them in the city's chariot stadium and locked the doors with guards stationed outside. "Death is common to all men," Herod told Salome and her husband, "but that I should go on without being mourned is a bitter thought. I have done too much for my people to die without their shedding of tears!" Then Herod drew the conspirators closer to his sickbed. "I know that the Jews will celebrate my death by a festival. Yet I can obtain a vicarious mourning and a magnificent funeral if you consent to follow my instructions. You know these notable men whom I am holding here in custody? The moment I expire, I want them surrounded by soldiers and massacred. Swear this to me!"

"We will do it, beloved," Salome promised as she squeezed Herod's sweaty hand, even as she vowed in her heart never to carry it through.

"Good . . . very good indeed," Herod wheezed. "So shall every household in Judea weep for me, whether they want to or not."

CHAPTER 20

WHO IS THE KING OF GLORY?

Six hundred miles to the east of where the diseased king of the Jews lay dying, in the land of Parthia, whose rulers had once before threatened Herod's reign through invasion, a far more dire menace to his royal legacy was preparing to return. A group of wise men known in Greek as *magoi*—influential scholars and astronomers from the Parthian territory of Babylonia—had witnessed a stunning new phenomenon. Despite being well-versed in the normal movements of the planets and stars, these men had no explanation for the brightness that had arisen to their west. It had followed no normal course through the heavens. In fact, it seemed entirely disconnected from the regular astronomical rhythms. *What can it be?* they wondered. Though they did not know, the curious scholars refused to quit searching.

A breakthrough came when one of these men chanced to examine a sacred Jewish text. Many centuries earlier, the great King Nebuchadnezzar had carried the people of Judah into exile, resettling them along the Euphrates River in Babylonia. Although some later kings had allowed many of those exiles to return to their ancestral lands, other Jews had stayed behind, creating a thriving Babylonian community that produced many textual scholars. Now the *magoi*, or the magi as they are known in Latin, consulted these Jewish sages for interpretive advice.

The mysterious text came from the Jewish book of Numbers (24:15–17). It was a prophecy from one of the Israelites' greatest seers:

> The utterance of Balaam the son of Beor,
> and the utterance of the man whose eyes are opened;
> the utterance of him who hears the words of God,
> and has the knowledge of the Most High,

who sees the vision of the Almighty,
who falls down, with eyes wide open:
I see Him, but not now;
I behold Him, but not near;
a Star shall come out of Jacob;
a Scepter shall rise out of Israel.

The magi marveled at these words, for they could see with their own eyes that the inexplicable western star stood over the lands of Jacob, whose God-given name was Israel. This was the country that Pacorus and Barzapharnes had invaded thirty-six years earlier, troubling the young prince Herod, who went on to rule the Jews for so long. Now something even greater than this was happening in Israel, something sent by the Wise Lord himself. Surely it would change the world forever![1]

"What do your people believe this prophecy means?" the magi asked the rabbis.

"It refers to the Messiah, the anointed one of God," was their unanimous reply. "Balaam 'saw Him,' though 'not near,' for his time had not yet come. Now, at last, it has arrived." This answer reflected the standard Jewish interpretation of the Numbers text. Many believers in Israel were anxiously awaiting their Savior because of these sacred words.

After taking counsel among themselves, the magi determined upon a bold course. "We must journey west and see this thing," they agreed. "We must visit the great King Herod, consult with his council of sages, and discover the meaning of this divine omen."

"Be careful, friends," the rabbis advised. "The hands of Herod are quick to shed blood."

The stunning news that Mary had received—*A virgin shall conceive a child! Who has ever heard of such a thing?*—continued to amaze her after the angel departed. She treasured his words in her heart, pondering their meaning while

1. The magi worshiped a god called Ahura Mazda, or the Wise Lord. They may have equated this being with the true God.

telling no one. Eventually, though, Mary realized she needed to talk with someone who could help her consider what God was doing in this extraordinary action. Only one person could truly understand, for she, too, had conceived a miraculous child. "Elizabeth your relative has also conceived a son in her old age," the angel had declared. "And this is now the sixth month for her who was called barren" (Luke 1:36). For so many years, Mary's elderly aunt Elizabeth had struggled with infertility. Now, incredibly, she was with child. Mary reminded herself again that with God, nothing is impossible.

The journey from Nazareth to Elizabeth's village didn't take long, for Mary's traveling companions were in a hurry. Joseph had arranged for her to travel with some of his kinsmen who were heading up to Jerusalem for Hanukkah. Since the eight-day Festival of Lights had already started, the travelers wasted no time and soon sighted the gleaming city on the horizon. Mary took leave of the caravan when it reached a village in the Judean hill country a short distance from Jerusalem. Elizabeth's house was there, providing easy access to the city. Her husband, Zacharias, was a priest who sometimes served in the temple.

Although the door to Elizabeth's house was closed, Mary could hear her aunt singing inside while she was grinding grain, her melodious voice contrasting with the gritty rasp of the mill. Smiling broadly at the joyous surprise she was about to give, Mary burst through the door and spotted her aunt in the house's courtyard. "Greetings, beloved!" she exclaimed.

Elizabeth's face lit up, first with a startled gasp, then with obvious delight. But as she rose to her feet, a different look came over her—a surprised expression accompanied by a sharp cry. Her hand went to her abdomen, signaling something surprising within.

"What is it?" Mary asked.

Instead of replying, Elizabeth rushed over to Mary and knelt before her. No pain darkened her visage. Whatever had disturbed her body had passed. Now Elizabeth's deep-set eyes and wrinkled face gazed up with wonder and awe.

"Blessed are you among women," Elizabeth cried with a loud voice. "And blessed is the fruit of your womb! But why is this granted to me, that the mother of my Lord should come to me? For indeed, as soon as the voice of your greeting sounded in my ears, the babe leaped in my womb for joy" (Luke 1:42–44).

Then Mary understood. The son she had been instructed to name Jesus had somehow communicated with the baby in her aunt's womb. The two miraculously conceived infants were rejoicing together in the coming work of God. Awed by these spiritual things, Mary placed both hands on her belly and spoke in hushed tones as she explained to her aunt what the angel had foretold. "'[This child] will be called the Son of the Highest; and the Lord God will give Him the throne of His father David. And He will reign over the house of Jacob forever, and of His kingdom there will be no end'" (vv. 32–33).

Elizabeth bowed her head, staring at Mary's feet. "Oh! Can you believe such good news about your son?"

"I believe he is the Messiah, the Son of God who is to come into the world."

Elizabeth nodded but didn't lift her gaze. "Blessed are you among women," she repeated, and "blessed is she who believed, for there will be a fulfillment of those things which were told her from the Lord" (v. 45).

"I am but his maidservant," Mary said demurely. "May his will be done in my life."

Sometime during Herod's final days, when he was cementing his legacy and making sure his name would be remembered forever, a caravan of visitors arrived in Judea on a frightful mission. These foreigners were known to him as astrologers from Parthia in the East. They were brilliant men—the leading scholars of their day, in touch with ancient science and mysterious magic. When they sought a meeting with Herod, he granted it despite his infirmities.

"Where is the newborn king of the Jews?" the magi asked him. "We saw his star as it rose, and we have come to worship him" (Matthew 2:2 NLT).

The question shook Herod deeply; for if some newborn king were discovered with divinely inspired claims to the throne, Herod's own sons might be dispossessed and his legacy would be shattered. Everyone in Israel was expecting God's Messiah to arrive at any time. According to an ancient prophecy in the book of Numbers, his "star" was supposed to arise in the sky. Now these wise visitors from eastern lands had received a heavenly omen about the anointed Savior. Something had to be done!

Herod must have been in Jerusalem when the magi arrived, for he was able to gather the chief priests and scribes of the city to inquire where the Messiah was supposed to be born. They pointed him to the words of the prophet Micah, "But you, Bethlehem, in the land of Judah, are not the least among the rulers of Judah; for out of you shall come a Ruler who will shepherd My people Israel" (Matthew 2:6; Micah 5:2).

Bethlehem! Though it was a tiny, no-account village, Herod immediately understood that some peasant child born there might have the power to unravel his legacy. He wanted to command the magi to slay the boy when they found him, but he knew these elegant easterners would do no such thing. Therefore, he slyly instructed his guests, "Go and search carefully for the young Child, and when you have found Him, bring back word to me, that I may come and worship Him also" (Matthew 2:8). Then the wise magicians departed.

———————————

For three months, Mary remained with her aunt Elizabeth near Jerusalem. But eventually, it was time to go home—a return that Mary dreaded. Though her virgin body had become the temple of the Lord, her fiancé, Joseph, didn't yet know of this holy indwelling. The baby that had been planted in Mary's womb by the hand of God himself was growing quietly in that hidden place. Mary often prayed a psalm over her unborn child. "You formed [my son in] my inward parts," she sang to the Lord. "You covered [him] in [his] mother's womb. I will praise You, for [this child is] fearfully and wonderfully made; marvelous are Your works, and that my soul knows very well" (139:13–14).

Would Joseph find the pregnancy so "marvelous" when he finally learned of it? Mary feared he would not.

Even after she reached Nazareth, she postponed telling him the news. Yet she couldn't avoid it forever. At last, she gathered her courage to tell Joseph about the unexpected life within her. "I am pregnant," she said simply, "but I have not lain with a man. The son within me is from the Holy Spirit. A messenger of God has told me this."

Though Mary had hoped for a tranquil response, it was not to be. Joseph's face registered an agonized expression that she would never forget. Weeping bitterly and striking his forehead with his fists, he cried to the heavens in shock and outrage. *The Original Gospel of James* describes him as saying, "With what countenance shall I look towards the Lord my God? What prayer shall I offer for this maiden? For I received her as a virgin out of the temple of the Lord my God and I have not protected her. Who has deceived me? Who has done this evil in my house and defiled the virgin? Has the story of Adam been repeated in me? For just as Adam was absent in the hour of his prayer and the serpent came and found Eve alone and deceived her and defiled her, so also has such a thing happened to me!"

"No, my lord!" Mary protested in a flood of tears. "Things are not as you think! I am pure and do not know a man!"

But Joseph, feeling the dagger of betrayal, couldn't accept these words. His eyes were hard and his finger accusing as he said, "Why have you done this, Mary? Why have you forgotten the Lord your God? You were cared for by God himself. Why have you humiliated your soul, you of all people, who were brought up at the Most Holy Place and received food from the hand of an angel?"

Despite Mary's tearful claims of innocence, Joseph refused to accept any excuses. Because he was righteous, he promised to divorce her without any public shame and send her on her way. Yet the thought of that, even if done quietly, was more than Mary could bear. She fled from his presence, not knowing when she might see him again.

For several days, Joseph drank the cup of bitterness to its dregs. His beloved Mary, the holy maiden of God, had fornicated with a man, then had the nerve to concoct some crazy story about an angelic announcement. She had opened her body to an alien invader, then blasphemed God by calling the child his. As if God plants children in a woman's womb apart from the seed of a man! Such a thing had never been heard of in Israel.

Or had it?

After Joseph had fallen asleep that night, tossing and turning on his bed as nightmares assailed him, everything changed in a flash. Instead of the demonic whispers, a glorious, shining angel came to him in a dream. "Joseph, son of David, do not be afraid," he said in comforting tones that banished the devilish lies. "Do you not recall what the prophet Isaiah said?"

Still in his dream, Joseph perceived himself reading the words from the book of Isaiah: "Behold, the virgin shall be with child, and bear a Son, and they shall call His name Immanuel" (Matthew 1:23).

A virgin with child—prophesied in Scripture!

"What does that name mean?" the angel asked.

"God with us," Joseph replied in awe.

"Yes," the angel agreed. "God with us." Then he took a step closer, staring down at the distraught man on his bed. "Joseph, son of David, do not be afraid to take to you Mary your wife, for that which is conceived in her is of the Holy Spirit. And she will bring forth a Son, and you shall call His name JESUS, for He will save His people from their sins" (vv. 20–21). And with that blessed promise, Joseph woke up.

Throwing aside his covers, the righteous stonemason hurriedly dressed by the light of the moon. Though it was the middle of the night, his words for Mary couldn't wait. He rushed to her house nearby and entered. Her room was on the floor above. "Mary!" he called.

After a moment, her face appeared at the top of the ladder, illumined by the flickering glow from the dying embers in the courtyard's firepit. "What is it, Joseph my lord?"

"Forgive me, beloved! Oh, forgive me! An angel has appeared to me this night, exactly like the one you described. He confirmed what you said. I should have believed you!"

Though Mary's face bore a look of shocked surprise, her voice was firm as she asked, "What did the angel tell you to do?"

"To take you as my wife, which I surely will! And I will raise this child as my own, even though he is from God and not me."

Now Mary descended the ladder, barefoot and wrapped in her cloak. Standing before Joseph, she took his hand in hers. "Did the angel tell you the child's name?"

"Yes. He spoke in Greek and said 'Jesus.' In our tongue, it would be 'Yeshua.'"

"Do you know why that is the child's name?"

"Of course," Joseph replied, nodding slowly. "Because he will save his people from their sins." He paused for a moment, then drew Mary to himself in a fierce yet tender embrace. A tremor of deep emotion shook his voice as he added, "Including, beloved, the sin of my own unbelief."

CHAPTER 21

SON OF MARY,
SON OF GOD

Mary drew her cloak closer about her shoulders, shivering against the chilly autumn winds. For several days, she had been traveling with Joseph from the Galilean lowlands to the hill country of Judea. The emperor in faraway Rome had recently come into power and he wanted to know who populated his lands. He had decreed an empire-wide census that required everyone to return to their ancestral homelands. For Joseph, that meant Bethlehem.

Though Mary's pregnancy was near full term now, the ride up from Nazareth hadn't been too arduous for her. Joseph had been so kind, leading the donkey by hand and caring for her every need. *But oh, those early days!* Mary couldn't help but recall that terrible day when she had broken the news to Joseph about her pregnancy. His shock and disappointment had been so awful until an angel had revealed the truth. *Then, how things had changed!* Mary shook her head as she recalled the humble way her husband had dealt with her after the angelic revelation. *He came to me in repentance and restored me to his side, to a place of honor. And during all the time we have been riding, how sweet and gentle he has been!* Those fond memories were in Mary's mind as she crested a ridge and gazed upon her destination for the first time. There, perched on a rugged hillside, was the city of David: Bethlehem of Judea, the House of Bread from which all nations would someday feast. In this place, Mary knew, she would bring forth her firstborn son, the Messiah, who would reign over the whole world.

Where, exactly, in Bethlehem was Jesus born? Modern people from the European tradition often picture the nativity happening in a stable, yet the Bible never states this. Luke 2:7 tells us only that "there was no place for them in the *kataluma*," so Mary laid the baby in an animal's feeding trough. The

Greek word *kataluma* can mean any kind of lodging place where someone would spend the night. Was this an "inn" with a stable out back like we so often hear?

The earliest Latin versions of the Bible started the confusion by translating *kataluma* with a word meaning an inn, that is, a public, roadside lodging place. John Wycliffe's first English version of the Bible in 1382 translated this same Latin word as "chaumbir" (chamber). But soon after that, William Tyndale's influential version, based not on the Latin but the original Greek, translated Luke 2:7 as "ther was no roume for them within in the ynne." All the early English versions after this, including the Coverdale Bible, the Great Bible, the Bishop's Bible, the Geneva Bible, the Douay-Rheims Version, and the original King James Version, followed the "inn" translation.

The problem is, while public inns for travelers were common across the landscape of medieval England when these translations were being made, the biblical situation was quite different. Our idea of an inn as a place where multiple sojourners find overnight lodging doesn't fit the context of Joseph and Mary at all.

The Romans did have two types of such lodging, but one was for imperial government travelers with official permission to stay there, and the other was associated with thievery, carousing, and prostitution. An upright Jew like Joseph never would have taken his pregnant wife to such a place, even if one had existed in Bethlehem, which was unlikely in a backwater village far from the main highway. And when the Bible wishes to speak of that kind of inn, it uses a different Greek word (a *pandocheion*, Luke 10:34).

The reality is, a *kataluma* in the biblical context refers to the guest room that most ancient Jewish homes kept available for visitors. It was a spare multi-purpose room for providing hospitality in that courteous culture. The same word was used of the "guest room" where Jesus' disciples celebrated the Last Supper (Luke 22:11). Almost certainly, Joseph first tried to bring Mary into his hometown of Bethlehem, where he could lodge in a village house among relatives who would provide their *kataluma* for the guests.

But due to overcrowding caused by other relatives arriving for the census registration, the Scripture tells us that when the time came for Jesus' birth, no private place was available for the laboring mother in the guest room (Luke 2:1–7). What could a godly husband like Joseph do? Although Scripture doesn't provide details, the ancient Christian traditions that have come down to us help us imagine the scene.

According to *The Original Gospel of James*, the holy couple was traveling along the road when Mary felt an urgency within her womb. She said to her husband, "'Joseph, take me down from the she-ass, for the child within me presses me to come forth.' And he took her down from the she-ass and said to her, 'Where shall I take you and hide your shame? For this place is deserted.' And he found a cave there and brought her into it, and left her in the care of his sons." In other words, the widower Joseph and some of his sons from his previous marriage nobly wanted to guard Mary's privacy by taking her into a nearby cave. After this account was written, several other ancient Christian sources likewise attested that the birth happened in a cave. Even today, the eastern Mediterranean depictions of the nativity (such as Greek Orthodox icons) always set the event in a craggy cavern, not a European stable made of wood.

Does a cave seem like a strange place for Jesus to be born? If it does, perhaps that is because our mental picture of Christmas has been conditioned by sentimental Victorian images instead of God's Word and a strong knowledge of Israelite culture. We need a new, more biblical image of Christmas!

Not many people today know that the region around Bethlehem was an important area where lambs were raised for a specific purpose. There, at the House of Bread, lambs were birthed for the following year's Passover sacrifice in the Jerusalem temple. All faithful Jews marked that annual holiday with a family feast of roasted lamb, unleavened bread, and bitter herbs.

In order to provide enough sacrificial lambs for the nation, special priestly shepherds raised sheep near Bethlehem. During the cold winter months, they sheltered their flocks inside local caves. Since the Scripture says the shepherds were outdoors at night during the first Christmas when an angel appeared to them (Luke 2:8–9), it couldn't have occurred in December.

Instead, the Savior's birth most likely occurred during the autumn festival of Sukkot, which marked God's provision for the Israelites during the exodus, while they wandered in the wilderness. Later generations of Jews commemorated the transient "booths," or shelters, that their ancestors had lived in while wandering, as well as the shelters used during the busy harvest when God's bountiful crop was reaped. Sukkot fell about nine months after Hanukkah, when lamps were lit to celebrate the restoration of God's worship at the temple. No longer were the people cut off from God; they had access to him again. That was the prophetic moment when the angel had announced Mary's virginal conception.

Do you see the intertwined themes here? A good Jewish woman like Mary couldn't have missed them as she reclined on the floor of the cave, reflecting between her contractions upon what was happening to her. Perhaps Joseph had piled up some straw to give Mary a soft bed as she tried to understand what God was up to. Scripture tells us that Mary pondered deep theological truths and treasured them in her heart (Luke 2:19). What truths? *Shelter in the wilderness . . . bountiful harvests . . . lamps of brilliant light . . . temple sacrifice . . . a restored relationship with God . . . a family feast of bread and flesh.* Somehow, in the mysterious will of Yahweh, all of these things were converging in the tiny fetus that pressed against Mary's womb and strove to enter the world.

At last, the birth pangs struck in earnest. The first-time mother's travails were fierce, not at all mitigated because the baby was destined to be the messianic king; for he was also a normal human. Yet even in the midst of her suffering, Mary's soul rejoiced in the good work God was doing.

After little Jesus had come forth, Mary nursed him, then swaddled him like one of the sacred lambs and laid him upon some soft grass in the feeding trough. In this beautiful way, the meaning of the ancient Israelite festival of Passover reached its fulfillment. When John the Baptist later saw the adult Jesus coming toward him, he exclaimed, "Behold! The Lamb of God who takes away the sin of the world!" (John 1:29). Peter likewise said we are redeemed by "the precious blood of Christ, as of a lamb without blemish and without spot" (1 Peter 1:19). And the apostle Paul wrote, "For indeed Christ, our Passover, was sacrificed for us" (1 Corinthians 5:7). Both the birth and the death of Messiah Jesus proved him to be the ultimate Passover Lamb.

The itch! God in heaven, make it stop!

Herod clawed his tickle-tormented skin, leaving long, red welts where his fingernails raked his flesh, but he didn't care. More than any of his pains—and they were many—his full-body itch had pushed him to the brink of madness. Indeed, the constant prickling sensation had driven him to attempt suicide. Only by death could he gain relief from the maggots that wriggled in his putrid groin and seemed to crawl beneath every inch of his skin. Flies had laid their eggs in his cankerous crotch, causing a persistent irritation that swept over his body and couldn't be stopped. As the king lay on his sickbed in the Jericho palace, the little knife intended for slicing an apple seemed to offer a final solution to all his troubles. Yet even in the glorious deed of noble suicide, Herod failed.

"Stop!" his cousin Achiabus yelled when the dying king raised the knife above his saggy breast. The man dashed over and seized Herod's wrist before he could plunge the blade into his heart. For a time, the two of them struggled, with one seeking death, the other seeking life—not the king's life but his own. Achiabus feared being blamed for the crime of regicide. The sound of lamentation filled the room as the doctors and servants watched the deadly struggle. Other mourners in the hallways took up the cry, assuming the worst.

At last, Herod's arm weakened. It was no use. He couldn't perform the deed. His strength, both mental and physical, had ebbed away. Herod let his arm go limp as Achiabus took away the knife. "Not today," the man muttered.

"But soon," Herod whispered, a statement of fact as well as a prayer.

In the end, Herod decided it was good that his suicide attempt had failed. He learned that when the cry of lamentation arose in the palace, Antipater, who was imprisoned nearby, had rejoiced. He had even started making plans for seizing the throne. Then the faithful jailer rushed to Herod's sickbed and reported this treasonous behavior. Disgusted, Herod beat his head at the thought that his ungrateful wretch of a son would outlive him and rejoice over his father's death.

With great effort, Herod raised himself on one elbow so his lungs could inflate enough for him to speak. "It is time," he gasped to the captain of his bodyguard. "Do the deed without delay." Herod knew he was within his rights, for Caesar Augustus had granted him the power of life and death over his treacherous son. Achiabus had just brought the imperial letter from Rome. Upon this command from Herod, Antipater was immediately strangled and buried without any ceremony to honor him.

Now that the son of disgrace had gone to the place he deserved, Herod decided his final act would be to rewrite his will. By rightly apportioning his royal power and massive wealth, he could shape his legacy and make an impact long after death.

The lawyers and scribes were summoned, each wearing a kerchief over his nose to guard against the fecal stench of the room, though their grimaces suggested mere cloths couldn't fully do the job. Herod divided his kingdom among three remaining sons: Herod Archelaus, Herod Antipas, and Herod Philip the Tetrarch. (Herod's fourth son by Mariamne II, called Herod II, wasn't included in the will because he was in disfavor.) The dying king also gave great wealth to Salome, along with some cities for her to rule. And to Caesar Augustus and his wife, Herod bequeathed the vast sum of fifteen million silver pieces, along with many gold vessels and costly garments.

"Now I shall be remembered as great," he consoled himself as he wallowed in his own filth. "My kingdom will have no end!"

For some time after her arduous labor and delivery, Mary rested and slept in the shepherds' cave near her newborn son. Only after the Roman census-taking was complete and the other relatives had left the Bethlehem house did Joseph and Mary return to the guest room in the village. Yet Mary knew she couldn't remain there indefinitely. According to the Mosaic law, she would be ritually impure for forty days following the birth of a son, after which she must go to the temple and make a sacrifice (Leviticus 12:2–6; Luke 2:22). Since the newly married couple lived far away in Nazareth, the local homeowner graciously invited them to remain near Jerusalem for a few more weeks, which they were happy to do. The guest room was a welcome change from the cold, dank cave.

The day finally came when Mary felt strong enough to make the short trip from Bethlehem to Jerusalem, a distance of about six miles. The holy family completed the trek in three hours, arriving at the temple after a steep climb. Mary brought her infant into the Court of the Women, accompanied by Joseph, who carried two newly purchased turtledoves in a sack at his side. In this courtyard, a priest from the inner sanctum would meet the couple and receive their sacrificial offerings.

Yet as they stood at the gate that led to the temple's lofty and awesome sanctuary, a strange event occurred. An elderly man named Simeon approached the couple, a fellow known to everyone in Jerusalem for his righteous character and devout life. He was awaiting the promised Consolation of Israel. In fact, the Holy Spirit of God had told this man he wouldn't die until he had seen the Lord's Messiah. Now he walked toward Mary with his arms spread wide and a look of radiant joy upon his face.

Mary wasn't sure whether to greet the prophet or simply await his words. To her surprise, he spoke no word of salutation, nor even seemed to register her presence at all. Instead, his eyes were riveted upon Jesus. When he reached to take the baby, Mary knew she should relinquish him to Simeon. Upon taking the child into his arms and cradling him to his chest, the prophet burst into song. "Lord, now You are letting Your servant depart in peace, according to Your word," he sang to the heavens. "For my eyes have seen Your salvation which You have prepared before the face of all peoples, a light to bring revelation to the Gentiles, and the glory of Your people Israel" (Luke 2:29–32).

"What can this mean?" Joseph whispered in Mary's ear. Since she didn't know, she made no reply but only waited to see what would happen.

Simeon drew close to Mary and gave back her son. Placing one hand upon Joseph's head and the other upon Mary's, he commended them into the care of Israel's God. Then his voice changed. Speaking in a more ominous tone, he cried, "Behold, this Child is destined for the fall and rising of many in Israel" (v. 34). Simeon even said that Jesus would be a "sign" whom many would speak against and oppose. Each person's response to Jesus would reveal the content of their heart.

These heavy words sobered Mary. Seeing her troubled expression, the prophet leaned in and met her gaze. "Yes," he said gravely, "a sword will pierce through your own soul also" (v. 35).

For the rest of her visit to the temple, Mary felt the burden of this dire prophecy. *What will it mean for a sword to pierce my soul? What pain do I have ahead of me?* It was a terrible prediction to contemplate.

Nevertheless, as Mary was about to depart the Court of the Women, she received some words of divine comfort. Another elderly messenger of God, this one a holy woman named Anna, drew Mary aside and spoke quietly to her. "These are matters for which to be thankful," she promised. "Your child is good news for all who long for the redemption of Israel." Mary pondered these words of hope and foreboding during the entire journey back to the house in Bethlehem.

It was to this very house that some strange visitors came not long afterward. They identified themselves as Parthian magi, led to this exact site by a miraculous star overhead. Joseph met the visitors at the door and invited them in. When they entered the house and saw the divinely chosen child in his mother's arms, they "fell down and worshiped Him. And when they had opened their treasures, they presented gifts to Him: gold, frankincense, and myrrh" (Matthew 2:11). These were great gifts, each worthy of a king.

Yet one of the eastern magicians offered a warning. "We have been told in a dream not to return to Herod," he said. "For although that tyrant's life is almost over, he will hate the true King of Israel until the end." After the magi departed, Mary's husband had a similar dream whose message he shared the next morning. "We must move to Egypt," Joseph announced. "Jesus is in danger from Herod, who seeks his life. Prepare your things. We shall depart at dusk tonight."

Only a few days after the holy family left for Egypt, fierce soldiers descended on Bethlehem. When the magi hadn't returned to Herod with news about their star-guided quest, he had forgotten about them. Yet as he lay upon his soiled sheets, those Parthian astrologers suddenly sprang to his mind. The lawyers and scribes who were preparing his will had given the papers to Herod Archelaus. That son would be sent to Rome with Herod's signet ring as proof that the documents were the king's valid last will and testament. These end-of-life preparations had gotten Herod thinking about securing his legacy.

My people must remember me as their greatest king, his tormented mind insisted. *But what about those eastern magicians? What if some "messiah" arose from the countryside and snatched the affections of the people?* Herod gagged at the thought of such a travesty, then spat out a wad of bloody mucus. *No fake king from a trifling town like Bethlehem can be allowed to tarnish my legacy!* He called once again for the chief of his bodyguards and explained what must be done. "Do it quickly and without remorse," he said. The man nodded and went out.

Immediately, a squadron of troops was armed and mobilized. The soldiers descended on Bethlehem, where around twenty infant and toddler boys were slaughtered by flashing blades—though not the one named Jesus.

Satisfied that all his rebellious sons had been executed and the Bethlehem problem had been dealt with, Herod was ready to die. His three descendants, the rightful rulers of the Jews, were about to take over his renowned kingdom. Each of them would glorify Herod's name.

And so, too, would his many constructions. All across the land of Israel, from the Jordan River to the Western Sea, from the Galilean farmlands to the sun-scorched depths of Jericho, stood monuments whose timeless stones spoke of Herod's greatness. His laws had been just; his errors few; his misdeeds necessary. Even on his befouled bed, Herod was able to puff out his chest with a sense of pride and accomplishment. *No one has ever reigned upon this earth like Herod the Great! And no one ever will again!*

The dying man consoled himself that even from the grave, his voice would be heard and his impact would echo across the land. The will and testament that ensured his wishes would be done was in Archelaus's hands, soon to be probated in Rome. That youth was also preparing a majestic funeral for his father. The desert monument of Herodium lay open to receive Herod's sacred body. His soul, of course, would ascend to heaven for a warm welcome.

I have been pious toward God, Herod assured himself as his vision dimmed and his breathing became shallow. *I gave that deity a magnificent temple. Now all that remains is to see what generous reward God shall give me!*

Yet as the moment of death drew near, Herod couldn't help but reflect on his sins as well as his accomplishments. So much killing, sex, pride, and greed! His family murders especially weighed on his mind: his sons who had been strangled, and worst of all, his beloved Mariamne. *Will I see her in paradise? Or am I doomed to perdition, lost from my beloved forever?* With his last ounce of strength, Herod lifted his bloodstained hands and held them before his eyes. *Will these instruments of murder prevent me from attaining eternal life?*

Was it all worth it? I have gained the whole world! But have I lost my soul?

Terrified now, Herod glanced around wildly for support, but the room was empty. No one stood by his bed to comfort him. No one cared that he was dying. In fact, everyone in the palace desired it. All of Israel wanted him gone. He was utterly alone.

"G-God!" he gasped to the ceiling, barely able to breathe. "R-r-reward me!" Yet even as he choked out his dying wish, he knew it would not be so.

I am lost, Herod realized as his mind darkened and his eyes fell shut for the final time. *God has rejected me.*

But so what?

I am Herod the Great, the rightful king of the Jews!

————————————

On the same day that Herod passed from this life, an angel appeared to Joseph down in Egypt. "Arise," he said, "take the young Child and His mother, and go to the land of Israel, for those who sought the young Child's life are dead" (Matthew 2:20).

This is all that Scripture tells us about the return home, so we have no way of knowing exactly what happened. Yet our knowledge of Mary's spiritual outlook and of ancient Jerusalem allows us to imagine what the journey might have been like. Presumably, Joseph informed Mary right away that they were going home to Nazareth. Just like the Israelites of the exodus, God's people were once again leaving the banks of the Nile to enter a promised land. Perhaps a word of prophecy jumped to Mary's mind, for she knew the Scriptures well. "When Israel was a child, I loved him, and out of Egypt I called My son" (Hosea 11:1).

Fatherly love, Mary thought as she gazed down at the giggling face of the baby Jesus. *What a fitting attribute of God!*

And also, she realized, *of his king.*

The trip back to the Holy Land didn't take long. The road between Egypt and Israel was well trodden, both by Gentile merchants and by many Jews traveling between the two lands. Mary couldn't wait to be home again.

Yet as the little family drew near to the outskirts of Jerusalem, Mary began to find her soul disturbed. Beggars tugged on her robe as she passed by, riding upon a colt. "Have pity on us, mother!" they cried. "Give alms!" She handed out a few pennies. But she didn't have enough coins for them all.

How numerous were these outcasts of Jerusalem! How many were the impure and unworthy who lurked outside the gate! The lame. The mentally ill. The prostitutes. The indigent. The blind. Mary felt overwhelmed by the enormity of their need. Suffering and anguish were etched upon each of their faces. Even when their voices remained silent in dejected despair, their hearts cried out for a solution more lasting than money. They didn't just need a coin for the day. They needed a Savior.

As Mary approached the walls of Jerusalem, the road ascended an ominous hill. Golgotha, the locals called it. *The Place of the Skull.* There, on top of its crags, the cruel Romans crucified criminals beside the highway. The condemned weren't lifted high above the ground and away from the gaze of the passersby. No, the crosses were at eye level—an up-close reminder of the indomitable power of Rome.

A lone man was enduring crucifixion as Mary went by. The shame of his nakedness could be seen by all. Blood ran down his arms from the nails in his wrists, while more blood soaked the wood beneath his pierced feet. He writhed in agony, arching his tormented body upward to snatch a breath, then sagging in exhaustion, then suffocating until he was forced once more to push against the nails. Each time he rose, he grimaced and groaned. After he had sucked in a breath and slumped back down, he quietly wept, knowing he would soon have to fight the nails again. Only death could deliver him from this inexorable cycle of pain. Yet on a Roman cross, death often took several days.

"H-help me," he whispered to Mary as she rode past his shuddering form. "S-s-save me."

Before she could answer, Mary felt a stirring within her garments. Her baby was tucked inside her cloak, wrapped in swaddling cloths for travel. She brought him forth. Not knowing what prompted her, yet believing the impulse was from God, she turned the child toward the dying man and held him out.

"Your Savior," she said as tears of pity trickled down her cheeks. "Your Savior and your King!"

"Wh-who . . . is he?"

"His name is Jesus," Mary declared.

The suffering victim had a simple reply. His final words expressed the universal need of the human heart. Looking straight at the infant in Mary's hands, he said with reborn hope: "I believe."

INTRODUCTION
TO THE CODAS

As Kathie and Bryan collaborated on this project, they quickly realized that the book's readers would profit from a peek into their discussions. Kathie's lively wit and the amazing stories from her vibrant, rich life needed to be captured and shared. Over the course of two weeks, Bryan interviewed Kathie about the subjects of each chapter. Special attention was given to Kathie's own biography as a parallel to the book's plotline. No doubt, the readers who remember spending their mornings with Kathie on air will hear her voice anew in these pages. More recent fans will likewise benefit from her winsomeness and warmth. Kathie's humble vulnerability about her family struggles adds a special, honest touch.

The reader is encouraged to use these codas to derive lessons from the lives of the tyrant king and the holy mother of the Messiah. The God who was at work back then is just as active today. Though His ways are sometimes hidden and His means are often surprising, even so, He is always nearby. We never know when His goodness and grace will suddenly burst forth! Kathie and Bryan unite in the prayer that their readers will discover a single, profound truth: that even the darkest of evils are infused with living hope. This hope can be found only in the God of light and love who sent His son, Jesus, to bring blessing upon the world.

CODA 1

A KING IS BORN

BRYAN: Tell us a little bit about how you got interested in King Herod.

KATHIE: The reason I initially got so fascinated with Herod was because I thought I knew about him. He's mentioned only a couple of times in the Scriptures, and you get such a finite picture of him. But when I went for my first rabbinical-guided trip with Ray Vander Laan, he painted a picture of Herod that was so vivid. And what I remember so much about that first encounter with the real story of Herod was thinking, if Jesus is the greatest story ever told, then Herod is the greatest story never told, because people do not know him. Maybe scholars do, but wow, what a story for everyone else to learn about! And when you combine it with all the historical background and all the characters he coexisted with—at times as a foe and at other times as a friend—the drama makes it feel like the *Real Housewives of the New Testament*! I mean, it's just extraordinary dramatic material.

One thing in particular I remember from that first trip was being at Herodium. I was blown away by how much they had redone or rebuilt, and how they had recently discovered Herod's tomb area. It was the highlight of my entire trip because the first five times I'd been to Herodium, everybody said, "Well, this is where Josephus says he's buried." And then all the great experts in the world would respond, "No, it can't be true. We would have found him by now. He's not here." You know, I love it when the so-called world experts are completely and totally wrong! You know what I'm saying? They have now found Herod's tomb! But that's not the point. The point is, I'm at Herodium. I'm up where his synagogue was.

How many people have lived lives like his? Nothing is like his life. Yet stories similar to his still can be found today—stories of people searching for power, becoming drunk on it and seduced by the world instead of by the Creator of the world.

You know, Herod was putting all his attention and all his powers and all his gifts into building the wrong kingdom. And it wasn't like Jesus building God's kingdom. It was Herod's kingdom come. And he said, "I'm not going to wait. I'm going to build it myself." And just like the Tower of Babel, these things do not work out well.

BRYAN: We will talk at the end of the book about the birth of the true King, but for now, can you give some preliminary thoughts about the contrast between a king like Herod, with all his privileges, and then someone like Jesus, the King of the world, who was born in an animal pen?

KATHIE: Well, obviously the Jews had been awaiting the Messiah for centuries and they were expecting a very different kind of king. They didn't like the lowly Messiah, the humble Messiah. They didn't like that concept. When you're living under that kind of brutal Roman reign, you want to be saved from it. You want somebody to come along on a white horse. We know that one day Jesus will be a champion in the overtaking of the government. And Scripture talks about how the government shall be on his shoulders (Isaiah 9:6). The ancient Jews didn't understand any of that imagery from Isaiah, though it was there.

But the Scripture that jumps out at me at this point is Micah 6:8, where it says, "What does the LORD require of you?" To love. To do justice. To love mercy. It's different in various translations but the essence is to walk humbly with your God. Well, in this case, Jesus, who we know was God before the dawn of creation, was God alongside His Father and the Holy Spirit for all eternity. God humbled himself before humankind. That concept was especially foreign to the Jews at the time because of the Shema: "Hear, O Israel: The LORD our God, the LORD is one!" (Deuteronomy 6:4). There's no other. They couldn't understand the idea of God in the personhood of Messiah coming as their humble servant, leaving the glory of heaven and being born in such a lowly environment and yet ordained to do it. I've always liked how somebody said (or maybe the Lord just told it to me the first time I visited Bethlehem): "Jesus was the only human being ever born with the express purpose of dying." That blew me away. He did that for you and me, and for the whole world. Amazing!

BRYAN: It seems like you have a close walk with Jesus. You know him in your heart, the way he talks to you and reminds you of his character.

KATHIE: I have always known him by instinct. But I had to grow to understand him through the Word. I wasn't willfully illiterate. I studied the Bible. I thought I followed Jesus, but nobody taught me the truth. And I remember getting angry. I said every day that I learned something new from the rabbis. I was thinking, *Why didn't I know this? Nobody told me.*

BRYAN: Tell me more about that.

KATHIE: When I was about ten years old, I was in Sunday school, and the teacher was talking about the story of when Jesus was going down the road from Bethany. He was hungry, and he saw a fig tree, but it had no fruit. So he cursed it. And I said to my teacher, "I don't believe that." Even at that young age, I could sense it. And she responded, "What do you mean, you don't believe it? It's there. I just read it." I said, "My Jesus would not curse something he created. He loves everything he creates. He loves all. So I don't believe that." She protested, "But it's right there in the Bible!" And I said, "I think it means something different." Even then, I knew!

Then I was studying this text many years later at the exact spot where it happened. And I thought, *Okay, buckle up. I'm about to figure this out.* And that's when they explained that in Jesus' day, in the first century AD, Jesus was followed constantly by people who were listening to his every word. In this instance, Jesus was using the cursed fig tree to symbolize two classes of people in Jewish life—the Pharisees and the Sadducees. They were watching him and following him too. And they knew that when Jesus cursed that tree for its lack of fruit, for its lack of feeding God's people, he was actually cursing the religious leaders for stealing from the people. And I thought, *Yes!* All those years later, I learned the truth behind what I suspected in Sunday school because I came to understand the cultural realities of that time.

The Bible gives us sketches but it rarely fills in all the details. To get the details, we have to study. We have to go and seek, as Jeremiah said, and we'll find it. So this is what keeps me fired up now. I'll say it probably a million times: I am not a scholar. I am not a biblical expert, but I have studied with the best in the world. And I want my readers to hear my heart. I want to share the fruit of my studies with them. I want the truth. That's what sets us free. I am answerable to the Lord and to what he has revealed to me as truth. Now, if I find out that I was wrong, then I must find a way to tell everybody, "You know what, guys? I believed this with all my heart when I wrote it, but I just discovered this new evidence that changes things." And that's what the searching of the Scriptures is all about. That's the thrill of it. But so often, people today don't study the Bible. They just don't. Or if they do, they study the wrong translations of the Bible or they follow some guru they believe in. I'm grateful that I've had so many different teachers who've made me question the way the rabbis do. And questioning the Word is not showing a lack of faith. That's exactly what God wants us to do.

CODA 2

THE GLORY OF ROME

BRYAN: In this chapter, you've got General Pompey coming to invade. You have this pagan general. You've got the defenders of the temple inside, wanting to keep him out. What do you think it must have been like to be a Jewish freedom fighter defending the temple against the Roman invasion of Jerusalem? And maybe you're going to die doing that. What are you dying for? What are you fighting for?

KATHIE: You know, many of my family members were lost at war. My father's stepfather was killed during World War II. So was my father's older brother, Paul. His other brother, Carl, was wounded. My father, who at the age of seventeen signed up the day after Pearl Harbor, served on a ship off the coast of Brazil. So he was the only one who didn't serve in actual military combat, but obviously he was extremely scarred by the experience of losing all these people that were precious to him.

I remember so well my grandmother, my father's mother, being a very bitter, unloving woman. And it was only later when I learned about how much she had lost and suffered in life that I really started to understand the cost of war. Usually, we just think about who won and who lost. But everybody loses in war. No matter what side of it you were on, everybody loses. There may be one elite person or someone who conquers and for a brief shining moment, it's Camelot. But ultimately, it's ashes to ashes, dust to dust. So that's why I look at things differently now. It makes me cry thinking about this, the cost of all that war and bloodshed.

But many Jewish people—and this is not just the Jews from back then but the ones who are truly Jews in their souls—still think of the temple as sacred and its destruction as the greatest tragedy in their history. I'm sure Orthodox Jews today would put the destruction of the temple as their people's worst tragedy—other than the Holocaust—not only in the time of Pompey but all the way to Emperor Titus's day in AD 70, when the sacrifices stopped. Because

167

their entire way of life was built around the temple and sacrifice. Am I wrong about that?

BRYAN: Not at all. But since then, for two thousand years, the synagogue has obviously played such a prominent part of Jewish life. So for contemporary Jews, they are more about the Torah and the synagogue. There's been a loss of temple worship, I guess you'd say, in the intervening centuries. But according to Scripture, blood sacrifice was essential to getting right with God. So those patriots were defending the temple because it was how you encountered God. That is the point. The freedom fighters were defending something that was essential, so it was worth dying for.

KATHIE: Yes. And that's what my step-grandfather was doing and my father was doing when they enlisted, knowing they could be sacrificing their lives. What totally breaks my heart today is that there's so little patriotism in America. Our kids have grown up spoiled and entitled. And I'm just ashamed of them. We can't even fill our quotas in any of our armed service divisions. We're woefully unprepared for war.

BRYAN: And in contrast, here were these Jewish freedom fighters ready to die for something bigger than themselves. But it wasn't just dying for stones or dying for a building or dying for a place that had a curtain or, you know, the structure itself. It was for the idea of the temple and for what happened there. And it was for the divine presence and the Most Holy Place, which Pompey was going to desecrate if he got in.

KATHIE: Yeah. And here's the thing. Buildings are not eternal, but God is. And that's who they were defending. That's who they died for. Because when God is not reverenced, when God is not honored, that is the deepest sin possible. That's the true blasphemy. That's the unforgivable sin. When you blaspheme the Holy Spirit, you blaspheme the presence and the holiness of God. That's what Pompey did. And God judged him for it!

But what I'm saying here isn't like the fire-and-brimstone message of some preachers. I'm just a defender of truth as I know it. I've still got much to learn, so that's the best way to describe it. At the end of the day, I hope I've learned something new, and I hope I can tell others about it and keep doing that until God calls me home.

CODA 3

A FATEFUL CHOICE

BRYAN: In the last chapter when Pompey went into the Most Holy Place, he desecrated it. But soon after that, in chapter 3, he's defeated by Julius Caesar, his rival, and the Egyptian pharaoh decapitated him and handed his head to Caesar. And I just wanted to think about that. What do you think about wicked rulers? Can they cross a line of no return, after which God brings them down? And are we right to celebrate the fall of a wicked ruler? Any thoughts about something like that?

KATHIE: Interestingly, what came to mind for me was King David. What he did was wicked beyond belief: the adultery and the murder and cover-up. And yet God said David was "a man after His own heart" (1 Samuel 13:14). And then God forgave him. Now, true, David had the baby who died. But look what God did. The next thing that happened was that David married Bathsheba, and the next baby, Solomon, became his heir. Yeah! So, no, I don't think anybody is wicked beyond saving. No one is wicked beyond the hope of a return. Because *repentance* means to turn around and go the other way, to go back. David did that and it was the prophet Nathan who said to him, "God sees you and knows your sin, but God will not hold this sin against you" (2 Samuel 12:13, my paraphrase). I believe that at any point you can return to God. Look at the sins of Saul in the book of Acts, at what he did in the name of righteousness. He thought he was being the best Jew around. He was going to get his seat on the Sanhedrin, boy, and get ahead in life. His name was Saul until he became a new creation in Christ. We know him as the great apostle Paul. Or I could think about the wicked King Ahab of Israel. Or I could think about Romans like Nero, or about Caligula. In modern times, I could think about Hitler. Who was more evil than him? No one! But even on his deathbed, Hitler could have claimed Jesus and accepted Jesus for salvation.

And lastly, I think of the two guys on either side of Jesus on the cross. One of them hurled insults and rejected him to the end. But Jesus said that the other one who called on his name would be with him that day in paradise. See? You're never too far gone for Jesus to save you. No matter what you've done, he'll take you back, or take you for the first time. Try it! He won't fail you.

BRYAN: Even up to the very last minute. And that's a great answer. I like your hopefulness that even wicked rulers can be saved. And you could apply that to just about anybody in Washington and have hope for even wicked rulers in our country today to change their ways because of the gospel. God judges people sometimes, but I like the hopeful tone you convey.

KATHIE: God is just, but at the same time, he is also merciful right to the very end. His mercies never cease; they are new every morning (Lamentations 3:22–23). Oh, that's why I have such a passion for the Word, Bryan! For a time in my life, I was dying without it, frankly. And I knew lots of verses, but I was like the Laodiceans; I was lukewarm. Then I encountered the real truths of Scripture, and I started living again. What bothers me is that it was not my fault. I was not being taught the Word, and that's like the Pharisees and the Sadducees who didn't teach the people, didn't love the people, didn't shepherd them. And Jesus' response to their behavior was the only time he got violent in any way, when he turned the money tables. Because those people turned God's temple into a place of thievery. They made it about laws and rules and money, instead of loving God and his Word!

BRYAN: Now I'm going to ask you about Galilee. Herod, as a young man, is appointed by Antipater to be governor over Galilee. What do you remember about the sights and sounds of that place? Maybe the sea or the land or the valleys of Galilee. Describe for us what it is like.

KATHIE: I think Galilee is my favorite part of Israel. First of all, it's so beautiful. The Jezreel Valley, which is wide and fertile. Or you go up on Mount Carmel and look down on the valley. One of my greatest experiences ever was on Israel's Independence Day, so it was in May. We were having a devotion on Mount Carmel, and all of a sudden, in the Jezreel Valley, all of these hangars opened up and Israeli jets went zooming into the sky. Wow! And we said, "There is a God in Israel!" It was just thrilling. I didn't even know that's where the jets were kept, but they were everywhere, in that same valley where the ancient Israelites battled the Philistines with their iron chariots. Nothing had changed except the technology! It was so thrilling to me that God is the same yesterday, today, and forever. He is the eternal God who does not change, and his faithfulness endures for all generations. And that was like a living vision of it for me. It's so beautiful, and yeah, I love that.

Another place I love is the spot where seven streams meet and feed into the Sea of Galilee; they come in right near Magdala. Today there's a little church there, but it's right on the water. And it's where streams of living water literally come into the Sea of Galilee in one spot. And they come from the mountains, obviously. Where these streams come together is where they believe Jesus called his disciples. Apparently it's the only place along the perimeter of the Sea of Galilee that this phenomenon of seven streams converging happens, creating an attractive environment for fish, if I recall correctly. So it makes sense that Jesus would have called his disciples there, the ones that were fishermen, because that's where they would be: where the fish are.

BRYAN: The inflow of the water and the turbulence of the water is a place that the fish love to congregate.

KATHIE: Yeah. And I didn't realize that fishermen didn't go way out in the Sea of Galilee because Jews have a very healthy aversion to water.

BRYAN: Because their lands didn't have much of a seacoast, originally. The Jews are not really a maritime people.

KATHIE: No, they're not. And the first time I went to the Sea of Galilee, I remember saying to Ray, my teacher, "Ray, this is some of the most beautiful waterfront property I've ever seen, and I've lived on the water in Connecticut and the Florida Keys. Why are there no houses here? There's the city of Tiberias, and that's about it." He said, "Oh no, the Jews don't like water. They're terrified of it. The worldwide flood from the story of Noah's ark, the parting of the Red Sea, you know, all these terrible things." And he said, "The thing is, people don't realize that the fishermen don't fish far from the shore. Right? They know that the storms come up quickly, the squalls, and they learned about that the hard way when Jesus told his disciples to go to the other side, and a storm hit them." See what I mean? I just love being in Israel and discovering the places where it all comes together to make sense. I always love it when truth reveals itself to you. That is the latest thing in my life. The last five or so years, it's been a season of God whispering to me, *Kathie, I will reveal it. Seek it. Seek me; seek the truth, and I will reveal it to you.* God is a revealer of all good things.

RULER ON THE RISE

BRYAN: Herod valued Mariamne's Hasmonean lineage as much as, if not more than, her physical beauty. He was marrying into a prominent family, and as so often happens, his marriage led to great grief. When the family is a prominent one, the grief is all the more public, which makes it harder to bear. Have you ever seen anything like that? Let's talk about that a bit.

KATHIE: You know, I really saw that one time with Ethel Kennedy on the day that her son Michael passed away in a tragic skiing accident in Aspen. Frank and I went to the hospital; it was around midnight. Ethel was there too, of course, in the hospital room with her son's body. The press had not yet found out about it. We all know that famous look of grief on Ethel Kennedy's face, right? We saw that when her husband was murdered, and we saw it when her son overdosed. That woman had known a lot of grief. Now, she was there, still in her ski suit, and she could not leave her son's body. She was so grief-stricken and traumatized. And believe me, I wish I could get the image of him out of my mind. Michael was a brilliant, brilliant skier. But that day, he'd hit the back of his head because he'd been skiing backward while also throwing a football—something he did often. The doctors had said there was no coming back from the terrible force of the collision, but he still had a pulse.

By the time Frank and I got there—we lived two hours away—it was just me, Ethel, Frank, and the body of her dead son. I mean, my whole life has been this kind of stuff, where I say to myself, *What am I doing here?* Well, I'll tell you what I was doing there. I looked over at Ethel, who was just inches from me on the right-hand side, and I said, "Ethel, oh, Ethel, honey, it's okay to leave. You can leave. Michael . . . . Honey, he's not there. He's not there, sweetie. He's with Jesus." And nothing happened. Finally, I said, "Oh, Ethel, sweetheart, to be absent from the body is to be present with the Lord." She stirred and looked over at me, very slowly turning her head and not even really focusing on me. But she said, "Wait, what did you say?" I said, "To be absent from the body is to be present with the Lord." She asked me, "Where did you hear that?" And I said, "Honey, it's in the Bible. It's in 2 Corinthians 5." And she murmured, "I've never heard that." I repeated, "Oh, honey, Michael is with Jesus and he's at peace and he wants you to be at peace that he's with Jesus. You can leave him, sweetie. He's not here. He's in the presence of the Lord." And it was exactly like that. And she was able to leave. But you know what? It wasn't religion that helped her in that moment. It wasn't her rosary. It wasn't her priest. It wasn't her confession. It wasn't anything man-made that helped her through that most difficult moment in her life. It was the powerful Word of the Lord.

BRYAN: Herod was an Idumean, but Mariamne was a Jew. She looked down on him for not being of the right race. Have you seen the ugly side of racism up close?

KATHIE: Racism is ugly wherever it raises its head. And nobody has a monopoly on racism; no culture is without it. Every society that exists has racism and jealousy and all those kinds of things. But I'm so grateful that I had a Jewish father and I knew where my mother came from. Her father was British and Germanic and French-Canadian. And I was always glad for their different backgrounds because I think I got the best of my lineage from my father and my mother. And I never found myself wishing I had a purely Jewish lineage.

I think a lot of racism is passed down in families. Big time. My last name was Epstein. My daddy's name was Aaron Leon Epstein. My brother became the pastor of the First Baptist Church in Manhattan, across the street from Carnegie Hall. And one of my favorite things to do is walk past it. And on the sign outside it says, "Calvary Baptist Church, Pastor David Epstein." And I'm thinking, *I think that's the only church in America that says that!*

BRYAN: Yeah, that is funny! It's not a very Baptist name, is it? It's obviously Jewish.

KATHIE: Can there be a Jewish Baptist pastor? But anyway, I've always hated racism. They stoned my father for being Jewish. He had rocks thrown at him several times when he was growing up because he was called a "Christ killer."

BRYAN: Oh no.

KATHIE: Yeah. And yet he was the godliest Christian man I've ever known; he was a follower of Yeshua. The original followers of Yeshua, which is the

Hebrew name for Jesus, were all Jews. And they called themselves followers of the Way. Because Jesus said, "I am the way, the truth, and the life. No one comes to the Father except through Me" (John 14:6). And people today say, "Well, that shows just how intolerant Christians are." My reply to that is, "The truth is, Jesus said it, so I believe it. But also, you don't realize what great news that is, you guys! The man who said no one comes to the Father except through him is the same man that died for you. He died for you; he left glory to hang on a cross for you. I think he's about the only person you'd want to see at the end of your life! You want someone like that, someone with so much love, to be the one claiming to be the only way to heaven."

CODA 5

DISASTER AND DESTINY

BRYAN: One of the first things that chapter 5 deals with is the Parthians, who comprised a major world empire in Persia nearly equal to the power of Rome. Out of the blue, a giant disaster hit Herod. He was on the run, desperate for help and at the end of his rope. My question is, Have you ever had a situation in your life where you're going along nicely and then suddenly everything blows up?

KATHIE: I wish I could say, "No, that's never happened to me." But it has. I don't know if you remember when I was accused of having sweatshops in 1996. That was about the most devastating thing that's ever happened to me. I couldn't declare the truth. Nobody was interested in the truth. Everybody wanted to believe that Kathie Lee—that sanctimonious, self-righteous phony—was a purveyor of sweatshops. Now, I had been an advocate for children my entire life. The first time I ever went on television, it was because I'd raised $58.52 for the Muscular Dystrophy Foundation. There was a contest one week where whoever raised the most money got to come on the show with Bozo the Clown. I won by putting on a carnival in my backyard. So I went on television and presented my check for advocating for children when I was about twelve, I guess. I don't know what year that was, but it was the first time I ever went on TV. And so, I have a history of caring about children that are not my own.

And years later, Frank and I built Cody House and Cassidy's Place. We gave millions of dollars, which we had earned ourselves. We didn't have millions from an inheritance. We had to earn $14 million to build Cassidy's Place. And we were just about to announce the opening of this center for children when this so-called human-rights activist stood up before Congress and accused me of having sweatshops in Honduras. Talk about being blindsided! I had literally given $14 million, and then I was blindsided and called a child abuser, which is the worst thing in the world. Does that make any sense? That I would be an advocate for children my entire life—long before I had any children of my own—and suddenly think, *You know what's a good idea? Why don't I start forcing kids in foreign nations to perform hard labor?* It's ridiculous. But everybody wanted to believe it in the mainstream press. I couldn't even get my own network—ABC at that time because this was during my time with Regis—to say something on my behalf. They felt like not firing me was the best they could do. "You know, we proved we love you, Kathie. We didn't fire you." What are you going to fire me for? I don't have sweatshops. Are you out of your mind?

You can tell even now how this scarred me. I mean, I had to testify before Congress. And as a result, I was able to get laws changed. I went up to Albany, where a law called the "hot goods" bill had been languishing in the local New York legislature. Nobody could get it passed. Nobody was interested. But I went up there and within nine days after testifying, they passed the bill, which basically said if a sweatshop is discovered, the government has the right to go in, take everything of value, and sell it for the benefit of the people who are being abused. And I said, "I'm all for that!"

The thing is, I didn't even know that sweatshops existed. You think it's a thing of the past, but it isn't. I got a very quick education on the fact that wherever greed and needy people exist, sweatshops do too. People who have no hope will go to work in these places because that's all they have. And greedy people will take advantage of them. Well, that's not what I'm about.

Around this time I was about to open a home for babies that had contracted AIDS and for drug-exposed infants in New York City. Certain interest groups fought us tooth and nail the whole time trying to keep us from building that place because nobody wanted to treat an infant with AIDS. And I prayed, *Lord, this is what you give me? I'm advocating for children, and suddenly I'm accused of sweatshops in Honduras.* So, yeah, I understand probably better than almost 90 percent of people in the world what it's like to be blindsided by something. And then you know what happened the very next year?

BRYAN: Tell me.

KATHIE: My husband meets some woman. He's on a plane and he has an illicit tryst with her in New York City. He kisses me goodbye after lunch, then he goes and does the dumbest thing he's ever done in his life. And it makes no sense. We had a great marriage. But that action of his was not about sex. So often, these things are not about sexual fulfillment; they're about power. I always say, "The one part of the male anatomy that people don't talk enough about is their ears." In other words, he's not being worshiped enough. "Oh, you're the greatest. Oh, I've never known someone like you." That's what catches a man's ears sometimes. So for whatever reason, Frank made the biggest mistake of his entire life. And that terrible discovery blindsided me right after the sweatshop thing. Those are the two worst years of my life.

So, yeah, I get it. And these things were all international news. I didn't deal with these things privately. I couldn't. I immediately went back to work the week after. I faced it head-on; I thanked everybody for their prayers and then went to work fighting it all. And I cannot tell you how influential that was to so many people. To this day, women come up to me and say, "Kathie, I watched you and how you dealt with your husband's infidelity. And I just want you to know that because you stayed in your marriage and saved your family, I stayed in mine." That's the real lesson here. God takes the ashes, the unbelievably ugly ashes in our lives, and he uses them for his purposes and his mercy and his kingdom—if we let him. It's like when Joseph said, "You meant evil against me; but God meant it for good" (Genesis 50:20).

BRYAN: That's so good, Kathie. Yours is a story that is related to Herod's because he also got blindsided. I think this opens up a window for readers to see how you responded and to realize that while much of your experience was different from Herod's, some things are parallel. When somebody gets hit out of the blue, we all have those emotions. Like you, Herod was a public figure. And so his trials and tribulations got put on public display. Thank you for being vulnerable in that.

I'll move on to another question here. In this chapter, we meet Anna, who is the mother of Mary. She struggled with infertility like Hannah did in the Old Testament, and that created doubt in God's goodness. And maybe this is related to what you were just saying about your blindsiding, but have you gone through seasons where you doubted God's goodness to you, or that he's there and he cares and he's involved? How have you dealt with that?

KATHIE: Here's how you survive those seasons, whether you're a plumber or you're a world-renowned entertainer or one of the most famous women in America. You never separate the secular from the spiritual. You don't think you're leaving one world to go into another one. I love the scripture that says, "In Him we live and move and have our being" (Acts 17:28). That means every nanosecond of our lives, not one hour on Sunday mornings when we go into a building and listen to God's Word and honor him, pray to him, and sing to him, but then we go home and forget about all that. No. It's every moment. Everywhere we go. Everything we do. We live in God. We move in God. We have our being in God. That's the way you have to live as a believer, so that you're ready when the crisis comes.

CHAPTER 6

THE KING COMES TO ZION

BRYAN: One of the topics that comes up for the first time in this chapter is, What do we mean by "Messiah"? And I know you want to weigh in on the meaning of the word and what it means to be the Messiah and how the Jewish people are waiting for the Messiah. But are they still waiting for Messiah? They certainly were during the time of Herod and Mary.

KATHIE: Well, the word means "anointed one," I believe, right?

BRYAN: Yes, that's right. And so does *Christos*. So that's a Greek form.

KATHIE: That's exactly right. *Christos*, meaning Christ, is the same thing. So yeah, I think it's almost like the Jews who were being held in concentration camps during World War II. They were waiting for somebody to come and redeem them. You know, whether it's the American Army or the British Army, they were saying, "Somebody come and save us; somebody come and save us from this evil!" I think the Romans were cruel taskmasters. And the Jews back then thought, "We have been through this already with Pharaoh for four hundred years." You know, so much of Jewish history is like that. A story of oppression under foreign powers.

BRYAN: The Greeks were oppressive, too, with the Jews under the Seleucid Empire in the intertestamental period, just before the time of Herod.

KATHIE: And also Babylon and Persia under Xerxes. Just oppression all the time. I mean, occasionally the Jews got a nice ruler who let them go back and start building their temple again. That's how it was in the days of Ezra and Nehemiah under Cyrus. It's God who raises up kings. God raises up kings and tears down kingdoms, and he has done it since the dawn of time. And he sends the rain on the just and the unjust, and his ways are not our ways. That's our biggest problem, believing his ways are like ours. And that was the problem with the Tower of Babel. They wanted to be God. And that was the problem going all the way back to Adam and Eve, who wanted what they couldn't have. They had everything, but the one thing they couldn't have set the world in motion toward disaster. We've never recovered from it.

But God created us for a garden. He made us in a garden and for a garden. I think that's still what he wants our lives to be: a garden, a place that we tend. A place from which we bring forth beauty. A place we nourish and a place where we worship and walk with him. I believe that. And one day, it will be here. It will be so. But until then, we have to make our own little gardens. I'm sitting here on my new farm in Tennessee and all I'm doing is tending the gardens here. And I've never had the kind of time I have now to do that. It's just so nourishing for me. It really is. I've got my little vineyard that is just sprouting, and we're not going to get good wine from those grapes. We might get a bad jelly or jam. I don't care. It's beautiful. And it makes my soul sing. It really matters what you put into your mind, what you put your hand toward, what you set your eyes upon. Think about it. If you eat junk food, your body's going to be junk. If you watch pornography, your life is going to be pornographic in nature, and every relationship will be pornographic. We reap what we sow. Whatever you put in is what comes out. That's not just true physically, but spiritually.

BRYAN: Also in chapter six, we see the bandits who were in the caves on Mount Arbel when Herod lowers down his soldiers from cranes and the troops jump into the fray. I believe you did the hike up from the bottom to the top of Mount Arbel, right?

KATHIE: Oh yeah, I did that. Just like they say, women never miss their period once it's gone. Well, I will never miss climbing up Mount Arbel again either.

BRYAN: I've done it too. It's so steep! But imagine being a soldier trying to get up there. I mean, the soldiers were supposed to attack those bandits, but they couldn't get to them for the very reason you're saying, which is this narrow path and the steep hike up to it.

KATHIE: There was no back road available, I guess. There is now, and you can drive close to the summit, but it wasn't there back then. The whole thing with Herod is that he figured out a way to do the impossible. He was always doing that, like in the case of Caesarea Maritima. And look at Masada, right? Whether it was a coastline needing a harbor or a desert needing a palace, he just found a way.

BRYAN: Talk about your admiration for Herod. He wasn't just some kind of hideous beast all the time, was he?

KATHIE: Not at all. I do admire him. I admire the artist that God created him to be. You see the remains of his beautiful mosaics and his architecture and everything. He loved beauty. Now the Greeks and the Romans did too. We can love the beauty of their art, but it should point us to the Creator. We're not supposed to worship the created thing. That's where we all go wrong. God commands, "You shall have no other gods before me" (Exodus 20:3). But we so often do. We worship beautiful things as idols. And God is a jealous God. We think of jealousy as a bad thing. But it means, "I will not share my throne with anyone. I am God, the sole Creator. I alone am God." What I admire about Herod is a lot of things. His intellect, his ability to solve problems—even major problems. I love his ability to come to agreement with people who disagreed with him. I like the way he dealt with the people who believed differently than him. He learned how to coexist with them, not because he was a great peacemaker but because he was smart. Yeah, he knew how to get ahead. He was a survivalist. He would win the show *Survivor* every time! Like all of us, he was a mix of good and evil. God wants to help the good win in all of us. But we have to let him do it.

CODA 7

MURDER IN THE PALACE

BRYAN: Herod is the king of the Jews, according to the Romans. But the Lord Jesus Christ—Yeshua Hamashiach in Hebrew—was a prophet, a priest, and a king. Those are the three offices that are ascribed to him. So I thought maybe we could begin by just thinking about Jesus. Who is he to you?

KATHIE: Also the Prince of Peace. I mean, everybody has such a personal walk with Jesus. I would never try to describe him except in my own personal sense of what he is to me. Oh gosh, I don't think mostly about the majesty of the Father or the majesty of Jesus because my picture of Jesus is that he is the lowly servant Jesus. And yet he is also almighty God. That is very true. But my personal relationship with him is incredibly intimate. So often, I want to crawl into my Abba Father's arms and let him hold me, to be still. But I want to walk with Jesus. He's the one who's on the move. He's the verb; he's the adventure. People who think being a Christian is dull have never lived one day following in Jesus' sandals. Never. It's the least dull life you can ever have because it's always a challenge. You're always learning something. So I think of Jesus as my rabbi. Yeah, I do. He's my rabbi. He's my teacher. He's my friend.

Sometimes when I'm in that tough terrain in Israel, he's the one that helps me down the wadis. He's the one that knows when I'm in trouble, where the dangers are. He's the one that reminds me to drink water like a good shepherd should do. He's that for me. That's my Jesus. And then he's teaching me the whole time. And he's funny and he's a lot of fun to be with.

There's mystery about the Father, I guess, is what I'm trying to say. So much mystery about the Father and yet I'm not confused about Jesus at all. There's no mystery for me. I know exactly who he is and what he did for me. It's crystal clear for me.

BRYAN: And you really kind of touched on him both as prophet and as priest. You described him as your teacher, which is to say he's your prophet, your rabbi, the one who instructs you. And he's the one who makes the mystery of the Father understandable. He's your go-between. He's your priest. So you really did bring out those things.

KATHIE: Jesus changed everything. He said, "Do not think that I came to destroy the Law or the Prophets. I did not come to destroy but to fulfill" (Matthew 5:17). And he gave us a whole new way of looking at the Law. He introduced something new for us to see. Although God has always been just and always been merciful and loving, that's not the main image we have of him from the Old Testament. But Jesus showed something new when he founded his church. But the church is not a building. The church is what Jesus meant when he said, "For where two or three are gathered together in My name, I am there in the midst of them" (Matthew 18:20). We are the church. Just as the early followers of the Way were the church. And that's *ecclesia* in Greek. It really gives it a whole new meaning, doesn't it?

BRYAN: That's right. The congregation, the gathering. Those who have been called out. And the beauty of the Jesus you're describing is really such a contrast with Herod, who in this chapter crossed a line and began to have his own relatives murdered, beginning with Aristobulus. And then you've got Cleopatra and her seduction and power. And I just wonder if you think that the world was more evil back in Herod's day in the Roman Empire, or kind of the same, or getting better?

KATHIE: I think evil is evil. There are degrees of it, I suppose. I mean, to me, it's hard to think that there's anything worse than molesting a child. I've been battling child abuse with an organization called Childhelp for forty years. And, you know, I can't even hear the stories. I want to throw up. Yeah, they revolt me; they just do. And in Capernaum—which was the millstone capital of the world back in Jesus' day and such a huge part of Jewish life and Middle Eastern life—Jesus stood right there in the synagogue, which you can see the bottom layer of today. I'm sure you've been there.

BRYAN: I have; I remember it. It's made of black stones.

KATHIE: Yes. And Jesus said it would be better that someone should have one of those millstones that were still lying around all over the place—and I love that Jesus taught them right where they were—put around their neck and be thrown into the sea than to hurt one of these little ones (Matthew 18:6). And the sea is what, a hundred yards from there? That's the Sea of Galilee. That's exactly where Jesus said it.

So there are certain kinds of evil like child abuse that are just horrific. But at the core of things, I think evil is evil. And one day, Jesus will show up on a white horse and throw the father of all lies into the pit for all time. And there will be justice for every little child who's been murdered or molested or had their soul stolen from them because their childhood was destroyed. And that helps me, just to know that one day it will all be made new. The crooked will be made straight, and everything will be redeemed. That's what I long for. People say, "Come, Lord Jesus! Come, Lord Jesus!" Yet he doesn't. We know that he said he tarries so more can be saved. But how many people have to be molested while he's tarrying? That's the hard stuff to understand. Jesus could in an instant change the whole world. He could make it so no one sins. But then, it'd be like we are all robots and all doing only the right and good. We have to have free choice, including the choice to do evil, in order to truly choose the good. And his ways are not our ways.

So all that to say, I don't know that we're any more evil today than we always were. It was evil in the garden when the Serpent lied; it was evil in every age and time when people shook their fists at God. But I think that today it's more in our face. We're more aware of it now. We're more aware of the bestiality of the world and the ugliness. We have visual pictures of it all the time, twenty-four seven, with cable television. So in that sense, not long ago, you could be an Iowa farmer for years and years going to your church every Sunday and live a very sweet, godly life and never know that any of this stuff existed in the world. But no more. We can't hide anymore. We can't get away from it. We can't not see it. And that's why it seems so much more evil. I don't think it's increased, because Satan can't be more evil than he is. We just are more educated about it.

BRYAN: One other thing we see in this chapter is how utterly dysfunctional Herod's family was. So just talk a little bit about family dysfunction, because we've been talking about cultural evil and child abuse and stuff like that. But what about family dysfunction, and how do we cut that off at the root, nip it in the bud? How do we heal from it, or what are its causes and solutions in terms of family dysfunction?

KATHIE: Well, it's really complex, of course, but I do have a simple answer to it. A friend of mine, a family counselor, when I was going through some stuff with Frank, said to me, "If you can't forgive your husband, forgive your children's father." And that changed everything. We see most of our lives only through our own selfish lens of what we need. But when we take our eyes off ourselves and put them onto what's truly much more important, which at that time in my life was my children and our family, it changes everything. And I really do believe that all things are possible with Jesus. He said, "With man this is impossible, but with God all things are possible" (Matthew 19:26). That's a simple answer to a really complex set of issues and questions.

HELL HATH NO FURY

BRYAN: In chapter 8, we encounter Cleopatra for the first time, and I wonder if you think of her as a villain figure, kind of like the biblical Jezebel or the Wicked Witch of the West, because she is decadent and cruel and wasteful of money. Yet she's also this figure who's at the top of Egyptian society, atop the pyramid of power in a very wealthy ancient kingdom. So what do you think of Cleopatra? Is she a misunderstood heroine? Is she an all-out Jezebel? Or a mixture? What are your thoughts about her?

KATHIE: I love the fact that suddenly, she's there in our book. It gives Herod so much more texture for me. It's like, *Wait, what? Cleopatra was part of his life?* We don't fully know Herod if we're looking only at the Bible. It doesn't tell us all there is to know. We don't know about this backstory with Julius Caesar and Mark Antony and Cleopatra and all of that. I just think it's such a rich story. A lot of people don't even know who was really real in history. But Cleopatra certainly was. She was born into royalty, right?

BRYAN: Yes, she was a descendant of the pharaohs. I mean, of the last pharaohs, which were Greek at that time. So she intermarried with the Greek dynasty that took over with Alexander the Great. They were called the Ptolemies. But she was a descendant of pharaohs. She was a princess. Blue-blooded. And we will talk about her more in the next few chapters.

KATHIE: We have to. Her story is essential to Herod's. Back then, Cleopatra had to survive. All women are smart, so back then they learned early on—back when they had no value in terms of the worlds that they came into and lived in—that you have to use whatever you can find to better your situation. And Cleopatra was clearly a brilliant politician. She used her beauty and her wiles to get herself to the top. I can appreciate that. I get it. There are people in this world that I can respect because of what they do with their lives, though I don't particularly like them. I won't name them. But there are lots of them. They're not good people, but they're smart and they're hard-working. And I always want to give those people their due, you know? I just think it's important. So I give Cleopatra her due. She made it to the top in a man's world, though I don't admire how she did it. Actually, I think Mark Antony is the one who was so unlikable in that whole thing. What a wimp.

BRYAN: He's a total wimp.

KATHIE: He's a complete and total wimp. She's not.

BRYAN: At the end of this chapter, we talk about Mary's—I mean the Virgin Mary's—father, Joachim. So these names and stories are just traditions; they're not in the inspired Scriptures, but there are many early Christian traditions about Joachim and his wife, Anna. And the chapter talks about what a good man he was. In fact, the quote is, "There was no man like him in the people of Israel." He was upright. He was a just man. What does that mean to be a good and upright man? What does that look like? Have you seen it in your own life?

KATHIE: Boaz is the first name that came to mind about being a good man. Or in my own life, my father was the godliest person I've ever known. He spoke very few words, but every time he said something, you never forgot it. He was wise. He'd been deeply hurt by his own father. He was one of the younger ones of the five children. His father left the family and went off and caroused and my dad's mother married again. So my father had to grow up fast. World War II changed everything. The crash in 1929 and then the Second World War, basically. And so, my father is an example of a really godly man.

CODA 9

HEROD ON THE FIELD OF WAR

BRYAN: So in this chapter, one of the things we see is how Herod was a good military leader. He gave a big speech, and he rallied the troops. I just wonder if you've ever had a situation—and maybe this is also advice for your readers—where you have this good leader who's also immoral? How do you navigate working under a leader who's got personality flaws and yet is a skillful leader?

KATHIE: Well, you just described me. Ha! I think we've talked about the fact that all my life I've been in the entertainment world. That's my mission field. And so there are very skillful people there who, morally, I knew were not doing so well.

For example, you know what? My mother used to have problems with gay people because she had never met a gay person before. And then she met some of my dearest friends who were gay. And she exclaimed, "Oh, but they're so nice!" I responded, "Hello, welcome to the kingdom of God! They're different from you, but they're beautiful people." You know, it's sometimes like that. The first person I ever wrote a huge song with was a gay friend. And I've written probably three or four hundred songs with him through the years. And I love him. I just flat out love him. And I realized that God had put me in that world not to condemn them any more than Jesus came to condemn. He put me into that world to love people and to show them that there is a better way, there is a more excellent way. That is just the way Jesus is, because he is the way, the truth, and the life. And when you follow Jesus, your sex life is God's business. It's not mine. If you cheat on taxes, I think that's lousy. But you know, that's between you and your accountant and God. I mean, I just don't have time for everybody else's sins. I'm completely overwhelmed by my own!

It takes all my energy to love people. Honestly, it's so easy to condemn them. *Boom!* Done, write them off. But to love them? Well, that takes commitment over the long haul. That takes determination. That takes time. But that's ultimately what God honors. He honors it when we love people in his name. He said, "Your love for one another will prove to the world that you are my disciples" (John 13:35 NLT).

BRYAN: If I can sort of segue, this relates to the idea that God was behind what you were doing. Herod did the same thing where he gave this speech and he said, "We're going to go into battle and we're going to win because we have God with us." And I wonder what you think about that. Can Herod claim that he has God on his side in battle, or can God be on the side of someone like Herod? He's on your side. He lifted you up in your showbiz career. But can he be on the side of someone like Herod as well? What do you think?

KATHIE: I think Herod said what was expedient to say on that day to rally his troops. He was brilliant that way. It wasn't that God was on Herod's side. God was on the Jewish people's side.

BRYAN: Well said.

KATHIE: That's where God is. He says, "You are my people." And his faithfulness endures for all generations. So that's what that was about. That was not about Herod. That was about the Jews. That was about God's people. God fought their battles, even through the bad leaders they sometimes had. And he still does.

A CHANGE OF ALLEGIANCE

BRYAN: Chapter 10 focuses on Mark Antony and Cleopatra. Everybody knows a bit about their love story and tragic deaths. And I just wonder if you think it is a beautiful story? Does it deserve a Shakespearean play or a movie with Elizabeth Taylor?

KATHIE: It deserves all the attention it got. It's like *Real Housewives of the New Testament* kind of stuff. It's got everything. But that doesn't mean it's a love story. The truth is, it's a lust story. There's a huge difference between making love and having sex. I've always said it. I've done both. And I know the difference. It depends, I guess, on the definition of *love*. Love can be true love. When I think of a true love story, I think of Ruth and Billy Graham. That's a love story. That is sacrifice. I think of my mother and father. That's a love story. But when I think about Cleopatra and Mark Antony, that's a power/lust story. Because those two things go together. It's full of sex. It's full of power. It's full of ugliness. You know, it's gotten down and dirty. And like I said before, Mark Antony is a total wimp in this story.

BRYAN: He's wrapped around her. He does her bidding. Loses his sense of independent manhood.

KATHIE: Yeah. And I get that. I've seen it. And she knew it, too, and they had something going, and she exploited it. But yeah, he comes off as just weak. You're not sorry when he gets his demise. Hers was sort of elegant and you could even say it was dramatic. And she did it her way, with the asp. She was a strong woman under intense pressures.

I don't know if I told you the story from years ago when Barbara Walters was being whipped terribly in the press because she was the first female prime-time newscaster. And she was working with Harry Reasoner, and she was just getting ripped to shreds because she was a woman. She was also

Jewish and had a lisp. You know, they called her "Babwa Wawa." She said it was just brutal. And suddenly, one day, a telegram arrived. That's how long ago this was. There was no email. There was no text messaging. No, a telegram arrived that said, "Dear Barbara, don't let the bastards win. Love, Duke." It was John Wayne! The great Western actor John Wayne had sent her this telegram. She said that changed her life. Because, she said, "He's right. I'm not going to let the bastards win. I'm the one getting a million bucks. I'm the one that's got this job. They're just jealous and mean-spirited and awful. I'm going to win an Emmy for it." That sort of thing changes the lens through which you see the world. She could have been totally discouraged by what all these people who didn't matter were saying. But then the biggest movie star in the world encouraged her out of the blue. I don't think they were even friends. But John Wayne recognized that it was wrong. She didn't deserve this. And he said, "Dear Barbara, don't let the bastards win. Love, Duke." Can you imagine?

BRYAN: That's the power of a strong man who can help. You know, the power of a strong, bold man. To come alongside and be an encourager in that setting is a beautiful thing.

KATHIE: That's my point. Now that's a leader. That's a leader who uses his power. Billy Graham did that for me, along with Kevin Costner. Kevin did that for me a couple of times, and then we became good friends from it. But I didn't know him at first. And when I was going through all the garbage with the sweatshops and stuff, I got a call one day, and my assistant said, "Kathie, Kevin Costner is on the phone for you." I said, "What?" I'm talking about years and years ago. So, anyway, he was on the phone and he said, "Kathie, just remember this: 'He who is in you is greater than he who is in the world.'" It was 1 John 4:4! So that's another example of how to use your power: to encourage, to lift up. I think of that scripture that says, "Do not let any unwholesome talk come out of your mouths, but only what is helpful for building others up according to their needs, that it may benefit those who listen." That's Ephesians 4:29.

I'm just so grateful for the people who were so good to me back then. And they continue to be. They're still great, great friends of mine. And I've tried to be that for other people. I've tried to be an encouragement to people because you should pass on what people have done for you, right?

BRYAN: Well, that raises an interesting parallel to Herod, where you're talking about friends like Kevin Costner or people that became lifetime friends. In Herod's case, he was allied with Mark Antony, whose fortunes went down and he had this demise. Then Herod realized that the guy opposite them, whom they just fought a war against, had won.

KATHIE: Herod picked the wrong team.

BRYAN: Exactly. And suddenly he realized that. But somehow, he managed—because usually the winner does a purge of the other guy's friends—but somehow, Herod flipped the script and got over onto the side of the new head power. So I just wonder if you have ever seen that kind of thing where somebody has to switch an allegiance? Or is that two-faced, or what do you think?

KATHIE: I don't think it was two-faced. I mean, he was a politician. He was not a godly man. You know what I'm saying? Not a godly man. And so, he was a survivor. Life forces you to make hard choices sometimes. And Herod did that. We all have to, sometimes. We may not like it, but we do it.

BETRAYAL AND BLOODSHED

BRYAN: In this chapter, we really get into Herod and Mariamne, and I know you like to talk about her. We kind of covered this with Antony and Cleopatra, but what about Herod and Mariamne? Do they have a love story or a lust story? Talk a little bit about how they relate, in your opinion.

KATHIE: I think they're very similar to Cleopatra and Mark Antony and that relationship. Very much so, because it's all about, What's the strategic alliance? You talk about these marriages that are arranged, and it's usually just, *What is going to consolidate things for me so I can continue my power?* They're more alliances than they are romances. For Herod, I think with Doris it was because she was attractive, and he needed to be married to be considered respectable for the role he was about to play.

BRYAN: A good Jew should be married, right?

KATHIE: Married and have children. Yes. And we were very clear with that in the book, how he married Doris for that reason. But then along came Mariamne, and she captured his attention completely. Even to the end of his life, at the point of his death. My teacher, Ray, he said that Herod cried out her name at the end of his life. That's what I remember. Ray pictured how Herod cried, "Mariamne!" And it was echoing up there at Herodium where he was buried. It was so powerful. I'll never forget that as long as I live. We're writing this book because of that moment.

BRYAN: Herod was obsessed with her, all the way to the end. There's a rabbinic tradition—this isn't found in Josephus, so it's not a confirmed fact—in the Talmud somewhere where one of the rabbis repeated the rumor that Herod had preserved her body in honey. That's not for certain; it doesn't come from a more reliable source like Josephus. It's just a scurrilous little rumor passed on by the rabbis. But it's not beyond what he would have done. And they even said he would copulate with the body.

KATHIE: Yeah, we have that in our book. That shows how depraved he was, how he was descending choice by choice into madness, like we talked about earlier. I think this guy had a good father, though. Antipater was a good man. And we don't hear much about his mother except that he kept her and took care of her. Cyprus was her name. I think he had a sense that family is everything, which probably came from his Middle Eastern heritage. I think he started out with lots of good stuff, just like Solomon did. But look how Solomon got to the point where he said it's all nothingness from nothingness (Ecclesiastes 1:2, my paraphrase). And nobody was given more gifts in all of history than Solomon was. And look what he did. Look what he did with his life. And Israel was never the same afterward because the kingdom was torn apart. That's the way I think of Cleopatra and Mark Antony, and I believe that Herod was just as confused as they were. Herod probably lusted after hundreds of women and had hundreds of partners, but he knew something was different; he felt differently about Mariamne. And for whatever reason, he called it love. I think he thought he loved her.

BRYAN: An obsessive love, it seems.

KATHIE: It's sick. There's a sickness attached to it. And then he murdered her. So is that love? No way.

BRYAN: It's such a tricky thing, because he does have this very strong feeling and he wants to love her, and he's desperate to be loved back by her. So he's like Mark Antony. He's pitiful in this one way where he's desperate. But she was a Hasmonean; she was all that he was not. He's wasn't, you might say, of the right race or ethnicity or legacy or family. And so, part of the dynamic was that she looked down on him and despised him for his low birth. And he was always aware of that. And it made him more desperate; it made her more arrogant, and she despised him. So was she a victim or was she the problem? Or is it just a great big mess all the way around?

KATHIE: I think it's like Abraham and Sarah and Hagar. It's a big old mess all the way around. It's hard to find somebody to like there, somebody to revere. I can't stand that story of Abraham and Sarah and Hagar. It's horrible. It's the low point of what we know about them from Scripture, for me. I don't think they knew what love is. They knew they felt a little differently about somebody. But that's just lust. And then we forget their name the next day.

BRYAN: Can you put yourself in Mariamne's shoes, where she's been forced into this marriage with a prideful man whom she looks down on and who is so obsessive? Can we think of her as a victim in that way?

KATHIE: I think we have to think of every woman who lived during those days as victims, because the culture victimized women. They weren't even worth the same value in a legal sense. They were less than men. They had no power unless they had some place in society like Mariamne as a Hasmonean or Cleopatra descended from the pharaohs. Other women had no rights at all. Think about Hagar. She was a slave. She was owned. We've come a long, long way in our world today, but unfortunately, so many women are still enslaved all around the world. In some ways, little has changed. Women are viewed as less than men in many places. So I think in that sense, Mariamne was a victim. And she was going to use every opportunity she had to make her situation better, to keep herself alive. Right? Of course.

BRYAN: It's important to talk about the oppression of women. And that's so true, whether you're a Mariamne at the top of the heap or you're a slave girl. Can you speak a little bit about Jesus coming on the scene, how his relationship to women was so different, and how he transformed the way that cultures are supposed to treat women?

KATHIE: I think the most radical thing in all eternity is him leaving glory to come to the earth and take on the form of a lowly human, to be tortured to death because of his love for us. Sometimes, I can't even think about it. When I think about his love for the broken, the sick, it amazes me. And his love for women was so radical. He was the most radical feminist the world had ever seen. Completely changed the way women would be seen from that moment on. I love that! He said, "You are every bit as precious to God as men. You are daughters of the king."

That's why most of the people at the tomb and at the cross were women. The only man there we know of was John. I believe all the others were looking on from afar, but only John was literally there saying, "Okay, I am with you." And yet he had left Jesus the night before. You know, they all ran. Every one of them ran. But the women didn't run. So you ask, "Why?" Because their lives had been so transformed by Jesus' love for them. It's women who have been maligned and devalued and raped and pillaged. Every culture in the world has been that way with women. It's going on with the women today being brought over the southern border by these coyotes. It makes me sick to my stomach.

But Jesus, he valued women. He went out of his way to find them. Like the Samaritan woman at the well. He went there on purpose to meet that woman right there. The first human being who saw Jesus after his resurrection was a woman who had been demon possessed. She loved Jesus the way none of us—who have never been demon possessed and then been freed from it—could. That's the point. We love the most when we've been healed the most and delivered the most. Jesus went out of his way to find those who needed deliverance. It wasn't just for me. It was for everybody.

The demoniac was the very first evangelist. Jesus said, "Go back to your family, and tell them everything God has done for you" (Luke 8:39 NLT). That man didn't know that Jesus was God, but it was Jesus who healed him, so God did it. That's why he was told to share that message. And if the world would just tell everybody what their God has done for them this day, we would not be living in the world we live in. We're so afraid. We isolate ourselves in buildings and we gossip about one another. And we send a check occasionally to somebody in Africa, but that's not what Jesus meant. He meant, "Go and tell the world what your God has done for you this day."

BRYAN: That's beautiful. That's powerful.

KATHIE: Breaks my heart, Bryan. It really does.

CODA 12

PAGAN JERUSALEM?

BRYAN: In chapter 12, we have some thoughts about Anna, the mother of Mary, or Saint Anne, as some people call her. But Anna, as she's called in the ancient sources, dealt with infertility, which we have sort of alluded to. Maybe begin by talking about women who struggle with infertility. Have you seen that in your life? What can you tell us about trusting God in times of infertility?

KATHIE: Well, I was so blessed when we got pregnant with Cody. It was on a European holiday, so I don't even know where we made Cody. Frank and I were on a beautiful sailing ship, so it could have been anywhere all over Italy. And so that's . . .

BRYAN: *Amore,* as they say.

KATHIE: That's *amore*! Right. And my favorite food in the whole world is Maryland blue crabs. So we came home from that holiday and I could not stand the look of it when we were having friends over for a big crab feast. I couldn't even look at them. And I said, "Oh wow, that's never happened to me in my entire life!" So then I knew I was pregnant, and I said, "Well, that's a good holiday when you can do that!"

BRYAN: That's quite a souvenir to come home with. Not with a T-shirt but a son.

KATHIE: I was never incapable of conceiving a baby. But I did lose two. I did have two miscarriages between Cody and Cass. That's traumatic. But I remember thinking, *Well, at least I have one beautiful child*. I always used to say that to Frank. I was not one of those women who all their life just dreamed of getting married and having babies, of holding my grandchildren in my arms. I was always about working because I loved my work. I do remember, though, the heartbreak of a miscarriage. I have so many friends that are infertile. I think the technology, the options, that people have today is so wonderful. I always try to find something to be grateful for when something else is going wrong in my life. God inhabits the praises of his people. Nothing can change your situation faster than praising God in the midst of it.

That's not our natural human response, to give praise. And yet we're told all through Scripture that that's what changes everything. Like when Paul talked about, "I've been hungry, and I've had my fill. I've been through everything. But I now can praise you for my weaknesses" (2 Corinthians 12:9; Philippians 4:12, my paraphrase). That's why I was even praising back then, saying, "Well, at least I have one beautiful child." And the Lord gave us, of course, our precious Cassidy. So I feel for people who long for this. You think about the abortions in the world and how people just, you know, can't wait to get rid of a baby while others just desperately want it to be there. The desire of their whole life is to be able to have a child.

BRYAN: I think you are reminding your readers to turn to God in praise and be grateful for what they do have, and to consider adoption, which is kind of what you were implying there. Those are all good things. I think that that made a lot of sense.

KATHIE: I wish they'd make adoption a lot easier for people. They make it so difficult and expensive. I can't even imagine my life without my children. Or now, without my little boys, my grandsons. They're just precious. I get to see Frankie this week.

BRYAN: Let's transition to that part where you're a mother and you're offering up your child like Anna had chosen to do with Mary at the temple. Maybe you've had that experience, or that moment, as a parent. Have you ever had to give your kids over into God's care and trust him—maybe sending them to camp, college, or something like that? What's your experience with that?

KATHIE: Well, no. I couldn't wait for Cody to go to college. I would have drop-kicked him out of the house if I could have! He gave me the hardest time for about five years. My counselor said, "You know, Kathie, that's not unusual for sons of really, really type A mothers." How did he say it? He said, "Boys will just make themselves obnoxious in order for them to separate psychologically from superstrong mothers." And I said, "Well, that I completely believe," because he was being obnoxious! Everybody else said, "Cody is just the sweetest kid." He was renowned in all of Greenwich, and still is, for being the nicest kid. They always said that Kathie and Frank's children are the two most unentitled, loving kids. They have such nice manners. And I said, "The kid that lives at my house? Are you describing that one? No, that is not my experience in the last few years!" You know Cody a little bit. You know what I mean.

BRYAN: What a fine gentleman he is. I love that guy.

KATHIE: Yeah, see? That's what I'm saying. That's most people's experience of him. And so anyway, no, he didn't want to go to school. He cried and cried and cried when we tried to drop him off at nursery school. But Cass was like, "Bye, Mommy! Bye. Now get out of here."

BRYAN: Maybe like Mary at the temple. "Bye, Mommy. I got work to do in my Father's house."

KATHIE: Maybe so.

BRYAN: So another question I have has to do with the way that Herod made Jerusalem into this Romanized city, yet he also wanted it to be a Jewish city. So it had to be a city for God, but also a city for the Romans. And I wondered if you have navigated issues where the Hollywood or the New York television community wants you to do one thing, but the Christian or the spiritual community wants you to do another. And how have you lived with one foot in the so-called Roman world, and one in Jerusalem?

KATHIE: I have always felt like, if you're a plumber, you're no less of a plumber if you're a Christian. You're a Christian first; you're a follower of the Way first, no matter what you do for a living. You stand up for Jesus in your work. And of course, I would not do nude scenes and I didn't do them. I remember I was offered something where they wanted me to sing this song, I guess it was on the show *Hee Haw Honeys*. They wanted me to sing a song sung by Sammi Smith that said, "Oh, help me make it through the night. I don't care what's right or wrong." And I said, "I can't sing that song because I do care what's right and wrong. But thank you." So I was always able to make choices pretty easily because I had such a sense of what was godly and what wasn't. Now, I did say the f-word when I was doing my Broadway debut. But I was playing a character. I didn't feel guilty about it. It's a man-made word. You know what I'm saying? But I would never take the Lord's name in vain. That's his covenant name that he gave to us, which he revealed to us about himself.

One of my favorite stories in my whole career was when I turned down the offer to take over for Carol Burnett on a Broadway show. And my agent said, "Why?" And I said, "Because I will not take the Lord's name in vain." And so he said, "Well, let me talk to Stephen Sondheim and see if he can change it."

And I said, "No. The only person that he's ever changed a word for was Barbra Streisand. I'm no Barbra Streisand, so I'm not even going to ask." He said, "Well, let me see what I can do." And he called me back. He said, "Stephen wants to meet with you." So we met over in the city and it was like 11:00 a.m. I'd just gotten off the show with Regis. And I'd been up forever, of course, but Stephen was rubbing his eyes like crazy. Like he was thinking, *Oh my gosh, I've never seen eleven in the morning before!* He was sitting on the sofa and I was in a chair opposite, and he said, "I understand you have some issues with the script." But I said, "No, I don't. I don't have any issues. I love the role. I could play it. I totally get this woman. I would love to do it for you, but I will not take the Lord's name in vain. It's a personal faith issue for me. I'll say the f-word or I'll simulate sex; I got no problem with that. It's a role. I'm playing the role of someone else. But I will not take the Lord's name in vain." And he practically fell off the sofa, just laughing at that. He said, "I've never in my life met somebody that would simulate sex or say that word, but would not say GD." And I said, "Some things are nonnegotiable for me. Yeah, that I will not do." So anyway, he said, "Well, I originally wrote the song for a character who was an English woman. So how about if you just say 'bloody'? Just say, 'Wait a bloody minute' instead of 'Wait a GD minute.'" And I said, "Okay!" I shook his hand and said, "Deal." It was done.

BRYAN: It's such a good story. There's a little bit of rawness to it, but it's such a perfect answer to the question that I asked about how you balanced "Rome" and "Jerusalem."

KATHIE: You live an authentic life. That's how you balance it. I'm not a different person right now than I would be on television. You just be authentically you. And if you're staying close to Jesus, if you're walking with him, I always say he will reveal what he wants you to do.

CODA 13

GATEWAY TO ROME

BRYAN: Can I ask you a question about chapter 13 as we move forward here a little bit? So, in this chapter we really explore Caesarea Maritima, and I just thought I'd get your sense of it. I know you've been there. What do you like about that place? Do you marvel about Herod's ability to bend nature to his will, or do you admire his giftedness? And what do you remember about the sights and scenes of Caesarea by the Sea?

KATHIE: Oh, it is truly one of my favorite places. Jesus said, "With men this is impossible, but with God all things are possible" (Matthew 19:26). Well, Herod thought of himself as God, so, you know, he made it happen. But I talked with you the other day about how much I respect his architectural gifts and his survival gifts. I mean, the world has rarely seen somebody as gifted as that man, nimble on his feet about everything. How many people can deal with being seduced by Cleopatra and survive angry emperors and shipwrecks and wars and all that he faced? He was truly a survivor in so many ways. When you go to Caesarea Maritima and you see the spot where the harbor was, you are reminded that Caesar's ships came there. Herod built it for Caesar's ships; he built it for having an army. He wanted that connection with Rome.

I have a specific memory of Caesarea Maritima. It was when I went with Frank, the one and only time that Frank went with me. It was in 2012, I believe. And you know the stadium that's there. It is just sitting there and it's still so clear what it was. And Frank went over to a little thing sticking up, and he jumped up on a rock and started in like he was calling the game.

BRYAN: Oh, that's great! He was a broadcasting legend. A sporting venue was what he loved.

KATHIE: That's what he knew, and this place was rocking that day. Everybody who was in our Bible tour group was laughing, thinking it was the most wonderful thing in the world.

BRYAN: I would have liked to have been there. To hear Frank Gifford do Monday Night Football live from Caesarea.

KATHIE: And so, every time I'm there, I go over to that exact same rock and do it. Yeah. In remembrance of a great man. You know, Frank is in eight Halls of Fame. Some he was awarded entrance into posthumously. But I mean, a lot of people have membership in one Hall of Fame. He is in eight. He earned every hall of fame that he was in, including best-dressed. He is in the Best-Dressed Hall of Fame. He is in the College Football Hall of Fame. Broadcasting. And all the rest.

BRYAN: Did he ever call any kind of racing like NASCAR or horse racing, or was it all football?

KATHIE: He and Bob Beattie were the preeminent ski-racing broadcast team. They called the major ski races all around the world. Like in Austria. I used to love to go with him. When he had those things in his life, he was doing what he loved, like *Wide World of Sports*. He called everything. There was hardly anything that was sports-related that he didn't do.

BRYAN: I ask because in Caesarea there's a venue that's right there by the seacoast that was used for chariot racing. It was a stadium for watching races.

KATHIE: Yeah, Frank would have been right there in the middle of that. It was his world. Sports are everywhere and have always been part of life. I'm sure that the cavemen had sports.

BRYAN: Maybe they had races or something.

KATHIE: Who can throw rocks the farthest, probably.

BRYAN: Frank Gifford would have been the best-dressed caveman in his furs, calling the game.

CODA 14

GREATNESS ACHIEVED

BRYAN: We talked in the last chapter about Caesarea by the Sea, but now we move on to chapter 14, where we talk about Masada in the Judean desert. Quite a different setting!

KATHIE: You know, I love water. I am not a desert person. I don't know why God made cacti. I just hate them. I despise them. I would never be the kind of person who would live in Phoenix or anywhere like that. Some people just love the desert. I've always been a water girl, and I remember being fascinated by the fact that Herod was a desert boy. I mean, he had his palace right there on the water in Caesarea with that gorgeous pool and everything, so how could he like Masada even more? I'm just totally the opposite of him in that respect. That's what I remember thinking. *Why wouldn't he love it more by the seaside?*

BRYAN: The ocean is really pretty at Caesarea. And he's literally got a palace on a peninsula, and at the end of it, the tip of the peninsula, was an area that faced west. So he could look out from there every day and watch a sunset over the Mediterranean Sea. And yet, like you're saying, he'd rather be in Masada. But you've been to Masada too. Have you ever hiked up the Snake Path?

KATHIE: Yes! The first time I went, I was seventeen. So I hiked up it pretty easily when I was young. That was different than my later trips with Ray Vander Laan and being like a goat going up that path, like one of those little animals—what do they call them? The ones that they call a *coney* in the Bible. The hyrax!

BRYAN: Yeah, I've seen those.

KATHIE: I was like one of those animals! I practically had to be carried up!

BRYAN: Well, they have the cable car to Masada now. A little easier than those hikes our friend Rod VanSolkema makes us do.

KATHIE: Oh no, no, no, no. I'm not doing that anymore. It's, like, our own little hell.

BRYAN: It's because of the time of day. Rod starts you in the morning when the eastern sun is beating on the face of that Snake Path, so you have sun as well as the steep hike.

KATHIE: I know. He's not a nice person, let's be honest.

BRYAN: He likes to be like the rabbi. You know, like literally walking in the same dusty, sweaty ways of Jesus. But it gives you a sense for the ancient soldiers, doesn't it? Imagine thinking if you're a soldier at the bottom and you've got the Jewish rebels on top or the enemies of Herod up there, and you're down below thinking, *How are we going to capture this castle in the desert?* It had to be intimidating, I'm sure.

KATHIE: Yeah. And yet Masada is still one of my favorite places to go to once you get there. Just for the sheer wonder of how the man had all those cisterns, how he had the pools, you know, enough water for a very long time.

BRYAN: You can look down into that giant, empty cistern at the other end from his palace. Yes. It's cavernous.

KATHIE: And you just think, *Who was this guy?*

BRYAN: And that water is pumped up there. It's not like it's just the rain collecting on top. He's getting it from the wadis below and somehow lifting it onto that plateau. Maybe some of it was from rain, but it doesn't rain enough. But the wadis, which were flooding down low, are collected and pumped to that height to fill that system. Not just for drinking but for gardens and baths as well.

KATHIE: Now, this is a man who did the so-called impossible at the time. Like I've said, I have enormous respect for his gifts. And you know, what does the Scripture say? "Every good and perfect gift is from above, coming down from the Father of the heavenly lights, who does not change like shifting shadows" (James 1:17 NIV)—one of my favorite verses. Every gift, whether you give it to Hitler or to Billy Graham, is a perfect gift. Every good and perfect gift comes from our heavenly Father. We can use it or we can corrupt it. But we were born in and were made to live in a garden. We were supposed to work it, make it bring forth life. On some level, Herod understood that, which is why he often turned the desert into a garden. There's something deep inside him that understood, *I'm supposed to use my gifts to cause the desert to bloom.* So this is why I'm so fascinated by the man. And Jesus said, "What profit is it to a man if he gains the whole world, and loses his own soul?" (Matthew 16:26). Well, that's exactly what happened to Herod.

BRYAN: It reminds us that we each have to steward whatever gifts God has given us.

KATHIE: God will use everything that he gives us. He told me that a long time ago. He spoke to me and said, *Kathie, there are no wasted crumbs on my table. I use everything. And if you will let me, I will use everything in your life for my purpose and for my glory. But only if you choose to walk with me.* That's what it is. It's a choice. And some days, it's a real hard choice—really hard choice. And other days, it almost gets to be like your DNA, and it comes naturally. I learned that a long, long time ago. The minute somebody would say something or write something nasty about me, I'd say, "Lord, I pray for that person." I pray for them because hurt people hurt people. Somewhere along the way in that person's life, that person was hurt, and that person has this wound, and this is the way they take it out. They take it out on other people. This is what they do. And so you need to pray for them. You can do this. It's a hard choice, but you can do it. God gives you everything you need to do the job he's called you to do.

BRYAN: Well, I think in some ways that's like the story we're telling with Mary, where she's only a young girl or she grows up a little bit and finds she has a calling from God. And in her case, it's to be the vessel of the Savior, which is really what you're describing. I mean, you're not saying to be his physical vessel like she was, but all that you've just been saying is a very Marian type of spirituality, where you say, "In what way can I be the vessel of the incarnation in the world today?" And so, I like how you're bringing out some parallels with that golden thread, that storyline we're developing with Mary against the story of Herod.

CODA 15

THE TEMPLE OF THE LORD

BRYAN: In chapter 15, we see Herod building the temple, and so we should talk about the Jewish temple. I know you've been to the Western Wall, and I know you've seen the Temple Mount. Nobody can miss it on the Jerusalem skyline today. But let's go back to the original Mount Moriah, where Abraham was willing to offer his son Isaac in Genesis 22. And then we learn in Hebrews 11 a little bit more about that incident. So maybe just talk about this as a father-son thing and the spiritual power of the moment when Abraham was willing to offer Isaac on Mount Moriah.

KATHIE: I think a lot of people are just aghast when they hear the story of Abraham and Isaac. But Abraham was a friend of God. We know that; God calls him that. And we also know that by that time, Isaac was not a baby. Right?

BRYAN: He was a young man; he could carry the wood. He was strong.

KATHIE: Yeah, he was strong. So Abraham knew that the promise of God had been fulfilled with a son. He had a good history of seeing God leading and keeping his promises. God told him what he was supposed to do, told him exactly what to do, and Abraham didn't even argue with God. He just left the next morning, early. And he saw the place in the distance. The hill of Moriah. And then Isaac said, "Father, we have the flint, and we have the wood. But where will we get the sacrifice?" And in Abraham's answer, he said, "The Lord will provide" (vv. 7 and 14, my paraphrase). That's *Jehovah Jireh*. The Lord Will Provide. I think in Abraham's heart of hearts, I'm sure he was questioning and quivering. I mean, I can't imagine being told to sacrifice my child. I can't imagine that moment when you bring the knife up to do it. And he either had such faith that God was going to provide something else like the ram or he was going to bring Isaac back from the dead. I don't know if he felt like it was a test of his love for God or a test of his faith in God. It was probably both. I just know I couldn't do it.

BRYAN: You'd have to be given the faith in the moment. You know what I mean? It would have to be a bequest of faith that gave Abraham the belief that, like you said—and that's what the book of Hebrews says—God could raise Isaac from the dead. And he knew the promise would come to that son. So he knew God was going to do what he said, right there in that place. And you have been up on the Temple Mount, I assume, at some point?

KATHIE: Yes, I've been inside the dome.

BRYAN: You've seen the rock there that's underneath the golden dome. They call it the Dome of the Rock. It's a Muslim shrine related to Muhammad today.

KATHIE: I remember seeing all the shoes on the floor. Nobody's allowed to go in with their shoes on. I don't know if they let people in anymore that aren't faithful Muslims. I'm not sure.

BRYAN: The most recent time I was there, I was not able to go in. But back in the early '90s while I was in college, I went inside.

KATHIE: I went in 1971 and pretty much could go where I wanted.

BRYAN: Yeah, I was one year old then.

KATHIE: Shut up.

BRYAN: Sorry, didn't mean to do that. Maybe the Western Wall is a better place to describe any spiritual feelings you've had or any sense of connection to the Holy Mount and the temple, or the provision of God, or the footsteps of Jesus. Or can you tell us anything related to spiritual experiences you've had at the Western Wall or on the Temple Mount?

KATHIE: Well, there's one story I could tell you. I almost died on the Temple Mount a couple of trips ago. I flew all night and went directly to the Temple Mount to shoot a show. Israel had asked NBC if I could come and do a five-part series, because so much of the tourism money had dried up because of all the negative press in the news. People always say, "Oh, it's a bad time to go to Israel." I always say, "It's never a bad time to go to Israel!" That's right. Ever since I've been going when I was a teenager, it has been safe. If you get a chance to go, you go!

BRYAN: The Mossad is the best security service in the world. They know what's going on there.

KATHIE: Yeah. So anyway, I got there. But I was dehydrated and hadn't really eaten. And there was this group of girls. It used to be that girls were not allowed to dance or sing or have any kind of expression on the Temple Mount. But they've been allowing it in recent times. They're expressing their joy in their Jewishness. Some people love it; others don't. But the girls loved it. And they're young teenage girls—I'd say around eighth through tenth graders. And they were singing and dancing in a circle. And Yael, my producer, said, "Kathie, go get among them. Go in the circle with them. Go talk to them." I said, "Oh, shoot!" because I had an interview to do; that's what I was there for. But in the meantime, they're saying I should go dance.

Well, I did. And it got more raucous and more raucous and more raucous. And the girls were spinning me around so fast that I said, "Oh my God! I'm going to faint! I'm going to faint!" And all of a sudden, one of them yelled into my ear such a piercing sound that it popped, as if my head had popped. And I said, "I've had a stroke or something," and I had the most blazing headache. I couldn't see and I had to sit down. I asked for somebody to get me some Tylenol but that didn't touch it. My headache lasted for three days. I ended up having to go to Hadassah Hospital, and I had to have a spinal tap at midnight. It was so awful. So that was my near-death experience on the Temple Mount.

BRYAN: That's an amazing story. And it lasted three days. I mean, I feel like there's spiritual significance in there somewhere. You know, like being underground for three days and coming up again. That's an amazing story.

KATHIE: You mentioned the Western Wall too. I love seeing people put their little prayers in the cracks. They've been doing it now for centuries. People are desperate for God to hear their prayers.

BRYAN: Have you ever put your prayers in there?

KATHIE: Oh sure, sure. Every time. Yeah, every time.

BRYAN: Solomon's temple was meant as a prayer house for the nations. And then of course Jesus came, and his message is for the nations. And maybe you can talk a little bit about how it's not just a place for Jews or Muslims but that the message of Yeshua is the message for the world, for the globe, for the nations, for everyone, right? The gospel is a universal message.

KATHIE: It caused quite the stir when Jesus said, "Destroy this temple, and in three days I will raise it up" (John 2:19). He was obviously foreshadowing his death and his resurrection, and after that the temple would be within God's people, not in a building. I think he meant it metaphorically—that he was going to tear down the old way of doing things and resurrect it to what it was originally meant to be, so that God would walk with his people. Remember, that's what he did when he created Adam and Eve. He loved spending time with them and walking in the garden in the cool of the evening. I love that picture of God wanting communion and intimacy with us. That was the original plan.

BRYAN: That raises a good segue here. If we consider, like you just said, how God walked with Adam and Eve in the garden and he wants that intimacy, but then in the time of the temple that Herod built, you had these different courts. You had the Court of the Women, and they couldn't go past that point. Someone like Mary, if we picture young Mary, if she did work at the temple as a singer or in some capacity, she couldn't have gone all the way in. She couldn't go into the Most Holy Place for sure, or even past the Court of the Women. You were talking about Jesus breaking down the old ways, such as how the temple had restrictions on women. But in Jesus, the full intimacy is restored, right?

KATHIE: Yes. As we know, women were not considered equal to men. And they still aren't in many, many places in the world. Jesus came along and said that women are "daughter[s] of Abraham" (Luke 13:16). And Paul talked in Galatians 3 about how there's neither Greek nor Jew, nor male nor female. We will ultimately be one. But what Jesus was teaching these women was something they had never been taught: they were valuable. Before Jesus, women were treated as chattel, or maybe an animal was worth even more than a woman when they were bargained for. The man would get more for a couple of camels than for a woman. Then Jesus came along and sat with women and befriended them. And he had an intimacy with them that was totally nonsexual and yet the most intimate thing they'd ever known. Because he looked at them and saw them and loved them. He treasured them in ways no one ever had. The way that only God can love.

BRYAN: That's such a beautiful picture, isn't it? Because what you're really imagining is that with the temple, for example, young Mary or any woman could go only to the Court of the Women, but she couldn't go all the way into the heart of God. She couldn't go to the altar, and she certainly couldn't go into the Most Holy Place, into the inner sanctum. But then the women at the tomb who met the risen Christ, or Mary, when she was in the upper room and received the Holy Spirit along with the disciples, they could all—each one of them, through Jesus—come into the inner sanctum. They could be in the bosom of God. No longer excluded by a courtyard or by the walls of men. Jesus did that.

KATHIE: Yeah, but here's the thing. Mary experienced something no woman ever did or ever will experience. God inhabited her womb. And a man, I don't care what they say, but a man couldn't have given birth. No way. What could happen? God made women to have that privilege of childbirth. And God honored a woman in that special way. He's like that, our God.

THE BEGINNING
OF THE END

BRYAN: Herod's getting older here. And so he's thinking about his legacy a little bit and his sons. What do you think about legacy? I mean, as you get to the later stages of life and you start to think about looking back and leaving a legacy, have you thought about your children as your legacy?

KATHIE: Oh, of course. Don't all parents have those kinds of thoughts from the moment you give birth? I believe I've always wanted to have a legacy, even if I wasn't going to have children, because I knew my life would have purpose and my legacy would be the people who I'd shared the gospel with. You know, I'd like to think of that as my legacy: my faithfulness to be as bold as I can be, to give an accounting of the hope that's within me. A hope that's free. A gift of grace that's free. And not because I'm any more spiritual than any other person, but because I was touched by the Lord at an early age to proclaim him. And I got a lot of flak for that in the broadcasting world. I was in circles that some people didn't approve of.

You know, Billy Graham got a lot of flak for what he was doing too. I came to know the Lord as a little twelve-year-old girl on the cusp of womanhood in a movie theater. Billy was criticized horrendously for making movies and having people come to the movie theater. But my mother and sister came to know the Lord by watching a Billy Graham crusade on TV. Now, do the airwaves belong to Satan? Only if we give them over to him! Does a movie theater belong to Satan? Maybe so, depending on what you show in it. But Billy knew his calling. And the last proclamation from Jesus was to go into all the earth, every corner of the earth, and tell all people the good news. And Jesus knew the internet was coming. He knew that would be possible in the blink of an eye. And now it is. Now the Scriptures have been translated into so many languages that it does actually reach every corner of the earth. The Scriptures that proclaim Jesus resurrected, ascended, and is coming again.

BRYAN: So I think you leave a legacy by who you touch for Jesus. And I like that you're focusing on your witnessing and your gospel focus instead of the things that a lot of people would say, things that aren't eternal. I think Herod thought, *Oh, my kids are going to be little mini-me's.* Have you ever seen that pattern where parents live through their kids?

KATHIE: Yes, yes, yes. But I told my children when they each turned twenty-one, "Now that you're an adult, I've done my job. I've raised you in love and obedience to the one true God who I will never forsake." You know, that was the main thing I had to do with my children besides feed them and love them—love them enough to tell them the truth about what's really important in life. And I saw so many trust-fund babies, and you still do. And they've been given nothing but stuff. Nothing but stuff. What did Solomon say at the end? Nothingness. Nothingness. It's all nothing. Look at the man who stood at the temple when it was finished, King Solomon, who gave one of the most amazing prayers and beseeched the Lord to take care of his people there. And that it would be, as you say, a place of prayer for the nations and all of that. Look how his descendant was somebody who said it's all meaningless at the end, that nothing matters. I mean, what does it profit a man to gain the world but lose his soul? I look at my stock portfolios and look at my bonds, but that's not living to me. Yeah, I'm going to live. I don't believe in leaving tons and tons of stuff to people. If I leave it all to our family foundation, then I'll put them in charge of it, and they can continue my legacy and Frank's legacy by knowing where to give it for the sake of God's work.

BRYAN: So there is a lot of wisdom here, and you're showing that it's okay to invest in your kids and provide for them and have them live after you and carry your name with honor, but not to live as if they are your idols or something like that. A lot of people idolize their kids, and in some way Herod did that because he thought they would be little idols of himself after his death. You're guarding against that, it sounds like.

KATHIE: Yeah, because I've been surrounded by people who've done the opposite. And it doesn't work. It really doesn't. It's actually just so simple. What does it say in God's Word? To act justly, love mercy, and walk humbly with your God. Yeah. If my kids do that, I don't ever have an issue with them.

BRYAN: In chapter 16, we talk a little bit about the Magnificat and if Mary was a singer in the temple. If that's true, then she would know about songs. And maybe this is a good place to talk about Luke 1 and that beautiful song of Mary, where she said, "My soul glorifies the Lord and my spirit rejoices in God my Savior" (vv. 46–47 NIV). Has that been a powerful thing in your life? Or, put another way, what do you find beautiful about Mary's singing to the Lord? And you're a singer, so you understand songs.

KATHIE: It's interesting that you quoted "my Savior," because that's who the Messiah is. And that is Jesus, right? The God who saves.

BRYAN: And *Yeshua* means Savior.

KATHIE: Yeah. Mary already knew, even before he was born. And she pondered all those things in her heart. I've always thought of Mary as a lyricist. She wrote a poem and other people put music to it afterward. I've been doing that for fifty years. It is beautiful. And I love thinking about that. I think the Jews have always expressed their feelings in music. I mean, every culture does because it is a universal language, so it would make sense. And boy, those girls were singing that day they almost killed me on the Temple Mount!

BRYAN: Yeah, Jewish girls have always sung. We don't know exactly what Mary did in the temple, or if she was even there. But what we do know from Scripture is that young virgins had a musical instrument or a vocal aspect of the worship of the Old Testament temple. Whether that was happening in Herod's temple, we don't know for sure. I think it's beautiful to think of Mary not just as a lyricist, like you said, but maybe also as one who sang out to God and set the words to music. Perhaps. We don't know for sure.

KATHIE: What I do know is that she held her baby in her arms and she sang to him. I'm sure the songs of the angels were what she sang to him, the same way I sang to my grandson Frankie the first day I met him. He was three days old and could already hold up his head. And he was a little fussy. And the minute I started singing "Amazing Grace" to him, he literally went still. What kind of an infant lies still while wide awake? He never lost my gaze. And then he started to make his little mouth move like he was singing along. And I thought, *Okay, he just came from there. He just came down from heaven. He knows this.* But you know what? I think every one of us has a song to sing. We just have to find our song, then send it forth.

CODA 17

LIKE FATHER, LIKE SONS

BRYAN: In chapter 17, we have this scene where Herod puts Mariamne's boys on trial, and it's like they're locked in a kind of death spiral, you know? He hates them, they hate him, and he has them executed. I wonder if you've ever seen this kind of tragic father-son relationship. How do you avoid that? Father-son relationships are so complex, and so important.

KATHIE: Frank's sons from his first marriage had very troubled childhoods. But Frank always said, "Yeah, but God gave me a second chance to be a good father." Of course, none of his kids would ever say he was a bad father, because he wasn't. He was just gone a lot because of the nature of his work. And as a result, they got a lot of their troubles because their father worked so hard. Frank did some things wrong, but he did a lot of things right too. For the right reasons. He was a good man who did some stupid stuff—but who hasn't? But that's another story. Frank never had a bad relationship with his children. They all loved him so much, as they should.

BRYAN: It's so powerful. I mean, it seems like there is a kind of parallelism between Herod's family with its dysfunctionalities and its lack of the saving power of God, versus yours, which has some struggles and some pains but also has this golden thread of Yeshua running through it. And maybe there's some kind of narrative quality where your story and your family are being paralleled along with Herod's family. In this book, I think we see the hopelessness of what ancient evil looks like, but we also see what it looks like to have a broken family, yet one that has the redeeming power of God in it. So I just love the material we're getting from your family stories. I think it's so powerful and a testimony to God's work in the Gifford clan.

KATHIE: Well, they all now know the power of prayer, and they see the change that took place in their father. They attributed it to me, but I said, "No, it's the Holy Spirit."

BRYAN: A woman can't change someone from the inside, but the Spirit can.

KATHIE: The Spirit can. But it's the ongoing walk with Jesus that is the most difficult. The walk with God is the renewing of our hearts and minds. That's the life journey we're on. Salvation is instantly instant. It's ours forever once we believe. It's eternal. But the other part is the hard one. That's the part that takes the hard work. It's the journey with Jesus. But oh, is it worth it!

CODA 18

A HOUSE DIVIDED

BRYAN: One of the things that comes up in chapter 18 are the traditions that suggest Joseph wasn't as young as we sometimes picture him. We often assume he was around twenty-one and Mary was sixteen or something like that. These ancient stories suggest Joseph was maybe an older man who was tapped to take care of Mary, almost like a guardian of this holy girl who'd been working in the temple. Does it change anything to think of their ages being different, and also him resisting at first, saying, "I'm not sure I want to take such a young girl. It seems like people will laugh at me." And then the rabbi said, "No, no, you have to do this. God commands it." Any thoughts about Joseph being a little bit older than Mary?

KATHIE: I think that tradition probably started because he just disappears in the story and the narrative of the Gospels.

BRYAN: Yeah, it would explain that, wouldn't it? If he was much older and he died before Jesus started his ministry.

KATHIE: I've always felt about Jospeh that he was more like a Boaz. He parallels Boaz from the Old Testament. Boaz was a good, godly man who took a woman under his care. I'm sure he was attracted to Ruth. I'm sure she was beautiful. People try to make it such a sexual thing that she lay down next to him on the threshing floor and she uncovered his feet. Well, I think all those things are just beautiful. And he was her kinsman-redeemer, which is what Jesus is to us.

BRYAN: So it's the idea of Joseph almost being a kinsman-redeemer to Mary, not like two young people out on their honeymoon of new love. Which is the current picture of most every nativity scene—where Joseph looks like he's about twenty-one and he's thin and the same age as Mary. They are like the young couple going off on their fun honeymoon. But maybe the dynamic was more like what you are saying, where he's her older kinsman-redeemer. He's her provision; he's a gift to her in that way.

KATHIE: That's the way I see them. And just the care he had for her, and the protection and the decency. He was a decent, godly man. It was naturally a shocking thing to find out she was pregnant, and he was disappointed and probably had questions about her character. But how many young women would be accepted like that if she were found to be pregnant while engaged in that day and age? And look at the girls that are stoned to death today in some cultures if they've been with a man. You know, the honor killings.

BRYAN: And the law of Moses would allow that back then.

KATHIE: Yeah, the law required it. But Joseph didn't do it because God was up to something new. Jesus, even in his birth, said, "No, I've come to redeem all things." While in prison, Paul would later write in Colossians 1: "God was pleased to have his fullness dwell in him, and through him to reconcile to himself all things, whether things on earth or things in heaven, by making peace through his blood, shed on the cross" (v. 19 NIV). *All things.* I think that's a beautiful message. That's the Christmas message.

BRYAN: So that really is a kinsman-redeemer type of role where stoning would have been her normal fate. Like Ruth was going to be an outcast or be sexually victimized in the fields. And Boaz covered her with his robe and protected her. And so, too, in this case, Joseph also protected Mary from a stoning by taking her as his wife, even though some would think her reputation had been violated.

KATHIE: It's just like Jesus, who later said to the woman found in adultery, "Woman, where are those accusers of yours?" (John 8:10). And to the angry crowd, "Let the one who has never sinned throw the first stone!" (v. 7 NLT). I studied with one teacher who said some people think that when Jesus got down in that earth and wrote on the ground—it's such an unusual thing to do during such a dramatic moment, right?—perhaps he was writing the accusers' names and reminding them of being with the town whore.

BRYAN: Like reminders that Jesus knows what they've done.

KATHIE: Of course, they never stone the guy. It takes two to tango, doesn't it? And these women in these cultures often had no choice about who they had sex with. But she's the one they wanted to stone. Well, Jesus is the stone you need. He was a stonemason. He is the chief cornerstone. He comes to release and forgive, not to punish.

BRYAN: Another thing in this chapter is how Herod started to torture people. What do you think it did to his psyche when he resorted to torturing people to find out what they knew? You can't come away from that torturing environment without being mentally scarred.

KATHIE: Yeah, I cannot take anything that has to do with torture. I've never been able to watch a rape scene or a torture scene. I think people who get off on that really have a mental health problem. That is demonic, right? That's so demonic.

BRYAN: Wherever there's torture, there are demons.

KATHIE: They come to steal and kill and destroy, whether they torture us emotionally or psychologically or physically. But that is the total opposite of God. Total opposite. In my work with Childhelp, I've discovered two of my favorite heroes in the world: two ladies who started it sixty-five years ago. They have battled child abuse every day since then. So every single day, I send them a video or just a picture of Frankie. They are now in their nineties and I cannot tell you the joy they get from seeing this child every day growing, being loved, being happy. Singing, clapping, throwing kisses, you know?

And when child abuse literally rapes a child of their soul, not just their body but their soul, that's when I want to say, "Come, Lord Jesus, come." These children, they've suffered enough. Yeah, they've suffered enough. "The Lord is not slack concerning His promise, as some count slackness, but is longsuffering toward us, not willing that any should perish but that all should come to repentance" (2 Peter 3:9). That's the only way I can deal with any of this stuff, any injustice, is that the God of justice is coming to make things right. Because that suffering is the complete opposite of his shalom. And the God of justice will reign for eternity, and there will be justice for every victim. And I believe that every child that's ever been aborted goes straight into the arms of Jesus, and so does every child who—oh, I can't even talk about it— about their organs being harvested and the torture of children. They're all God's children. The God of justice will make things right.

BRYAN: I mentioned about the torture that it was more like judicial torture to find out secrets, who's got a plot in the palace or something like that. But it also relates to the pain and suffering of children when we consider the killing of Mariamne's sons and then later the killing of Antipater, his firstborn son, where Herod was just this person who resorted early in his life to violence. We talked earlier in the book about how he made a choice not to follow Torah but to follow the Roman way and put a bunch of bandits to death. And it put him on a path in life where he used violence to find solutions to his problems. Thus he became immune to inflicting pain, so he could then one day kill his own sons. He'd built up a pattern that hurting other people is the best way to help yourself in life.

KATHIE: Once it solves one problem, it's going to establish in your brain, *Well, that solved that. Let's do it again. Yeah, that works.* And so you get inured to things. Just emotionally, the human psyche can take only so much. You get accustomed to it, to the point where once you've lost your soul to sin, you start to enjoy it. You start to get off on it.

BRYAN: Don't you find that to be an exhortation to your readers in this book to watch their choices? Because maybe it's a little choice, but it's going to hurt somebody. Like, *Hey, it'll get me ahead in life.* Better me than them, right? And then you might think you got away with it. But what you really started yourself down is a path of pain that destroys you as well the people around you.

KATHIE: You don't realize that every cheeseburger you eat is going to just put more junk in your life. And it's like if you have a constant feast of junk food, your body becomes junk food. If you have a thousand sexual partners, you won't remember a face, you won't remember anything about anybody but you. If you have a thousand pornographic images before your eyes, you can't see your wife's face anymore. And whether you know it or not, your body will start having maggots and larvae and all those things.

BRYAN: Like Herod, your private parts will be infested with larvae. Even if you can't see them or you don't see them until late in life, it's eating you away from the inside.

KATHIE: Yes. What does it profit a man to gain the world but lose his soul (Mark 8:36)? That's the main thing. Don't let that happen to you. It's a tragedy. But it's preventable, even now, with repentance and faith.

CODA 19

HOPE IS ON THE WAY

BRYAN: Well, in chapter 19, we relate the annunciation to Mary, and we've already been talking about Mary, but what an amazing, surprising thing it was to hear this news because she didn't know she was pregnant. And she probably didn't know it was an angel at first. Just a really handsome man, because angels are always described as handsome. And he had this news that she was going to be pregnant. She probably wasn't happy at first because she knew she would have shame, but still, she said yes to it.

KATHIE: The first emotion would be shock. "What are you talking about?" I don't even think she was upset about it at first. You hear something like that, you have to say, "Wait a minute. Whoa, whoa, whoa. Back up there. The birds and bees."

BRYAN: Like, this doesn't work. This doesn't happen like that.

KATHIE: Right. "How can I be with child?" And then the angel said, "The Holy Spirit will come upon you, and the power of the Highest will overshadow you" (Luke 1:35). And in the book of Matthew, the angel of the Lord told Joseph, "You shall call His name JESUS, for He will save His people from their sins" (1:21).

BRYAN: Mary is often referred to in the language of grace. If you look back in the original Greek, *charis* is used several times for "grace," or forms of that word. And Catholics will be familiar with the term "Hail Mary, full of grace." We're not trying to say she's the dispenser of grace like Jesus, but she is still a woman full of grace. I mean, Scripture uses the word *grace* about her. What do you think of that? That she's this person full of grace, but it's the grace that came to her from the Lord.

KATHIE: Well, she gave birth to Grace himself.

BRYAN: Oh, that's good. That's going in the book.

KATHIE: She gave birth so that grace would have a face.

BRYAN: That's going in the book too.

KATHIE: And I think, yes, God showed great favor to her. Great favor and great honor.

BRYAN: *Favor* is a word I like. That's often how the angel's words are translated: "Rejoice, highly favored one." But if you look back in the original Greek, *favor* is actually the same word for *grace*.

KATHIE: That makes total sense to me. And I think she was the picture of grace in the way she received the message and humbly bowed before it. She said in her heart, *This is bigger than me. And if this is of you, Lord, let it be done to me.* Basically, she was saying what Jesus said in the garden: "Not My will, but Yours, be done" (Luke 22:42). Every single one of us will have to say that same prayer in our lives, not once but probably hundreds of times. "Nevertheless, Lord, your will be done and not mine." We can pour our hearts out to him. But at the end of the day, you've got to end up saying, "All right, Lord, I've told you what I want. I've told you what happened. It's killing me. But your will be done. Lord, give me the grace to receive your will." And the irony of it is when people talk about "God says he'll give you the desires of your heart," the condition is "Seek first the kingdom of God and His righteousness, and all these things shall be added to you" (Matthew 6:33). The truth is, if we put him first, if we seek him, if we love him, he's going to give us a new desire.

BRYAN: So it's not, "Lord, I want a big yacht. Why aren't you giving it to me?"

KATHIE: That's why it takes so long for these things to come true. Because he's changing us until we go, "Oh, now I see. That is what I wanted all along, Lord."

BRYAN: I like the parallelism that you just mentioned. I don't know if I've ever quite thought about the idea that when Jesus said, "Not My will, but Yours, be done," it was coming from Mary, who asked for God's will to be done to her. So how did Jesus in the garden of Gethsemane know to respond that way? You could say, "Well, he's God, so of course he's going to respond like that," right? But he's also a man who was taught things, and his mother probably taught him the spiritual lesson that when you're feeling this way, respond like this. So Jesus said, "Not My will, but Yours, be done" because his mother taught him how to have a spiritual life that has that reaction. You know, I think that's a beautiful idea.

KATHIE: Yeah. That's why the song "Mary Did You Know?" is so power-ful. You can see me and Kenny Rogers singing "Mary Did You Know?" if you look it up on YouTube. That's another fun thing I did. I was always blessed to know and work with these people. I mean, just blessed beyond belief to know them. I've known Kenny since 1977 when I did *Hee Haw Honeys*. I met Dolly Parton, then I met Kenny Rogers, then I met the Gatlin Brothers. And they've been my friends ever since.

BRYAN: You've had quite a life in showbiz, and I think a lot of the fun of this book is going to be how we can bring in some of these stories and relate them to Herod and to Mary. And you've lived quite a life. Not that it's over, but even so far, you've lived quite a life in showbiz and knowing various movers and shakers everywhere.

KATHIE: I'm Waldo. I'm everywhere. And there's no reason for it on the surface. I was called, that's all. And if you're faithful, you are favored. I've tried to be faithful, and I have failed on so many occasions that I can't even count. But the story of my life, and I would bet yours as well and all these readers of ours, the story of our lives is not our faithfulness to God. It's always the other way around. All our stories are of God's faithfulness to us. When we lose track of that, that's when we spiral, right?

BRYAN: Absolutely. And here's another question relating to Mary, and I think you've probably covered this kind of topic when you talked about the sweatshop accusations. Mary wasn't guilty of having sex outside of mar-riage, yet her culture would have assumed that about her. And she had to endure shame even though she was innocent. And they tried to shame you even though you were innocent of sweatshops. So what would it be like for Mary to walk through unfair shame? It's one thing to be shamed because, "Oh, I sinned, and I know I did."

KATHIE: Right. "And now I deserve this."

BRYAN: But in Mary's case, it was unfair.

KATHIE: Oh, it was completely unfair. But she also had history with God at this point. She had a history of God's faithfulness to her. She knew she'd never had sex with a man. And yet there she was—pregnant. She knew that she could have been stoned, but her faithful betrothed, her kinsman-redeemer, married her anyway. You know, she surely told Joseph about what the angel had said to her. And Joseph said, "Maybe it was the same angel that came to me." And so she had community with Joseph. She had his support. He might have been the only one who believed her. But that was enough, right?

BRYAN: He believed her, though maybe not at first, until the angel came to him and said, "Joseph . . . do not be afraid to take to you Mary your wife, for that which is conceived in her is of the Holy Spirit" (Matthew 1:20). The Greek word here is *ek*, which means "out of" or "from the source of" the Holy Spirit. It's a simple preposition. But it means from the source of the Holy Spirit. He is the source of what is in her. Then Joseph was okay with how things were going to be. He wouldn't put her aside; he would take care of her.

KATHIE: Other people, I'm sure, like Anna and Joachim, believed her. They were godly people. And we know that Elizabeth and ultimately Zechariah did too. So she had enough people in her inner circle saying, "This is of God, this is the Messiah, so you must go forward with this. What you have within you is the long-awaited Messiah, the Anointed One whom we've longed for." And she probably was just overwhelmed with that and thought, *Why me, Lord? Why me, of all people?* That's exactly what bursts forth from her in the Magnificat.

BRYAN: I have the text right here. She says, "My soul magnifies the Lord, and my spirit has rejoiced in God my Savior. For He has regarded the lowly state of His maidservant; for behold, henceforth all generations will call me blessed. For He who is mighty has done great things for me" (Luke 1:46–49).

KATHIE: "All generations will call me blessed." See? She knew.

BRYAN: And that's why it's okay to call her the Blessed Virgin. Catholics use language like that, but it's not just Catholic talk. It's Bible talk. She said it herself. "All generations will call me blessed." That includes our generation today.

KATHIE: She was the blessed child of God who happened to be a virgin when she was given the greatest calling of all. Not just to believe in the Messiah. Not just to know him personally. But to carry him inside her own body, the way only a woman can.

BRYAN: You have a real tender heart toward the women of Scripture, don't you? Women like Mary, like Hagar, like Hannah.

KATHIE: All of them. They are the daughters of Abraham. And best of all, they are the daughters of the King.

CODA 20

WHO IS THE KING OF GLORY?

BRYAN: In chapter 20 we meet the magi. So often, you hear about them in songs or see them in a manger scene. You see these three kings sort of sentimentally pictured, but that's not really who they were, right? Who were the magi, from what you understand?

KATHIE: Well, the big controversy is where did they come from. We have decided that they come from Babylon. And they make this journey all the way across the desert. They come over and find the Messiah by following the star. So why do we pick the number three?

BRYAN: I think that goes off of the three gifts they brought, right? Gold, frankincense, and myrrh. But the Bible doesn't say there were three magi. And it doesn't say they were kings, either.

KATHIE: That's right. They were what we call "wise men." Could you say, "learned men who studied the stars"? Yes, that's exactly what we have here: astrologers. Yes. Astrologers.

BRYAN: Therefore, you'd say pagans or unbelievers. We don't do astrology.

KATHIE: What's upsetting about that? The Bible is very good. It tells us to respect the stars. You know, there's wisdom in the skies! There's all kinds of knowledge from there, and yet we as Christians in the Western world misunderstand so many things. I don't mean putting your faith in the stars, getting your astrological sign, and going to get your fortune read by an astrologer. Believing in the stars in the sky like that is never taught in the Scriptures. Of course not. It was not that. You seek the Creator of the stars instead. God said to seek the stars, and you will find that I'm the One who created them, and I store wisdom in the skies.

BRYAN: The heavens pour forth speech. They declare the glory of God.

KATHIE: That's right. So they might have been pagan without the knowledge of Yahweh in their lives, but they were doing something that was actually from the Lord. They were being very, very faithful to Scripture. And a star is what led them! God used it to get them to leave their lands.

BRYAN: Now, of course, you're not saying that casting horoscopes and astrology is something we should do today, right?

KATHIE: No, God never meant it for that purpose. I mean, it's like everything that God does. This goes for every truth: a counterfeit always arises. That is a counterfeit to what God said. What he actually said was "Go, look at the stars and meet me." You see how he said to Abraham, "Look up at the sky. Look at the stars. I will make you a great nation and more fruitful than all the stars in the sky" (Genesis 15:5, my paraphrase).

BRYAN: Yeah, so the stars are actually a very Christian thing, and we should look at the stars is what you're saying.

KATHIE: Well, I wouldn't say it's a Christian thing because, you know, I'm Jewish. I would say it's a very Scriptural thing.

BRYAN: Okay, good clarification. Hmm, I like that. And what do you think their journey was like as they traveled across the countryside to their destination?

KATHIE: Dusty and dry! I've never been to Babylon. I've never been to Iraq or Persia or any of those places, but I've seen enough pictures to know it's very similar to Israel. There's a lot of desert to cross and a lot of mountains, and a lot of it is so beautiful. But there were no superhighways, that's for sure! And they had to come with a bountiful supply of food because you know, they're not hunters, these men. They are learned men, and they had to probably come with a whole group of people who were serving them along the way. They were men of accomplishments, wherever they came from, and if they had gold and frankincense and myrrh, they were men of means. So we have a beautiful picture of a group of people supporting them on camels and donkeys, carrying their supplies. And they probably had a couple of people to guard against bandits because they were ever-present. There were always bandits coming out of the hills, so these wise men had their posse with them!

BRYAN: It's a beautiful picture, isn't it? Maybe we picture it in this Hallmark way, where we picture three people trudging along. But really it was a whole group of foreigners basically coming to Yeshua, coming to Messiah, coming to Israel. It must have been amazing to discover Israel's Messiah, even though they were at the height of learning in ancient Babylon, the very origins of human civilization. What a humbling thing for them.

KATHIE: And they found it in the old Jewish Scriptures, in the book of Numbers, like we say in this book. I love that.

BRYAN: They didn't really know what they were going to find, did they? I mean, they followed where they were led, but they didn't exactly know the outcome.

KATHIE: No, they didn't know anything except to go. There was this scripture, and a star, and a Savior arising. That's all. That's pretty amazing. You can imagine how curious they were. It's similar to Abraham when God said for him to leave. "I will show you your new land." Abraham had no idea where God was sending him. And we don't actually know how God spoke to him. Did he speak audibly? Maybe there was an angelic appearance, or maybe Abraham just heard it in his heart.

BRYAN: And he came from the same land that the magi were coming from, because Ur of the Chaldees (Genesis 11:31, 15:7) was essentially the same place as Babylon. And also the Israelites came to the promised land, led along by a pillar of fire, which is a similar concept, isn't it? Have you ever had that in your life, where you've had a clear sign to go but you didn't know exactly where you're going? You just know there's a good promise at the end, and you had to sort of wander with expectation and wonderment. Have you had stuff like that in your life?

KATHIE: Oh, sure. One would be when I left my home as a young woman, and I went to California to pursue my career. It's not like I had any showbiz prospects at home. Nobody was knocking on my door! So I was going into a foreign land, and I had no idea what was at the end, but I had a true calling on my heart. The latest one was when I moved here to Tennessee. My old home in Connecticut had become a morgue to me, like a mausoleum devoid of sound because Frank had died. My kids were in California with their own careers, and the house was no longer full of music and fun and parties and animals. I still had my dogs, but that's it. It was desolate to me. For years, Frank and I would always toast the sunset on our porch. And then when we had our children, they had their little sippy cups, and Frank and I would toast the sunset. And then everybody was gone. I remember the first time I went out there to toast the sunset with just me and my dogs, and I couldn't do it. So the Lord specifically led me to a whole different culture down here in the South. This is not nirvana by any means, but to me, it seems like a huge culture shift, and it is! You hear church bells. There are more churches than there are gas stations in Nashville. God is honored here, and you go into stores and they're playing praise music over the speakers.

BRYAN: I hear you. I grew up in Memphis and went to college at UT Knoxville. So I definitely know what you mean! And now I'm back in Virginia, which is like that too. So I know what you're talking about, and it's a whole new experience for you as someone who had been up in New England. And when you left, did you have any kind of "star," like a symbol of your going? Or when you were led to go to California for your career or to come to Tennessee and you were being pushed out from your comfort zone, did you have a star or a sign to push you forward?

KATHIE: No, it was just a quiet, inner way of God speaking to me, like when I first listened to him at that movie theater as a girl. I just felt him speak to my young heart, "Kathie, I love you. And if you'll trust me, I will make something beautiful in you."

BRYAN: Yeah, that's so good. Well, I have one more question. This one has to do with Mary in this chapter. We show her telling Joseph her secret. Of course, when he hears that his betrothed is pregnant, he would normally assume she cheated on him. And we know he didn't believe her explanation because he planned to divorce her. Then the angel tells him the truth, and really, he probably had to repent because he should have had faith. When she said, "Hey, my beloved, this came from God," he shouldn't have jumped to the wrong conclusion like that. So there's a beautiful reconciliation that happens in this chapter.

KATHIE: Yeah, but you know, there's all this Scripture that he should have known. There's not a lot of Scripture, but there's enough to say, "Blessed are you, Bethlehem Ephrathah, for out of you the Messiah will arise" (Micah 5:2, my paraphrase). There's pretty much no doubt that the Messiah was going to come from Bethlehem. And then in Isaiah 7:14, it says the Messiah would come from a virgin. We have seen petri dish births today. We've seen all of that from science, but not one has happened that didn't have a sperm.

BRYAN: Right, and especially back then, it would have been shocking. The baby just came spontaneously in her womb, so Joseph was shocked. He knew of those verses, yet he didn't believe.

KATHIE: And she had to have been so crushed. Mary must have felt, "Joseph will protect me. Joseph will protect me! He's a good man!" But then, Joseph was going to leave and who's she going to have? And you have to remember that in those days in Israel you could be stoned for adultery. You know, for being pregnant outside of marriage. And to be betrothed in the Jewish sense was basically a marriage. It just hadn't been consummated yet. Although they had not been intimate with one another, they were considered a married couple. When she got on the donkey and they left Nazareth to go to Bethlehem, they traveled as husband and wife.

BRYAN: And so for her to have been rejected by her husband must have been really painful for her.

KATHIE: Yes, because he was going to put her away and divorce her privately. He was a good, godly, decent man. He didn't want to hurt her, and I think he probably loved her. They probably spent a lot of time together. I don't know in the Jewish tradition how much time they were together once the betrothal was announced between the families. I don't know how much time they might have spent together, but probably a lot.

BRYAN: I think they probably did spend some time together in a small village or something like that. They couldn't have missed each other, I suppose, but they wouldn't have cohabited, and he was making a home for her. That's what Mary thought she would have until this estrangement. So how much more beautiful it is when they come back together, and the grace and the forgiveness and the reconciliation happen. Maybe we can conclude with that idea, because obviously you've had estrangement in your marriage with Frank, yet you saw beautiful reconciliation. What is it like when there's been an estrangement that Jesus overcomes? What is it like to have that restoration happen?

KATHIE: Well, it sure beats a divorce! Because divorce destroys your home, destroys your children, destroys your future. I mean, God is a God of reconciliation, the God of forgiveness and all those things, but we still have to be proactive in that whole situation. It doesn't just happen. If you have a root of bitterness in you, it doesn't happen. It doesn't happen unless you want it to, and it takes both parties to want it. And I wanted to save my marriage and my family, and he wanted to be forgiven, you know? Only God can do that.

BRYAN: It's a picture of the gospel. That's a beautiful thing when we see it and we can all be grateful for God's grace.

KATHIE: There's so much grace, for sure. Yet I was never the same after it happened. When the one person in your life who you think is the most trustworthy, the most important person in your whole life is your spouse, you have a good marriage. But then, the next thing you know, all of a sudden, you're sleeping with the enemy. I forgave Frank instantly because that's what we're supposed to do. But then it took years to heal, because you have a wound, a deep one. Scars are exactly what we need sometimes. They are there to remind us of what we've been healed from.

BRYAN: Aren't you glad you had Jesus in your life during that time?

KATHIE: Yes! I bet I would have divorced his ass so fast. Yeah, I surely would have. And I would have had every right to. The biblical pronouncement would be, "Yes, you have a biblical right to divorce."

BRYAN: But instead, you found healing and hope and unity. And look at the good that came out of it. I mean, your two beautiful children and their children who are just now being born, and what a legacy of hope was given because you persevered at that time and didn't give in to bitterness.

KATHIE: I knew I was completely right to stay in my marriage. I felt the Lord say in that still, small voice he speaks to me with, very gently and tenderly, he said to me, *Kathie, do you want to be* right *or do you want to be* righteous? And I said, "I want to be righteous, Lord." He answered, *Then let it go.*

CODA 21

SON OF MARY, SON OF GOD

BRYAN: Let's talk about the first Christmas. The real story of Jesus is different from the way we often imagine it, isn't it?

KATHIE: It really is! I am so passionate about not doing the tinsel and the Hallmark Christmas story movies anymore. It just wasn't like that. I don't believe at all that Jesus was born in a stable. They didn't have stables the way we think about them today. There's also no way it was in December. I have been in Israel so many times, and every time I've been there in December or in January, I get pneumonia! Why? Because that's the rainy season and that's when they put their animals in caves. The shepherds' fields in Bethlehem were all there to take care of the animals that were going to be prepared for sacrifice. And every one of those shepherds was a priest, a Levite priest. When you go to Bethlehem today and you see these young kids tending their flocks, it's not those kinds of people who were there in Jesus' day. Those guys had a priestly purpose, which was to birth lambs, and when they were born, they wrapped them in swaddling cloths. Why? So they would be perfect. So they're not wobbly and vulnerable when they're first born. They stand right away, but they fall, and they hit the ground and it's all rocky. You're going to have a lamb that's not good for anything on the Temple Mount, though it'll make a nice dinner. But the Jewish sacrifices required perfect lambs, just like Messiah Jesus was perfect. And so those shepherds had an express purpose, which I think was so clear when the angel appeared to them, probably in October during the festival of Sukkot. That would mean Jesus was conceived during the Feast of Lights, or Hanukkah, in December. Then the baby was born the following fall during Sukkot. So when the shepherds heard they would find the child lying in a manger wrapped in swaddling cloths, that's not a normal thing to wrap babies in, right? That was a sign you have got something special

230

going on, and they were Levite priests, so they knew the Word. They knew the Scriptures. They knew it was the Messiah, unlike the fishermen, who didn't really understand when they heard stories, or the regular shepherds. But these Levites knew what was happening.

BRYAN: It really gives new meaning to the Christmas story when you see the Jewish background.

KATHIE: Yes! So much of what we assume about the early believers in Jesus is not accurate. We really need to change our cultural views of Jesus and try to better understand what was going on in those days. For example, we need to make sure that people realize Bethlehem was a tiny, tiny little village. Then when people talk about Herod's "slaughter of the innocents," they know it wasn't thousands of babies that were killed but far fewer. Some scholars have said it was like maybe ten or twenty, if there were a hundred people in the village. But still, those Roman soldiers, they went out and they slaughtered all the children. They didn't pull down their pants to see if it was a male. They slaughtered every child they saw. Just for expediency so they could get back to their warring, you know?

BRYAN: Roman soldiers were bad news.

KATHIE: Yeah, they were. They were not a godly group. Except for the centurion. Except for Cornelius.

BRYAN: There were a few God-seekers among the wicked and the dominant.

KATHIE: Everywhere. God always has his followers. He really does. It's just that they are sometimes few and far between. But it was still hard for Cornelius to do it. I'm talking about what kind of orders Cornelius had to carry out. He was a man who loved the Jews and even built a synagogue for them. But I'm sure he was asked to oversee slaughters and oversee crucifixions. You don't become a centurion by, you know . . .

BRYAN: By being a softy.

KATHIE: Right! And if you ask me, "Have I in my life and in my career, have I ever had to do things that I don't believe in?" Well, I have had the ability to say, "No, I don't want to do that," "I can't do it," "I don't believe in it." But those guys were answerable to Caesar and Rome, and they lost their jobs and almost always lost their lives if they refused. And their families were slaughtered too. So they had much more at stake. And the more we heighten that kind of thing, the more we create an understanding of just how brutal life under the Romans was, the more the readers will understand the contrast of Jesus and the goodness of what he brought. Life back then was hard. And not just under the Romans. Life under the Sanhedrin was hard too. Those religious leaders made six hundred laws, in addition to the Mosaic law. They made the common people keep a bunch of laws that were not from God; they were man-made, just so they could retain control.

BRYAN: It's really oppressive to live under that.

KATHIE: Oh my gosh, nothing but oppression! And then Jesus came and walked among them and said, "Consider the lilies of the field, how they grow: they neither toil nor spin; and yet I say to you that even Solomon in all his glory was not arrayed like one of these. Now if God so clothes the grass of the field, which today is, and tomorrow is thrown into the oven, will He not much more clothe you?" (Matthew 6:28–30). Yeah, and he's going to take care of you too. Jesus simplified everything. He got back down to the essence of God's love for people and how important the Torah was. It wasn't about rules but about relationship. Even King David ate the unleavened bread; he ate the Bread of the Presence. That was breaking a rule, but it was okay because of why he did it. And Jesus healed on the Sabbath because, he said, "The Sabbath was made for man, and not man for the Sabbath" (Mark 2:27). For doing good, and for rest! But if your donkey falls down in a ditch, are you not going to lift it out and do good (Luke 14:5)?

BRYAN: You do good to God's creatures even if it violates a man-made rule.

KATHIE: Yes. So Jesus came to fulfill the Law and emphasize the mercy element to it. And that's the way I want to end our whole book. I want to focus on that point. Herod didn't live a life of grace and mercy. He claimed to be a king of God's chosen people. But he didn't live out the main thing that characterizes God, the essential thing God wants from his people. God isn't about elevating our own power and prestige. He is about love. What did Jesus say is the greatest commandment? To love. To love the Lord your God with all your heart, soul, mind, and strength. And what flows from that? To love your neighbor as yourself. Herod did the exact opposite. He loved himself first. But Jesus gave his life for the lowly shepherds, and for the centurions and emperors, and for you and me, and for the whole human race. God's real King doesn't spread domination and violence. He's the King of kings because he's the King of love!

ACKNOWLEDGMENTS

First, I must thank my cowriter, Bryan Litfin, who graciously agreed to use his prodigious talents to help us bring this story to life.

Second, I want to thank my very gifted and visionary literary agents at UTA in New York: Albert Lee and Pilar Queen. They caught the enthusiasm for this very different kind of book immediately because we all share a passion for the power of an amazing story, and they helped us bring it home.

And finally, a big thanks to Stephanie Newton, my very brave editor, and her amazing team at W Publishing.

ABOUT THE AUTHORS

KATHIE LEE GIFFORD is the four-time Emmy Award–winning former cohost of the fourth hour of the *TODAY Show* alongside Hoda Kotb. Prior to her time at NBC News, Gifford served as the cohost of *Live with Regis and Kathie Lee* for fifteen years. In 2015 she was inducted into the Broadcasting and Cable Hall of Fame, and recently she was awarded a star on the Hollywood Walk of Fame.

A playwright, producer, singer, songwriter, and actress, Gifford has starred in numerous television programs and movies in her forty-five-year career. She has written several musicals, including Broadway's *Scandalous*, for which she received a Tony nomination for Best Actress in 2012. In 2019 she made her directorial debut with *The God Who Sees* oratorio, shot in Israel and based on a song she cowrote with Grammy-nominee Nicole C. Mullen. She has written and directed three more oratorios and will be releasing the collection of four as *The Way*.

Gifford has authored six *New York Times* bestselling books, including *The God of the Way*; *It's Never Too Late*; *The Rock, the Road, and the Rabbi*; *Just When I Thought I'd Dropped My Last Egg*; *I Can't Believe I Said That*; and the popular children's book *Party Animals*. She has also recently released *Hello, Little Dreamer* (2020) and *The Jesus I Know* (2021).

Gifford lends support to numerous children's organizations, including Childhelp, the International Justice Mission, and the Association to Benefit Children. She received an honorary doctorate from Marymount University for her humanitarian work in labor relations.

Gifford is on Twitter/X and Instagram @KathieLGifford.

DR. BRYAN M. LITFIN is a professor of Bible and theology at Liberty University in Lynchburg, Virginia. Previously he was head of strategy and advancement at Clapham School, a classical Christian school in Wheaton, Illinois, after serving for sixteen years as a professor of theology at Moody Bible Institute in Chicago and three years as an editor and writer at Moody Publishers.

Bryan received his PhD in religious studies from the University of Virginia, where he focused on the field of Christianity and Judaism in antiquity. His area of expertise is the early Christian writers of the ancient Roman era. He has a ThM in historical theology from Dallas Theological Seminary and an undergraduate degree from the University of Tennessee in print media and communications.

Litfin has published six adventure novels—three set in an imaginary future (*The Chiveis Trilogy*) and three in the ancient church (*Constantine's Empire* series). His nonfiction books include *Getting to Know the Church Fathers*, *Wisdom from the Ancients*, and *Early Christian Martyr Stories*. His book *After Acts* describes what happened to Jesus' apostles after their biblical stories ended. In addition, Litfin has published many book chapters and journal articles of academic scholarship. He is a member of the Evangelical Theological Society.

Bryan is married to Carolyn, and they have two adult children. He enjoys taking students on annual trips to Greece, Turkey, and other Mediterranean lands. The Litfins worship at Rivermont Evangelical Presbyterian Church in Lynchburg.

Bryan can be reached at his website, bryanlitfin.com.

OTHER HCCP BOOKS BY KATHIE LEE GIFFORD

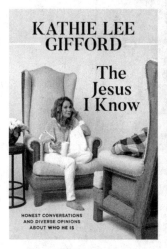

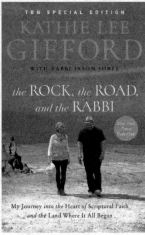

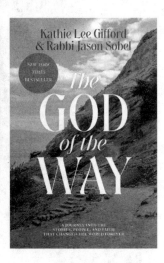

Kathie Lee Gifford reveals heartwarming, entertaining conversations between people and personalities who both agree and disagree about who Jesus is, his role throughout history, and his presence in our lives today.

Journey with Kathie Lee Gifford and Messianic Rabbi Jason Sobel into Israel and explore the deep roots of the Christian faith.

Dig deeper into God's Word, from the creation of the world through the desert and empty places, the Hebrew nation, and meet Jesus, the disciples, and his followers.

Connect with Kathie Lee on Twitter/X and Instagram @KathieLGifford.

OTHER BOOKS FROM BRYAN LITFIN

Historical Nonfiction about the Early Church

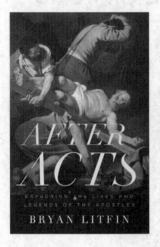 

The Chiveis Trilogy: Christian Fiction the Way It Was Meant to Be

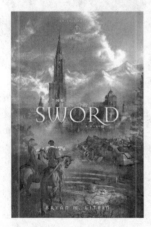  

Nuclear war has ravaged the earth. Centuries from now, an alpine society has achieved a culture of swords and horses but has lost all memory of Christianity. Then a courageous army scout and a beautiful farmer's daughter find the ancient Scriptures of God. Can the one true faith reawaken in Chiveis?

For more information, visit bryanlitfin.com.